Commission of the European Communities

XXth Report
on Competition Policy

(Published in conjunction with the
'XXIVth General Report on the
Activities of the European Communities 1990')

Brussels • Luxembourg • 1991

Cataloguing data can be found at the end of this publication

Luxembourg: Office for Official Publications of the European Communities, 1991

ISBN 92-826-2314-9

Catalogue number: CM-60-91-410-EN-C

Printed in Belgium

Contents

Introduction

Internal market

Since the very beginning of the creation of the common market competition policy has been an important Community instrument used both to promote economic integration and to ensure an efficient allocation of resources. Effective competition is the main stimulus to innovation and higher productivity which underpins policies designed to increase economic growth and welfare. Not only does competition lead to higher output but it also enables consumers to obtain a fair share of this growth. Living standards therefore depend on the maintenance of effective competition.

This traditional role of competition policy has been given increased importance by the completion of the internal market by 1992. The full benefits of the internal market in terms of higher output, growth and employment can only be attained if competition intensifies as a result of the dismantling of the barriers to trade that still remain. The increase in competition expected as a result of this integration process can be thwarted in a number of ways so the Commission must be vigilant to guard against any such attempts. Member States must not be allowed to replace forms of protectionism abolished in the market integration process by State aids or exclusive rights accorded to monopolies. Companies must not be allowed to thwart integration (e.g. to create cartels to split up markets, to block exports and imports, to abuse local dominant positions, to block new entrants or to create new dominant positions through anti-competitive mergers). In all these areas where anti-competitive measures threaten the market integration process the Commission will reinforce its policy. In choosing the priorities in which to concentrate its efforts the Commission will increasingly bear in mind the areas where effective competition is not fully developed. It is precisely in the areas where the least progress has been made in market integration and where trade between Member States is the least developed that the greatest gains can be produced by the application of an effective competition policy. As a result the impact and effectiveness of the application of competition policy on market integration and consumer welfare will be maximized.

It is clear that the removal of the remaining technical, fiscal and physical barriers to trade will not bring about on its own a real internal market. Trade and competition between

Member States must develop along lines dictated by economic efficiency and this will not be an overnight process. It may take some time both for consumers to become aware of the availability of alternative supplies from other Member States and for producers to gear themselves and their distribution system to sell to areas in which they traditionally did not sell. The Commission's aim is to ensure that anti-competitive behaviour by enterprises or structural changes in the market do not put a brake on this process. The entry into force of the Regulation on merger control in September 1990 completed the range of instruments with which to prevent anti-competitive behaviour or structural changes from hindering market integration.

Deregulation

Regulated sectors and those in which companies enjoy exclusive rights will have to be subject to the rules of competition if the internal market is to function properly. Whilst the Commission recognizes that account must be taken of the need to supply services of a general economic interest, this must be done in the manner least restrictive to competition. With the aim of opening up the possibilities for competition, the Commission will apply the rule of proportionality in deciding whether these services of a general economic interest can be effectively provided in any other way than by granting exclusive rights to particular suppliers. Such services of a general economic interest are usually found for basic utilities (e.g. gas, water, electricity, telecommunications, etc.). Exclusive rights given to a company which are necessary to provide these services of a general economic interest should not be allowed to extend into other areas which are not essential to the provision of the service in question and for which competition is possible. A further consideration is that many of these services necessitate a near universal network in each Member State and the Commission has to see to what extent the principle of open access to the network can allow competition without prejudicing the provision of the service. However, to make the possibilities of competition a reality, it is important that networks which are essentially national be linked up physically.

In addition to the utilities of gas, electricity, telecommunications and post, the Commission is also examining other markets where competition between Member States is not yet fully developed. This situation is found notably in the transport sector (air and maritime), banking and insurance and the audiovisual sector.

International aspects

The proximity of the internal market in 1992 should not be allowed to obscure the wider international context of competition policy, which is also becoming of increased importance. This trend is bound to continue with the growth of international trade and the increasing internationalization of certain markets. It is important that the Community, in completing the internal market, should not adopt a protectionist attitude *vis-à-vis* the rest of the world, thereby isolating itself from international competition. Only if companies are subject to normal competitive pressures both from inside and outside the Community will they prove dynamic and strong enough to innovate, grow and compete on international markets. In its recent communication on industrial policy the Commission recognized that a healthy system of competition was one of the most effective ways to promote industrial change and improve the competitiveness of European industry. Protectionism and sector-specific measures are seen as increasingly counterproductive and greater efforts must be made to open up and strictly implement the rules of the multilateral trading system.

At the same time the Community is increasingly using its influence to extend the application of the principle of competition policy among its trading partners both in multilateral forums and through bilateral contacts. Competition policy in the past has been of only limited importance in international trade. Trade patterns tended to be based on import and export legislation, rather than competitive advantages. Developments over the last couple of decades have led, however, to the lowering of tariffs as well as the gradual decrease in the number of non-tariff barriers. This has greatly enhanced the possibilities for competition. It has also led to a spectacular increase in the number of international strategic alliances and has helped to spread phenomena such as international sourcing.

This has had important consequences for the implementation of competition policy. Anti-competitive behaviour within the Community may involve companies established in a third country or be linked to similar behaviour in non-Community markets.

The international implications of these issues are addressed in a growing number of multilateral forums in which the Community plays an increasingly active role. In addition, competition policy is also becoming an important element in the Community's bilateral relationships with its major trading partners.

The main multilateral framework for discussing competition policy issues was once again the OECD and more particularly its Committee on Competition Law and Policy. The contracting parties to Unctad underlined their interest in competition policy issues during the review conference on the set of multilaterally agreed equitable principles and rules for the control of restrictive business practices. The discussions taking place in the Uruguay Round of multilateral trade negotiations within GATT have also stressed the importance of workable competition conditions for the development of international trade and of an active competition policy to combat anti-competitive behaviour.

The discussions between the EC and the European Free Trade Association on a European economic area (EEA) entered into a decisive phase during 1990. It became clear that competition policy should be a crucial element of the EEA. The EEA, once established, will be the world's largest single market. An active competition policy will ensure that economic resources within this market are allocated on the basis of competitive advantage and that the EEA will benefit consumers throughout the entire area.

The Commission has taken a major initiative which should lead to a legal framework for intensified cooperation with the anti-trust authorities of the USA. At the same time, increased cooperation with the authorities in Canada, Japan and other countries is also under consideration.

Finally, the process of change from centrally planned to market economies in Central and Eastern Europe has shown the need for an active competition policy. Although competition authorities now exist in several countries in this region, they still lack the necessary experience and often even the basic legislative instruments to help them perform their job. Several of them have therefore turned to the Community with requests for technical assistance.

Competition policy

Articles 85 and 86 of the EEC Treaty

Even though greater efforts to reinforce the internal market are being made in markets previously protected from competition (notably regulated industries), this should not be allowed to obscure the continued vigilance of the Commission against any anti-competitive behaviour of companies that split up markets. A good example of this was the decision of the Commission to impose a record fine of ECU 48 million for illicit agreements designed to partition markets and abuses of dominant position to eliminate competition. The Commission's resolve in such matters should not be doubted. This is particularly important in sectors which directly affect consumers since such action helps demonstrate to a much wider audience the relevance of competition policy to their welfare and the success of the internal market.

Merger control

The year 1990 was very significant for competition policy with the entry into force of the merger control Regulation. Even though in operation only three months, 12 cases have been notified. In a full year this is expected to be around 60. Although it is still too early to draw many general conclusions from the cases considered so far, it is already evident that the Regulation is essential to prevent the strengthening or emergence of dominant positions as a defensive and negative reaction by companies to the opening up of the internal market. This may be particularly so where an already tight oligopoly is further narrowed by mergers between companies in the same geographic markets. On the other hand mergers can be an important way in which companies react positively to the internal market process. As long as dominant positions are not created or reinforced, mergers may serve to facilitate greater interpenetration of geographic markets that may not have previously been subject to the full effect of the competition from other Member States. The Commission must distinguish between these situations and ensure that effective competition is always safeguarded.

State aids

The distortive effects of State aids will not only be made felt keenly in the new context of the single market, but also risk endangering the unity of that market. For macroeconomic policy reasons, as well as for reasons of competition policy and the overall economic cohesion of the Community, there is a need to significantly reduce the level of spending on subsidies in the Member States.

Commission action, previously focused almost exclusively on new notifications, will now be extended to all existing aid systems. Only a complete review of the existing mass of aid schemes, many of which have been operating for years, can bring about a situation in which those aid schemes which are allowed to function in the future are fully in line with the needs and requirements of the single market. The review process will lead to proposals for the abolition of certain schemes and important modifications to others. Initial proposals made by the Commission in 1990 have, on the whole, received a favourable response from Member States which have either agreed to phase out or make major reductions in their application. The review process will be intensified in the coming months.

This intensified activity in the field of State aids necessitates greater transparency. Steps have already been taken to increase transparency including the publication of the second survey of all aids, the publication of details of all decisions taken in the State aid field and the holding of regular multilateral meetings with experts from Member States to discuss general policy issues. Greater transparency in this field will facilitate the cooperation of the Member States as well as making a comparative analysis of the aims, results and justification for State aids easier. As such it is a prerequisite for both Member States and the recipients of aid to understand the reasons for a stricter policy towards certain types of aids that are harmful to the market integration process. Finally the link between an effective State aid policy and economic and social cohesion described in more detail below, cannot be underestimated. In fact, unless State aid policy is effectively applied these goals, which are an essential element in the political agreement of the Single European Act which underpins the internal market, will be seriously compromised.

Transparency

In order to maintain the momentum of and support for competition policy, it is essential that this policy becomes more transparent thereby facilitating awareness of Member States, companies and private individuals in this field. In addition to the specific measures designed to increase transparency described above, the Commission is review- ing the different means of publicizing activities in this sphere with a view to making understanding of the issues more accessible to all interested parties. Progress has already been made in this respect but should be considered as an on-going process rather than a one-off exercise. Public awareness of the relevance of competition policy both for the wider aims of market integration and economic growth as well as to protect individual companies from restrictive practices is vital if it is to enjoy widespread support and application. This increased transparency facilitates the moves towards decentralized application of the competition rules by national courts and authorities. The Commission has neither the administrative resources nor, because of subsidiarity, the desire to intervene in every case where the rules of competition apply. The Commission is therefore currently examining the best way to encourage this decentralization in a manner that will best lead to both a strengthening and wider application of the rules of competition. The Commission considers in this way that the goals of market inte- gration with undistorted competition will be achieved more successfully than by the Commission acting on its own.

Link to other policies

In addition to competition policy's role in bolstering the internal market and inter- national competitiveness, it has both an input into, and an impact on, other Community policies. Competition policy is not a marginal instrument of Community policies, isolated from the mainstream of events; it is an integral and essential element of a whole range of Community activities. In most areas of Community endeavour, if a policy runs against market forces and competition, it not only has less chance of success, but is also unlikely to benefit consumers. For example, in technology policy, whilst some cooperation in research may be desirable, elimination of effective competition would take away the main spur to innovate and apply new technologies. In the application of anti-dumping duties, European industry has a legitimate right to be protected against unfair and illicit trading practices, but the intensity and duration of such protection should not put into question the rules of the Treaty on competition. Economic and social cohesion is an essential part of the internal market programme. The Community's structural Funds reinforce the effectiveness of Member States' aid schemes in the disadvantaged regions. However, it is essential that aids given outside these areas be closely monitored;

otherwise richer Member States with greater budgetary resources to fund State aids might implement policies which undermine Community cohesion. Cohesion and competition policy in the form of reinforced aid disciplines are therefore complementary.

Unification of Germany

The year 1990 saw the unification of Germany. Here, just as with the moves towards the completion of the internal market, it would be wrong to think of competition policy as having only a negative policing role. An active and efficient competition policy is of primary importance in promoting integration and efficiency. In the case of German unification competition will be the main instrument in transforming a centrally planned economy into an efficient market economy. The Commission's role is to ensure that the new *Länder* are open to all Community investors on a non-discriminatory basis. It must ensure that the sale of State monopolies leads to a competitive economic structure, not the strengthening of any dominant positions. It is clear that some State aids are necessary to ease the transition towards a market economy. Nevertheless these aids and their duration must be kept to a minimum in order to avoid an aid-dependence mentality replacing the protection enjoyed by the former State enterprises which ware sheltered from market forces.

Part One

General competition policy

Chapter I

The contribution from socio-economic and political circles

§ 1 — European Parliament

1. Parliament devoted considerable time to competition matters in the course of 1990.

In its resolution on the Nineteenth Competition Report, [1] which it adopted on 24 January 1991, Parliament put forward suggestions and requests regarding the structure and content of the Competition Report itself, and commented on recent developments in the competition sphere and their consequences for the administration of competition policy.

At the end of the resolution Parliament asked the Commission to provide a written response to its proposals. The Commission sent Parliament its replies. [1]

Parliament noted the complexity of the issues involved in competition policy, and the challenges represented in particular by the unification of the Federal Republic of Germany and the implementation of the merger control Regulation.

In its reply the Commission said that it had been following the effect of German unification on competition in the Community very closely; and it welcomed the fresh scope opened up by the merger control Regulation, which completed the body of legislation allowing effective competition to be maintained in the Community.

Parliament also considered that Community policy on State aid should be tightened, and that there was a need to ensure the fullest possible transparency of aid granted by national and regional authorities.

The Commission shares Parliament's view that competition policy cannot be carried on in isolation and holds a central place in the completion of the single market and the process of strengthening industrial competitiveness. State aid policy is also an important factor in the establishment of greater economic cohesion in the Community.

Parliament stressed that the process of completing the single market gave ever greater significance to competition policy; a proper balance had to be achieved between

---

[1]   See the Annex to this Report.

competition policy and the Community's other policy objectives.

Parliament also delivered opinions on competition questions in air transport,[1,2] insurance,[3] and State aid to shipbuilding[4] and the steel industry.[5]

In the course of 1990 Members of Parliament submitted 154 written questions to the Commission on competition matters (162 in 1989); a further 61 questions were submitted for oral reply (54 in 1989).

§ 2 — Economic and Social Committee

2.   On 19 December the Economic and Social Committee, in plenary session, delivered its opinion on the Nineteenth Report on Competition Policy.[5] The Committee said its opinion was offered in a spirit of cooperation, and was intended among other things to support and stimulate the Commission in its conduct of competition policy. The Committee put forward generally favourable assessments of certain specific aspects of competition policy, and drew attention to:

(i)   the need for clarification of the grey area between the Community competition rules and national competition rules;

(ii)   the need to ensure that State aid was transparent and degressive;

(iii) the importance of comparing prices in different Member States, taking account of objective differences in the circumstances of different regions.

The Committee pointed to the need for closer collaboration between the Commission and the competition authorities in the Member States. It also thought that close contact with the anti-trust authorities of non-Community countries was always useful and indeed necessary.

The Commission greatly appreciates the support the Committee has given to its competition policy. It is aware of the concerns expressed in the report, and particularly the need to strengthen contact with the authorities of the Member States and of non-Community countries. It has already taken several steps in this direction, which are explained in more detail in other chapters of this Report.

---

[1]   Opinion adopted on 18 May 1990, OJ C 149, 18.6.1990.
[2]   Opinion adopted on 15 June 1990, OJ C 175, 16.7.1990.
[3]   Opinion adopted on 11 September 1990, OJ C 260, 15.10.1990.
[4]   Opinion adopted on 24 October 1990, OJ C 295, 26.11.1990.
[5]   See the Annex to this Report.

In 1990 the Economic and Social Committee also delivered opinions on air transport,[1,2] insurance,[3] merger control[4] and aid to shipbuilding.[5]

§ 3 — Advisory Committee on Restrictive Practices and Dominant Positions

3. During 1990 the Advisory Committee met 10 times to consider preliminary draft Commission decisions applying Articles 85 and 86 of the EEC Treaty in individual cases. It delivered a total of 16 opinions. It was consulted in four cases where the Commission envisaged sending the companies concerned an administrative letter clearing their agreements informally, following the publication of a notice under Article 19(3) of Regulation No 17. The Committee was also kept informed of progress in a number of important cases under investigation.

§ 4 — Conference of National Government Experts

4. In the course of 1990 three meetings of government competition experts were held at the invitation of the Commission. The first was the annual meeting of senior civil servants responsible for competition matters in the Member States, which took place on 5 July; it considered the role of domestic authorities and domestic courts in the application of Community competition law, and ways in which closer cooperation might be secured between the Commission departments and the competition authorities of the Member States.

This was followed by a meeting of government competition experts on 25, 26 and 27 September, which made a technical assessment of working papers drawn up by the Commission. These included a draft Commission notice on the application of Articles 85 and 86 of the EEC Treaty by the courts of the Member States, which is intended to encourage more intensive application of Community competition law. There was also a thorough discussion of two working papers on closer cooperation with national competition authorities.

Lastly, at a meeting held on 5 December, the Commission submitted the draft of an updated version of the 1962 notice on commercial agents.[6]

---

[1]   Opinion adopted on 28 February 1990, Bull. EC 3-90, point 1.1.26; OJ C 112, 7.5.1990.
[2]   Opinion adopted on 20 November 1990, Bull. EC 11-90.
[3]   Opinion adopted on 30 May 1990, Bull. EC 5-90, point 1.2.33; OJ C 182, 23.7.1990.
[4]   Additional opinion adopted on 5 July 1990.
[5]   Opinion adopted on 19 October 1990.
[6]   OJ 139, 24.12.1962.

§ 5 — Meeting of national experts on State aids

5.   In previous years the Commission has held on an *ad hoc* basis multilateral meetings with experts from Member States to discuss draft proposals in the field of State aids, often for policy frameworks. The aim of these meetings was to obtain the views of Member States which were then taken into account when the Commission decided on its policies. In order both to increase the transparency of application of State aid policy for Member States and to provide a forum for the exchange of views between the Commission and the Member States, the Commission has decided to hold multilateral meetings on an systematic basis, normally at least twice a year to discuss current policy proposals from the Commission or other points of importance in the field of State aids. During 1990 two subjects were discussed — aids for public enterprises and for rescue operations. [1] Meetings to discuss a number of proposals before they are adopted by the Commission are already envisaged during the course of 1991.

§ 6 — Advisory Committee on Concentrations

6.   After the merger control Regulation entered into force on 21 September, the Advisory Committee met twice to consider administrative and legislative questions arising out of the application of the Regulation.

---

[1]   See also point 169 *et seq.* of this Report.

Chapter II

International contacts

§ 1 — OECD

7.   The Committee on Competition Law and Policy met twice in 1990. At the first meeting, the Commission presented Committee members with the final version of the draft Regulation on merger control eventually adopted by the Council on 21 December 1989. The Committee also approved a summary report on competition policy and deregulation, whilst the various working parties continued their activities.

One of the matters dealt with by the working parties was the preparation of a study on the economic aspects of anti-dumping and a report on franchising.

8.   The Industry Committee completed the first stage of its work on identifying and quantifying aid to industry with the drawing-up of a summary report. It then started the second stage which consisted of updating data collected and calculating the net amount of aid granted.

9.   Following the proposal of the United States of America of June 1989 in the OECD Working Party No 6 on Shipbuilding for the introduction of the 'standstill, roll-back' principle in the respective policies of the OECD member countries, the Council authorized the Commission to participate in negotiations in the OECD for an international agreement on adherence to normal and fair conditions of competition in the commercial shipbuilding and ship-repair sectors in consultation with the Article 113 Committee.

In the Negotiating Directives it is stated that the Commission will ensure that the Agreement's provisions provide complete transparency with regard to the existing obstacles, a real balance of obligations for the different parties to the Agreement and prevent the introduction of new obstacles. In particular, the Commission should ensure that private practices which constitute barriers to normal conditions of competition, e.g. unfair pricing, fall within the scope of the agreements and that there is an appropriate instrument for detecting and remedying such practices. The Commission will have to secure a balanced phasing-out period as regards the subsidies for the industry. ·

The OECD Working Party No 6 on Shipbuilding met six times in 1990. The parties in this group are Japan, South Korea, the United States of America, the Community, Finland, Norway and Sweden. Yugoslavia and Canada have observer status in this group. A final agreement between the different parties is not yet in sight, although progress has been made in the negotiations on the outline of the Agreement.

§ 2 — Unctad

10.   The ninth session of the Intergovernmental Group of Experts on Restrictive Business Practices was held from 23 to 27 April 1990. The session was essentially devoted to preparing for the United Nations Conference which took place in Geneva from 26 November to 7 December 1990.

Work concentrated on a review of the set of multilaterally agreed principles and rules for the control of restrictive business practices.

11.   The Conference, in which the Commission took part for the first time on the same basis as Member States (but without voting rights), ended with the adoption of a Resolution on strengthening the implementation of the 'set of principles'. The strengthening would be achieved principally by increasing consultations within the Intergovernmental Group of Experts and expanding the technical assistance offered by members of the Group in response to the many requests addressed to the Unctad Secretariat by Group 77 countries and in general by all countries anxious to strengthen the governing role of the market in their economies.

It was agreed in principle to hold another conference to review the 'set of principles' in 1995.

It is interesting to note that the Commission was asked, in connection with the abovementioned technical assistance, to take part in training projects organized in Nairobi, Kenya, by the OECD, and in Lima, Peru, by the *Deutsche Stiftung für Internationale Entwicklung* on behalf of the Andean Pact countries.

§ 3 — GATT — Uruguay Round

12.   The negotiations which continued throughout 1990 confirmed that their successful conclusion was crucial if world trade and commercial transactions in goods and services were to avoid being subjected to unfair and distorted competition.

The Commission played an active part in the negotiations, formulating proposals aimed at strengthening international competition, in particular as regards trade-related investment measures (TRIMs), trade-related aspects of intellectual property rights (TRIPs), services, safeguards, subsidies and countervailing measures.

The Community's resolve to implement a Community competition policy is one of the reasons which explains its determination to achieve an agreement favouring the liberalization of international trade as soon as possible, despite the suspension of negotiations at the end of the ministerial conference held in Brussels in December 1990.

§ 4 — European economic area

13.   The launching, on 20 June 1990, of negotiations with the EFTA countries on the creation of a European economic area rapidly brought to light the need for comparable and equivalent conditions of competition within the area.

14.   As a result, preparatory work was undertaken by experts to identify the content of established Community practices, as regards both the competition rules applicable to enterprises and State aid schemes, as well as national monopolies of a commercial nature.

15.   As a result of further work by Negotiating Group No I, the Community concluded that in order to maintain equivalent competition conditions within the area, the EFTA should create a 'second pillar' with equivalent powers to those exercised by the Commission in regard to competition.[1]

The EFTA countries are therefore considering the possibility of setting up a second pillar as requested by the Community. Two operating conditions should be fulfilled: the allocation of individual cases should be based on objective criteria agreed by the contracting parties, and all decisions adopted by one of the two pillars should apply to the entire area, unless they are questioned by the competent monitoring or judicial body. Discussions in this vein are continuing, the Community hoping that objective allocation criteria for individual cases will strengthen legal certainty for operators, and that the structure responsible for applying the competition rules within EFTA will have the same safeguards as the Commission.

The exchanges of views also revealed the need for mutual information and cooperation to ensure that the system runs smoothly once the two analogous monitoring structures have been set up. This aspect, which is not limited just to competition rules, is being examined in depth by Negotiating Group No V.

---

[1]   Meeting of the high-level Negotiating Group on 20 and 21 September 1990.

§ 5 — Cooperation between the Commission and the anti-trust authorities of non-member countries

16.   The annual meeting between the Japanese Fair Trade Commission and the Directorate-General for Competition (DG IV) took place in Brussels in October. In particular, the talks gave the Japanese authorities the opportunity to discuss their efforts to make their distribution rules more transparent and to seek the Commission's opinion of their draft guidelines concerning exclusive import agents. At the request of the Japanese officials, the DG IV representatives described the Commission's policy on fines and explained in detail the procedures provided for in the Regulation on merger control.

17.   The annual bilateral talks with the Department of Justice and the Federal Trade Commission of the United States were held in Washington in November. In addition to the usual exchange of information that traditionally takes place, exploratory talks were started on the possibility of concluding an administrative agreement on bilateral cooperation, as proposed by Sir Leon Brittan in his speeches given in February 1990 in Cambridge and to the New York Chamber of Commerce.

This objective, which accords with the spirit of the 1986 OECD Council Recommendation on cooperation in the field of restrictive business practices affecting international trade, would provide a more detailed framework for relations between the Community anti-trust authorities and those of the United States, similar to those the latter has already established with Canada, Austria and the Federal Republic of Germany.

The adoption of the Regulation on merger control in the Community increases the need for such cooperation, inasmuch as a number of transactions with a Community dimension are scrutinized twice, once on each side of the Atlantic. It was therefore agreed that preparatory work would start immediately on the feasibility of such a project, with due regard for existing constraints such as confidentiality and decision-making times.

18.   A meeting in Ottawa with the Canadian anti-trust authorities (Bureau de la politique de concurrence) allowed participants to compare their respective approaches to merger control. The Canadian authorities asked the Commission for its views on the draft Merger Enforcement Guidelines drawn up in November 1990.

Chapter III

Small and medium-sized enterprises

19. The Commission believes that the competitiveness of small and medium-sized enterprises may be hindered, both on their own markets and upstream and downstream, where such markets either become highly concentrated or are impeded by a large number of restrictive agreements, or again are unbalanced by abnormally high levels of State aid. As regards aids for small and medium-sized enterprises, the Commission maintained its generally favourable attitude.[1] Thus a positive view is usually taken of aids to SMEs, especially those which improve their competitiveness. The Commission also continued to take account of the impact on SMEs of its decisions relating to competition.

As part of this favourable attitude the Commission decided to modify its decision of 19 December 1984 regarding the assessment of aids of minor importance which are aimed primarily at SMEs.[1] The main change involves increasing the size of company eligible for such aid.

In principle, the Commission will not object to aid schemes of minor importance notified pursuant to Article 93(3) of the EEC Treaty and will approve such schemes by an accelerated procedure. The Commission takes this favourable attitude because of the lesser impact of these schemes of minor importance on intra-Community trade and competition.

Schemes of minor importance are now defined as those where the beneficiary enterprise does not employ more than 150 people, has an annual turnover of not more than ECU 15 million, and where the aid intensity does not exceed 7.5%, or when the total volume of aid a beneficiary may receive is not more than ECU 200 000, or when the aid is designed to lead to job creation and it amounts to not more than ECU 3 000 per job created. The Commission will also approve under the same accelerated procedure prolongations or budget increases of less than 20% of schemes in operation and previously approved by the Commission.

All aids to exports in intra-Community trade or operating aids are excluded from the accelerated procedure, as are aids to certain sensitive sectors, which must be notified in the normal way.

---

[1]   OJ C 40, 20.2.1990.

In 1990, the Commission approved 36 schemes under the accelerated procedure for aids of minor importance.

In addition, it approved eight aid schemes designed to assist, above all, small and medium-sized enterprises, in specific activities. Among these, there were projects for energy saving and exploitation of renewable energies, research and development, encouragement for enterprises to cooperate, and for anti-pollution and tourist infrastructure.

Part Two

Competition policy towards enterprises

Chapter I

Main developments in Community policy

§ 1 — Merger control

20.   The year saw the new Regulation[1] on the control of concentrations between undertakings[2] enter into force on 21 September 1990 and start to be implemented. The Commission regards the Regulation as a vital additional instrument made available to it by the Council in order to ensure a system of undistorted competition in the Community. The Regulation will contribute to the construction and completion of the internal market. The assessment criteria set out in Article 2 indicate clearly that merger control is to be based on the principle of protecting free competition. However, assessment of the impact of a merger takes account of a series of other specified factors that may guide the Commission in its appraisal. So as to provide a 'one-stop shop' and give effect to the principle of the division of jurisdiction between the Commission and the Member States that is at the heart of the Regulation, the Commission will, with the Member States, ensure strict application of exceptions to the exclusive competence conferred on the Commission in the case of mergers above the thresholds laid down in Article 1 of the Regulation.

The Commission's exclusive competence is a fundamental principle clearly established from the outset of proceedings, but these will be carried out in close and constant liaison with the competent national authorities. [3]

Legislative measures

21.   The Council Regulation was followed up by legislative and interpretative implementing instruments. The guidelines required for their implementation were adopted

---

[1]   Council Regulation (EEC) No 4064/89 of 21 December 1989, OJ L 395, 30.12.1989; corrigendum OJ L 257, 21.9.1990.
[2]   Nineteenth Competition Report, points 14 to 16.
[3]   See Article 19(2) of Regulation No 4064/89.

following wide-ranging consultations of the various sectors concerned. The Commission adopted them on 25 July 1990 after the Advisory Committee on Mergers had helped to finalize them.

22.   Commission Regulation (EEC) No 2367/90 of 25 July 1990 on notifications, time-limits and hearings[1] covers the various aspects of the merger control procedure. Its various provisions are largely modelled on the terms and formulation of the other Commission Regulations implementing the basic Council Regulation setting out the competition rules (Regulation No 17). However, the novelty of the merger control procedure has meant that a number of new rules have had to be introduced.

23.   In the case of notifications, Regulation No 2367/90 provides for the compulsory use of 'form CO'. This sets out all the information which firms must provide to the Commission to enable it to examine each case properly and to prepare the decisions to be adopted under Regulation No 4064/89. Following the consultation process, when the Regulation was being drafted, a balance was established between, on the one hand, the need for the Commission to have full information available from the start of a case and, on the other, the need to avoid imposing a heavy administrative burden on firms.

In replying to the questions in the form, particularly in the case of mergers affecting a large number of firms and markets, firms must provide the Commission with a relatively large amount of information. Nevertheless, a single notification form comprising from the outset all the information requested was preferred to a 'two-stage approach'.

The aim is to enable the Commission, from the first stage of the procedure, to assess whether a merger involves serious doubts as to its compatibility with the common market and thus to ensure that decisions to initiate proceedings are not taken merely in order to allow a more detailed examination, due to a lack of initial information. This would have run counter to the rapid procedures provided for in Regulation No 4064/89. At any rate, the Commission intends to review the notification form in the light of experience gained during the first year of its implementation and, if necessary, to make any amendments and relaxations required after a further round of consultations.

Nevertheless, so as to reduce some of the inconvenience involved in the wide-ranging information requirement and provide some flexibility, the implementing Regulation allows firms to provide additional information in respect of incomplete notifications *a posteriori* and the Commission to dispense the notifying parties from the obligation to provide any information required by form CO which it does not consider necessary for the examination of the case (Article 4(3)). This dispensation option has already proved of considerable practical importance.[2]

---

[1]   OJ L 219, 14.8.1990.
[2]   See point 147 *et seq.* of this Report.

Furthermore, so as to allow notifying firms to retain the legal advantages involved in a notification, the implementing Regulation provides for the possibility of converting a notification submitted under the merger control regime into a notification under Regulation No 17 (Article 5), where it emerges that the operation notified does not constitute a concentration within the meaning of Article 3 of Regulation No 4064/89, but is an operation to be assessed under Articles 85 and 86 of the EEC Treaty. In such an eventuality, the Commission will endeavour to respond within the shortest possible time in examining under Articles 85 and 86 cases initially notified as mergers. One of the possible arrangements, where such an arrangement is legally feasible, is to send the notifying firms, within shorter time-limits than at present, a comfort letter stating that the Commission has no reasons to oppose the operation concerned in so far as it comes under Articles 85 and 86 of the EEC Treaty.[1]

24.   So as to provide greater legal certainty, the implementing Regulation also contains detailed provisions allowing both firms and the Commission to calculate the time-limits laid down in Article 10 of Regulation No 4064/89. The formulation of the provisions is essentially modelled on Council Regulation (EEC, Euratom) No 1182/71 of 3 June 1971 determining the rules applicable to periods, dates and time-limits.[2]

25.   Lastly, the implementing Regulation lays down the arrangements for the hearing of the notifying parties and of third parties, as provided for in Article 18 of Regulation No 4064/89. It gives the parties in particular the option of making known their views immediately after provisional decisions and prior to final decisions concerning the compatibility of merger operations. In this same area of the rights of the defence, the basic Regulation explicitly gave firms the right of access to the file. It thus continued the practice which the Commission has been following in proceedings under Article 85 and 86 of the EEC Treaty.[3]

In addition to the implementing Regulation and the notification form, the Commission has adopted a number of other implementing measures, including two notices on the interpretation of specific concepts contained in the basic Regulation, namely:

(i) the definition of mergers covered by Regulation No 4064/89 and of situations involving coordination which continue to be subject to Articles 85 and 86 of the EEC Treaty (Article 3(2) of Regulation No 4064/89);[4]

(ii) the concept of restrictions ancillary to a merger, which are subject to the same rules as the merger itself under the Regulation (Article 8(2)).[5]

---

[1]   This was done in the Renault/Volvo case in respect of the operation relating to cars.
[2]   OJ L 124, 8.6.1971.
[3]   Eleventh Competition Report, points 22 and 25.
[4]   Commission notice regarding concentrative and cooperative operations, OJ C 203, 14.8.1990.
[5]   Commission notice regarding restrictions ancillary to concentrations, OJ C 203, 14.8.1990.

The two notices set out the main considerations determining the Commission's views on whether or not notified operations come under the Regulation and under what conditions restrictions associated with a merger are to be considered ancillary.

The variety and complexity of the operations or restrictions concerned are such that the principles laid down cannot provide a definitive answer for all the situations which may arise in practice. However, they can provide useful guidelines for firms and their legal advisers in assessing the fundamental concepts underlying the basic Regulation.

The actual application of the basic guidelines set out in the notices will essentially come into play as the Commission develops its corpus of decisions, subject to review by the Court of Justice and the Court of First Instance.

Administrative measures

26.   So as to enable the Commission to fulfil its new responsibilities deriving from the introduction of merger control for Community-scale mergers, a Merger Task Force was set up within the Directorate-General for Competition. The Merger Task Force is responsible for examining notifications and drawing up the decisions to be adopted by the Commission under Regulation No 4064/89 and to provide all information and advice on the applicability of the provisions of the Regulation to mergers before notification. The Task Force has three operating units and comprises 45 officials, including 25 case-handlers — half of these, in accordance with the agreement reached when the Regulation was adopted by the Council, being officials seconded from the national authorities.

The allocation of human resources to the Task Force and its operating methods were determined in such a way as to provide sufficient flexibility in meeting the expected workload.

So as to be able to meet the strict deadlines laid down under the new rules, the Commission, acting under an internal decision, authorized the Commission Member having special responsibility for competition to take certain decisions and certain procedural measures provided for in Council Regulation No 4064/89 and the implementing Commission Regulation No 2367/90. However, final decisions on the compatibility or incompatibility of mergers under Article 8 of Regulation No 4064/89 must be taken by the full Commission.

In addition, various appropriate administrative measures have been taken to ensure that information is kept confidential and that the business secrets of firms involved in merger proceedings are not divulged.

Lastly, an adviser to the Director-General for Competition was appointed. He is responsible not only for organizing and chairing merger hearings, but also for ensuring close and constant liaison with the national authorities. In addition, he looks after the security aspects of confidentiality and business secrecy.

The first cases of implementation of the Regulation

27.   By 31 December 1990, the Commission had received 12 notifications under Article 4(1) of Regulation No 4064/89.

It adopted one decision on the non-applicability of the Regulation and five decisions not opposing mergers and declaring them compatible with the common market pursuant to Article 6(1)(b). In all these cases,[1] the Commission found that the operations concerned, although falling within the scope of the Regulation,[2] did not raise serious doubts as to their compatibility with the common market.

28.   In addition, some 50 informal contacts prior to notification took place. Where the applicability of the Regulation is obvious, such consultations essentially involve helping the firms and their advisers to determine the necessary content of the notification, bearing in mind the possibility of dispensing with certain information in form CO in the light of the foreseeable impact of the merger on competition.

In a number of cases, it emerged from such consultations that the operations planned did not reach the thresholds set in the Regulation or did not constitute a concentration within the meaning of Article 3. In most of the other cases, notifications are already being drawn up or will probably be drawn up during the first few months of 1991, depending on how the merger negotiations between the parties go. A rough extrapolation of the number of cases examined during these first three months of implementation of the Regulation suggests that the Commission's current forecast of around 60 notifications a year will be borne out by the facts.

29.   Informal preliminary contracts, such as the requests for information received by the Task Force, point to three main types of question raised by the Regulation. The Commission will endeavour to clarify them through the decisions it adopts.

The three main types of question are:

(i)   the concentrative or cooperative nature of joint ventures;

(ii)   the technical procedure for calculating turnover;

---

[1]   See point 147 *et seq.* of this Report.
[2]   In the Renault/Volvo case, this finding was restricted to the truck and bus sector. In the Arjomari/Wiggins Teape case, it emerged that the concentration did not have a Community dimension, since the threshold set in Article 1(2)(a) was not reached: it was not sufficiently established that the main shareholder of one of the parties to the concentration had the power referred to in the third indent of Article 5(4)(b) such that its turnover had not to be taken into account.

(iii) the definition of the relevant geographical market.

30.   As far as the internal procedures adopted by the Commission in order to comply with the strict deadlines to be observed in implementing the Regulation are concerned, experience so far — even if limited to the initial stage of proceedings — shows that they satisfactorily meet the requirements set by the Regulation.

31.   The Decisions adopted so far have already provided the Commission with an opportunity to give a ruling on certain questions of principle. These include:

(a) the concentrative nature of an operation in the light of the existence of a single economic management, the level of financial holdings exchanged and the degree to which functions are integrated (Renault/Volvo);

(b) in calculating the turnover of an insurance company, the taking into account, in addition to the value of gross premiums, of the turnover achieved by legally separate real estate subsidiaries (AG/Amev);

(c) the concentrative nature of the acquisition of exclusive control in an undertaking previously placed under joint control, since it changes the nature and intensity of the influence which the acquiring party enjoys (ICI/Tioxide);

(d) the condition attaching to the existence of the power to appoint more than half of the members of the board or other bodies of an undertaking within the meaning of the third indent of Article 5(4)(b), which is established only where the main shareholder has been able to make such appointments by exercising more than half the voting rights present or represented at the last general meeting of shareholders (Arjomari/Wiggins Teape);

(e) as regards the relevant markets in retail distribution, the specific character of supermarkets and mini-supermarkets in relation to small specialized shops, and the taking into account in geographical terms of a set of local markets (Promodes/Dirsa);

(f) in connection with a case involving the marketing of agricultural products, the importance of whether or not there are barriers to entry in defining the relevant geographical market and in determining the significance of the market shares of undertakings involved in a merger (Cargill/Unilever).

32.   Although Regulation No 4064/89 does not provide for decisions adopted pursuant to Article 6 to be made public in any other way than through notification to the undertakings concerned and to the competent authorities of the Member States, the Commission has, from the outset, so as to ensure transparency, adopted the practice of sending copies on request to third parties who can show that they have a sufficient interest. At the request of the undertakings concerned, it removes from such copies any information which it deems to be business secrets.

§ 2 — German unification

33.   The unification of the Federal Republic of Germany has been of particular importance for Community competition policy. Two German States having totally different economic systems have been united: on the one hand, a decentralized market economy based essentially on private enterprise and, on the other, a centralized planned economy under State control.

The objective of Community competition policy was to underpin the difficult transition to a market economy. The main concern was the removal of the existing monopolistic structures so that the necessary conditions for the development of competitive capacity could be created. At the same time, the aim was to prevent powerful firms in the industrialized countries, particularly those in the neighbouring part of the Federal Republic of Germany, from gaining rapid hold of former State undertakings and thereby establishing themselves in an advantageous position that would be difficult to catch up with. There was a danger of this happening particularly in service sectors requiring a strong local presence (distributive trades, banking and insurance), transport and energy supplies.

The Commission took action on several fronts; from the start of the year, it entered into close cooperation with the Federal Government and the German anti-trust authorities. After the parliamentary elections in March, this cooperation was extended to include the Democratic Government of East Germany and the *Treuhandanstalt*, the State holding company set up to administer former public undertakings.

In this connection, agreement was reached on the basis of the abovementioned objectives. The German authorities accepted the Commission's suggestion that the sale of firms being privatized should be made public, so as to facilitate market access for interested parties from other European countries. In addition, the Commission used its powers of investigation in appropriate cases. These were based on a number of complaints from non-German competitors fearing that they would be placed at a disadvantage compared with West German firms.

Application of the competition rules, particularly Articles 85 and 86 and Article 37 of the EEC Treaty

34.   The three stages of the German unification process (the opening up of frontiers and the formation of a legitimate democratic government, the creation of economic and monetary union on 1 July 1990 and the achievement of unification on 3 October 1990) defined the legal framework within which the Community could act. Only the final stage brought the Community competition rules fully into force in the former German Democratic Republic. Before that date, the Commission could act only if there were substantial effects on competition and trade within the Community. The Commission took the view that any such impact was more probable after economic and monetary union than before.

The Commission also required the rapid dismantling of State monopolies of a commercial character. Although it was initially planned to allow a transitional period for certain import monopolies to enable the German Democratic Republic economy to adjust, the elimination of all State monopolies of a commercial character had already been achieved before official unification.

Major individual cases

Allianz/Staatliche Versicherung der DDR

35.   Allianz's majority shareholding in the former East German insurance monopoly, which it acquired before 1 July 1990, raised the question of whether a possible dominant position by Allianz on the West German market had been reinforced. The parallel investigation carried out by the Commission and the *Bundeskartellamt* did not provide sufficient evidence of an abuse of a dominant position on the market. Furthermore, it is to be expected that the measures taken to facilitate market entry for Allianz's competitors and the special rights granted to policyholders insured under the former German Democratic Republic monopoly to terminate their policies will substantially help to improve business opportunities for Allianz's national and foreign competitors.

Deutsche Bank/Deutsche Kreditbank

36.   A similar situation arose with the Deutsche Bank's intended purchase of a majority shareholding in the Deutsche Kreditbank. The Deutsche Kreditbank was originally the only credit institution having the power to grant loans to industry. This restriction was lifted by the government of the German Democratic Republic during the first half of the year. Furthermore, the Deutsche Bank stood back to allow other competitors to acquire a considerable part of the existing subsidiaries of the Deutsche Kreditbank. Subsequently, the subsidiaries were taken over by competitors of the Deutsche Bank, thus enabling them to enter more easily on to the market within the former German Democratic Republic.

Verbundnetz Gas

37.   Verbundnetz Gas is the owner of gas pipelines situated within the territory of the former German Democratic Republic. During the first half of 1990, Ruhrgas and its associate company VEB Erdöl und Erdgas acquired shareholdings of 35% and 10% respectively. Having been informed that a number of Ruhrgas's competitors who had been interested in partial acquisition or construction of gas pipelines within the territory of the former German Democratic Republic had been refused such possibilities, the Commission began a formal investigation in July 1990 based on the presumption of the creation of a dominant position in the former Federal Republic of Germany. While the investigation was being carried out, the *Treuhandanstalt* as owner of Verbundnetz Gas began negotiations with interested Community companies and with non-Community countries. The objective of the negotiations was to allow other gas producers and transport undertakings to acquire holdings in Verbundnetz Gas and to use its gas pipelines for the transport of their own gas.

Deutsche Lufthansa/Interflug

38.   The Commission monitored the planned acquisition of a minority shareholding by Deutsche Lufthansa in Interflug in order to ensure that it did not lead to the creation or reinforcement of dominant positions in transport into and out of German territory. The Commission also wished to ensure that facilities which are essential to all airport users (air-traffic control, ground handling) were not controlled by a company in a dominant position.

Application of the competition rules and merger control after 3 October 1990

39.   Since 3 October 1990, the competition rules and, in particular, Articles 85 and 86 of the EEC Treaty have been fully applicable in the territory of the former German Democratic Republic. Agreements already in force which are incompatible with Article 85(1) may be brought into line with Community law within three months of that date. If firms wish to claim exemption for existing agreements under Article 85(3), they must submit an appropriate notification to the Commission within six months of the above-mentioned date.

40.   Council Regulation No 4064/89 of 21 December 1989 on the control of concentrations has applied without restriction since 3 October 1990 in the territory of the former German Democratic Republic.

§ 3 — Application of the block exemption Regulations

41.   In the present economic context, with growing interpenetration of national markets and closer contacts between firms in the run up to the completion of the internal market in 1992, the number of agreements liable to be caught by the ban laid down in Article 85 of the EEC Treaty has been increasing steadily. This situation has highlighted the need to be able to provide rapid exemption for agreements which are acceptable from a competition policy point of view.

With this in mind, the Commission has in recent years adopted eight block exemption Regulations. The objectives pursued were, firstly, to provide firms with legal certainty while at the same time avoiding the burdens and delays inherent in any individual notification and, secondly, to allow the Commission to concentrate on cases involving more serious restrictions of competition.

It is probably too early to say at present whether these objectives have been fully achieved, especially since there have so far been few instances in which the Court or the Commission have had to interpret the Regulations. Nevertheless, if practical experience were to reveal particular difficulties resulting from overdetailed provisions or indeed from the overlapping of the scope of application of various Regulations in the case of particularly complex agreements, the Commission, which has completed most of its legislative programme, could in future look at ways of adjusting the Regulations.

However, contacts with firms and their advisers indicate already that the parties concerned generally bring their agreements into line with the requirements laid down in the Regulation. This would explain the fairly small number of notifications of agreements of the type covered by the Regulations, either on the basis of Regulation No 17 or through use of the opposition procedure, which is provided for in most of the Regulations.

Exclusive distribution agreements

42.   As in previous years, during the period covered by the Report, the Commission examined exclusive distribution and exclusive purchasing agreements falling within the scope of Regulations (EEC) Nos 1983/83 and 1984/83.[1]

In some cases, the Commission asked the parties to amend some of the provisions in their agreements so as to bring them into line with the conditions laid down in the two Regulations.

---

[1]   OJ L 173, 30.6.1983.

The Commission informed Community agricultural machinery manufacturers that their products were not covered by the exemption of exclusive and selective distribution arrangements granted under Regulation 123/85[1] to manufacturers of motor vehicles intended for use on public roads and that they had no justification for restricting imports or exports between Member States. Agreements restricting the right of distributors to sell to any customer anywhere in the common market are, in many cases, prohibited under Article 85(1) of the EEC Treaty. In view of the repeated restrictions of competition which have been found to exist in the Community in the case of agricultural machinery, the Commission thought it necessary to take action in order to ensure freedom of movement within the internal market. The Commission asked the manufacturers to adjust their agreements accordingly.

Specialization and research and development

43.   In 1990, the Commission received two notifications asking for the opposition procedure to be applied under Regulation (EEC) No 417/85[2] in respect of specialization agreements between firms whose combined turnover exceeds ECU 500 million. In one of the cases, the Commission did not oppose the agreement; in the other, the six-month period has not yet ended, and the case is still being examined.

44.   Four notifications were received asking for the opposition procedure to be applied under Regulation (EEC) No 418/85[2] in respect of research and development agreements. In one of the cases, the Regulation cannot be applied, since the agreement covers the joint marketing of products; it is intended to terminate proceedings by sending a comfort letter. In another case, the opposition procedure could not properly be requested since the agreement contained clauses preventing the application of the block exemption (blacklisted clauses). At the Commission's request, the parties amended their agreement as follows: the duration of the non-competition clauses was reduced to the period in which the research and development programme was being carried out, and the restrictions imposed on each of the parties regarding the use of the know-how outside the area covered by the research and development programme were confined to the know-how communicated by the other party. In a third case, concerning the notification of a research and development agreement between 13 companies under the RACE programme, the Commission did not oppose exemption since there were no major restrictions of competition. In the fourth case, Quantel International (Continuum)/Quantel SA, the Commission found that Regulation No 418/85 was not applicable to agreements which, in particular, prevented one of the parties from having access to the Community market for an indefinite period. The parties lodged an initial appeal

---

[1]   OJ L 15, 18.1.1985.
[2]   OJ L 53, 22.2.1985.

(Case T-29/90) to the Court of First Instance of the European Communities against the letter in which the Commission informed them that their agreements did not qualify for exemption under the Regulation. A second appeal (Case T-36/90) was then lodged against a letter confirming the first letter and announcing the initiation of proceedings under Article 85(1) of the EEC Treaty. In the second case, the Commission adopted a position essentially identical to its position in the first case, arguing that the appeal was inadmissible since it was directed against an act that was merely preparatory to a final decision and that it was in any case unfounded.

Patent and know-how licensing

45.   In 1990, the Commission continued to examine notifications of know-how agreements and mixed know-how and patent licensing agreements coming under the provisions of Regulation (EEC) No 556/89 on know-how agreements [1] or Regulation (EEC) No 2349/84 on patent licensing agreements. [2] It sent some 30 letters to the firms concerned asking them to bring their agreements into line with the conditions laid down in the two Regulations; in most instances, the Commission was able to terminate examination of the case by sending a comfort letter.

46.   No notification requesting the opposition procedure provided for in Article 4 of Regulations Nos 556/89 and 2349/84 was received by the Commission in 1990.

47.   During the period covered by the previous Report, the Commission was unable to accept a request for the application of the opposition procedure under Article 4 of Regulation No 2349/84, since the information provided by the parties in their notification was incomplete. Following contacts with the parties, the Commission was able to grant individual exemption to the agreement by means of a comfort letter. Another request concerned the provisions of Article 4(2) of Regulation No 556/89 in respect of the second source of supply. The Commission pointed out that such a clause related to the situation of a customer wishing to have a second source of supply for the same products and not, as in this instance, for competing products manufactured by other processes. Accordingly, the quantitative and customer restrictions resulting from the agreement could not be covered by the opposition procedure; the notification is being examined on an individual basis.

The other notifications submitted in 1989 under the opposition procedure and still to be examined were dealt with on an individual basis; in most of the cases, since the parties had amended their agreements, proceedings were terminated by the sending of a comfort letter.

---

[1]   OJ L 61, 4.3.1989.
[2]   OJ L 219, 16.8.1984.

Franchise agreements

48. In 1990, the Commission received four notifications requesting the opposition procedure under Article 6 of Regulation (EEC) No 4087/88 on franchise agreements. [1]

In two cases, the Commission found that the agreements did not significantly affect competition in the common market and trade between Member States. The opposition procedure was therefore not applicable, since the agreements were not in accordance with Article 85(1) of the EEC Treaty.

In the other two cases, the Commission ruled that the opposition procedure could not be applied, notably because the agreements contained the following blacklisted clauses: the requirement that the franchisee accept the prices set by the franchiser, and the requirement that the franchisee, in providing services, use only products manufactured or services provided by the franchiser or by third parties designated by him, where, for reasons other than the protection of his industrial and intellectual property rights or maintaining the identity and reputation of the franchised network, the franchiser refused to designate as producers or suppliers third parties proposed by the franchisee. These cases are at present being examined on an individual basis.

The Commission was also able to terminate examination of four of the five notifications received in 1989 after the parties had brought their agreements into line with the conditions laid down for block exemption. The fifth notification is still under examination.

Motor vehicle distribution

49. In line with its intention to monitor prices in the motor vehicle sector, [2] the Commission sent a request for information to 16 motor vehicle manufacturers and has received a large number of replies. The purpose of these investigations is to check whether the exemption granted in respect of the ban imposed on selected distributors from selling new vehicles to non-authorized resellers should — in accordance with Article 10 of Regulation No 123/85 [3] — be withdrawn because of large-scale price differentials between Member States.

The main question is whether the price differentials have been maintained over long periods in such a way as to exceed the 12 or 18% margins provided for in the 1985 notice [4] annexed to the Regulation. The question is also whether motor vehicle distribution

---

[1] OJ L 359, 28.12.1988.
[2] Nineteenth Competition Report, point 21.
[3] OJ L 15, 18.1.1985.
[4] OJ C 17, 18.1.1985.

agreements and the restrictions of competition which they may contain must be held mainly responsible for the situation.[1]

The manufacturers argue that prices charged to the final consumer, which are recommended by the manufacturers in each Member State, cannot be compared without certain adjustments being made. Some manufacturers state that vehicles must be manufactured with different engines or different specifications since there is not yet any Community system of type approval. They also put forward a series of other arguments to justify price differentials, including differences in taxation on purchase or on registration, the control of prices in one of the Member States and the differing degrees to which national markets are open to imports from non-Community countries.

The Commission has on a number of occasions pointed out that recommended retail prices exclusive of VAT in the various Member States must as far as possible be kept in line with the ranges specified in its notice and that product differences must be limited to real market requirements.

50.   On 26 March 1990, the Commission ordered interim measures against the PSA group so as to allow the motor vehicle purchasing intermediary Ecosystem to maintain its volume of purchases from Peugeot's Belgian and Luxembourg networks. PSA had instructed its network to stop accepting orders placed through Ecosystem. Ecosystem is a service-sector company which acts as an agent within the meaning of Regulation No 123/85 for its French customers so as to assist them in the purchase of their vehicle in other countries in which they can obtain better terms than in France.

Following a complaint from Ecosystem, the case is currently under examination, and it was to ensure that the complainant did not suffer serious and irreversible damage as a result of a boycott that the Commission decided to allow interim measures enabling Ecosystem to continue to import Peugeot cars on behalf of French consumers, up to a limit of 1 200 each year, whereas it would otherwise have had to stop such imports completely. The interim measures, which are without prejudice to the final outcome of the case, will continue until examination of the substance of the case has been completed. The Court of First Instance rejected PSA's appeal that the interim measures ordered by the Commission be suspended.

51.   After having sent the company Automec a statement of preliminary observations,[2] followed by a letter based on Article 6 of Regulation No 99/63, the Commission rejected by decision the Italian distributor's complaint that BMW Italia had committed an infringement. The Commission pointed out in its decision that, in assessing the information in its possession within the meaning of Article 6 of Regulation No 99/63, it had

---

[1]   Answer given by the Commission to the Written Question by Sir James Scott-Hopkins, Member of the European Parliament (not yet published).
[2]   See judgment of the Court of First Instance of 10.7.1990 (Case T-64/89), point 153 et seq. of this Report.

discretionary power to attach degrees of priority to the cases brought to its attention. The only duty incumbent upon it under Community law was to examine the facts and arguments put forward by the parties, to adopt a formal position on a complaint and possibly to pursue the case in the Community interest. The Commission took the view that, in the case in question, the Community interest did not justify action on its part, especially since the facts had already been brought before the national court.

Transport

52.   During the period covered by the Report, the Commission received nine requests for application of the opposition procedures provided for in the Council regulations applicable to transport, namely four relating to air transport (Regulation No 3975/87),[1] four relating to sea transport (Regulation No 4056/86)[2] and one relating to land transport (Regulation No 1017/68).[3] In one of the cases, the Commission notified the parties that there were serious doubts as to the applicability of Article 85(3) of the EEC Treaty. The Commission also raised objections in one case which had been the subject of two requests[4] during the previous year.

The Commission adopted three new block exemption Regulations in the field of air transport[5] and sent the Council a proposal for a Regulation authorizing it (the Commission) to adopt a block exemption in the sea transport sector.[6]

---

[1]   OJ L 374, 31.12.1987.
[2]   OJ L 378, 31.12.1986.
[3]   OJ L 175, 23.7.1968.
[4]   The requests were not included in the last Report.
[5]   See point 69 *et seq.* of this Report.
[6]   See point 78 *et seq.* of this Report.

§ 4 — Underpinning the internal market

53.   The Commission has also been intensifying its activities in areas where a more rigorous application of the rules of competition will most facilitate the breakdown of barriers to intra-Community trade and competition. Its policy therefore underpins the moves towards completing the internal market. Of particular importance are the Commission's efforts in the field of telecommunications, postal services, energy, transport, assurance, and the audiovisual sector. The major developments in these fields as well as for software and the beer market are described below.

Whilst many barriers to intra-Community trade and competition are created by companies themselves, and competition policy will as in the past continue to tackle these problems, it is felt that at the present stage of economic integration in the Community the barriers are greatest in markets currently subject to State regulation. Unless the rules of competition are effectively applied in the area of regulated markets there will be no real internal market for those products which account for an increasingly large share of national income. Furthermore the potential gains to consumers from introducing more competition into these regulated sectors is greater than in sectors where workable competition already exists.

For various public policy goals, such as ensuring security of supply or ensuring the provision of a basic service to the whole population, governments in most Member States have intervened to regulate the markets for certain products, notably utilities (energy and water), telecommunications and broadcasting. This desire for the provision of public services often led to the establishment of public undertakings in many cases with statutory monopoly protection. Such a public undertaking was also seen by governments as the best way to regulate sectors where, because of the costs of duplicating an expensive distribution network (e.g. cables for telephones and electricity), it seems that the service in question could only be provided economically by one company which owned the network and which would therefore have a 'natural' monopoly.

The Commission's aim is to find a solution that is the least restrictive of competition whilst at the same time not prejudicing the operation of services of general economic interest (in the sense of Article 90(2) of the EEC Treaty). An examination will have to be carried out to see if a statutory monopoly with certain exclusive rights is the only feasible way to provide certain key or reserved services or if a less restrictive way is possible. Furthermore the definition of these reserved services where a statutory monopoly may be permitted will have to be drawn as tightly as is possible and competition will be introduced for non-reserved services. In addition, in cases where it is uneconomic to duplicate the network it may be possible to allow providers of competing services to use the network, thereby opening up the possibility for competition. In other cases technology is making the construction of alternative networks a feasible way of competing with a hitherto unique network and the rules of competition must be applied to ensure that market regulation puts no brake on this development. This problem in telecommunications and electricity supply have also been the subject of investigation under the studies programme.[1] Unless the services provided by these statutory monopolies are of general economic interest covered by the derogation of Article 90(2) of the EEC Treaty and exposing them to competition would prevent them from providing their services, these monopolies are subject to the rules of competition (Article 90(1) of the EEC Treaty) and cannot use these statutory rights or any abusive behaviour in the sense of Article 86 of the EEC Treaty to protect themselves from competition.

The Commission has had increasing recourse to Article 90 of the EEC Treaty either through Directives or decisions to tackle problems raised by statutory monopolies and apply the rules of competition. Although each case will have to be studied on its merits, the Commission expects activity in the field to increase. In this respect it is important to realize that the privatization of a State monopoly may be a neutral operation from a competition viewpoint and does not in itself increase competition. The rules of competition with respect to dominant companies (Article 86 of the EEC Treaty) will therefore be applied without discrimination regardless of whether a company is nationalized or privatized.

(a) Telecommunications[2]

54.   Following up its Directive of 28 June 1990 on competition in the markets for telecommunications services,[3] the Commission pursued a very active policy of implementing Articles 85 and 86 of the EEC Treaty in the telecommunications sector in an effort to put an end to restrictive practices and abuses of dominant positions in the sector. As a result, an end was put to restrictions on the use of telecommunications circuits imposed by telecommunications organizations or recommended by associations of them and to agreements on prices within such associations.

The Commission also adopted a position on various forms of cooperation which have been introduced and laid down certain principles to be complied with in this respect so as to ensure effective competition on the market.

Pursuing this active policy of implementing Articles 85 and 86 of the EEC Treaty in the telecommunications sector will be even more necessary once the regulatory obstacles

---

[1]   See Part Four, Chapter II of this Report.
[2]   See also Public undertakings — Telecommunications, point 355 of this Report, and Studies, Part Four, Chapter II of this Report.
[3]   OJ L 192, 24.7.1990.

have been removed as a result of the application of the abovementioned Directive of 28 June 1990. The Commission will set out its policy in greater detail in guidelines on the application of the competition rules in the telecommunications sector.

RTT

55.   Following a complaint against an abuse of a dominant position lodged by a private supplier of value-added telecommunications services regarding the conditions under which lines are leased by the Régie des télégraphes et téléphones (RTT) in Belgium, the Commission made representations to the RTT. The RTT agreed to stop applying the general contractual conditions governing the access of third parties to an international data-transmission network. In the Commission's view, such conditions contained restrictions that were liable to affect competition. The RTT also agreed to stop imposing on its existing or potential customers wishing to lease the abovementioned international lines any restriction other than that they should not carry out a simple transfer of data.

CEPT

56.   The Commission contacted the European Conference of Postal and Telecommunications Administrations (CEPT) following the revision in April 1989 of its Recommendation on the general principles for the lease of international telecommunications circuits. In the Commission's view, the recommendation constituted a price agreement that appreciably restricted competition within the Community. The Recommendation provided, amongst other things, for the imposition of a 30% surcharge or an access charge where third-party traffic was carried on a leased international telecommunications line or a leased line interconnecting to a public telecommunications network. The Recommendation also provided for the application of uniform tariff coefficients for the establishment of the price of leased international lines. Cooperating with the Commission, the CEPT abolished the Recommendation; competition between telecommunications organizations in the supply of leased international lines was thus restored, to the benefit of users and particularly of suppliers of value-added services.

CCITT

57.   The Commission made representations to the meeting of the International Telegraph and Telephone Consultative Committee (CCITT) in May 1990 at which the review of two important CCITT recommendations concerning the general principles and

particular conditions relating to the leasing of international telecommunications lines was discussed. In the Commission's view, the recommendations and some of the proposals tabled at the meeting with a view to revising them were liable to constitute agreements between undertakings on prices and other business conditions that were likely to restrict competition between the telecommunications organizations. The Commission therefore drew the CCITT members' attention to the possible application of Article 85(1) of the EEC Treaty to the recommendations. As a result of the Commission's representations, the CCITT members were able to continue their work on reviewing the recommendations taking fuller account of European competition law.

MDNS

58.   The Commission indicated what were the essential conditions for granting exemptions under Article 85(3) of the EEC Treaty to cooperation agreements between telecommunications organizations in the supply of non-reserved telecommunications services such as managed data-network services (MDNS). A draft agreement of this type between 22 telecommunications organizations had been submitted to the Commission. Although the draft was finally abandoned, the Commission took the opportunity of giving its views on the possible exemption of this type of agreement. The Commission indicated that, although such agreements restricted competition, they could nevertheless offer benefits to consumers, namely a one-stop shop, a speeding-up of the standardization process, a reduction in costs and an improvement in the quality of services. However, exemption could in principle be granted only under certain conditions that would prevent any discrimination by the telecommunications organizations against private suppliers of telecommunications services or cross-subsidization of MDNS activities performed by the telecommunications organizations.

ECR 900

59.   On 27 July 1990, the Commission granted negative clearance to a consortium of three large European electronics and telecommunications companies — the German company AEG Aktiengesellschaft, the Franco-Dutch company Alcatel NV and the Finnish company Oy Nokia — to develop a pan-European mobile telephone system. [1]

In 1987, the European telecommunications administrations signed an agreement within the framework of the CEPT (European Conference of Postal and Telecommunications Administrations) on the establishment of a pan-European digital cellular mobile telecommunications system in their respective countries by 1991. The only potential

---

[1]   OJ L 228, 22.8.1990.

purchasers of the system (known as the GSM system) are at present the national network operators in the CEPT member countries or the undertakings acting on their behalf.

In order to participate in this new project, AEG, Alcatel and Nokia set up a consortium known as ECR 900, whose task is to develop, produce and distribute jointly the pan-European digital cellular mobile telephone system and parts thereof. Most of the other undertakings operating in the telecommunications sector have also combined in order to be able to respond efficiently to the invitations to tender published by the network operators (PTTs). More than half a dozen consortia are involved in the current development of the pan-European system.

The Commission concluded that, in view of the very particular circumstances surrounding the development of the GSM system, the cooperation agreement was not in accordance with Article 85(1) of the EEC Treaty: the companies pursuing the project could not, given the very heavy investment required and the very strict timetable imposed by the invitations to tender, be actual or potential competitors for the project if they acted alone.

Eirpage

60.   On 24 November 1990 the Commission published a notice pursuant to Article 19(3) of Regulation No 17 announcing its intention to grant an exemption pursuant to Article 85(3) to the joint venture set up by Bord Telecom Eireann (Irish Telecom) and Motorola Ireland Ltd (Motorola) for the purposes of setting up, promoting and operating a nation-wide paging system interconnected to the public telecommunications network. [1]

Following a number of amendments to the agreements notified, which had initially been considered as restricting competition, the Commission took the view that the cooperation between the two potential competitors could be exempted. This was after Irish Telecom, as the operator of the public network, allowed equal access for competitors to the facilities necessary for providing a similar service. The joint venture allowed the rapid introduction of a new telecommunications service of direct benefit to consumers and was likely to promote business development. Interested third parties were given the opportunity to comment on the Commission's proposed decision, and their comments will be taken into account in the final decision, which will be the Commission's first formal decision on a cooperation agreement between a telecommunications organization and a private company.

---

[1]   OJ C 294, 24.11.1990.

(b) Postal services

61. At its meeting on 12 September 1989, the Council stressed the need to think about laying down European rules defining the central core of services which would be reserved for the national postal administrations (entrusted with the operation of services of general economic interest) and the services which should be open to competition.

The Commission accordingly began work on a Green Paper on the postal services which would involve wide-ranging consultations with the sectors concerned.

Parallel to this, the Commission continued, as in the past,[1] to examine existing monopolies in the light of the Community competition rules.

The Community interest requires the development of an efficient Community postal system. The delivery of written correspondence, including cross-frontier delivery, is of crucial importance to the proper functioning of the internal market and the growth of both intra-Community and international trade.

The Community postal system must be developed in line with the general objectives of the EEC Treaty, notably those stated in Article 3(c) and (f) with regard to the abolition of obstacles to freedom of movement for services and the institution of a system ensuring that competition in the common market is not distorted. At the current stage of its thinking, the Commission considers that a public service monopoly is justifiable only in so far as satisfactory service is provided for all users and in so far as the technical and economic development of the sector concerned is maintained; if that is not the case, reserving such services to the national postal authorities alone would be liable to constitute a State measure incompatible with Articles 90(1) and 86 of the EEC Treaty.

Such incompatibility could also arise if certain postal services that have traditionally been open to competition with the private sector or have been developed by the competing sector were, for reasons other than the non-economic public interest, reserved for the national monopolies.

(c) Energy[2]

62. In 1990, the Commission pursued the process of completing the internal energy market both through legislation and by tightening up the application of the competition rules.

Thus, a Directive facilitating the transit of electricity and a Directive improving the transparency of gas and electricity prices for industrial consumers were adopted by the

---

[1]   Fifteenth Competition Report, point 259; Nineteenth Competition Report, points 228 and 229.
[2]   See also Studies, Part Four, Chapter II of this Report.

Council of Ministers. In addition, the procedure for adopting a proposal for a Directive facilitating the transit of gas was nearing completion at the end of 1990.

63.   The Commission continued its work on the desirability of and arrangements for possibly allowing third parties access to the gas and electricity networks. For this purpose, four Advisory Committees were set up on which both the Member States and the parties concerned were represented; once the work of these Committees has been completed, the Commission will decide, before the end of 1991, on the degree of openness that is desirable in these areas.

64.   The Commission continued the investigation begun in 1989[1] on the vertical agreements between coal producers and electricity generators. In this context, it examined the compatibility of the *Jahrhundertvertrag*, notified on 1 June 1989, with Article 85 of the EEC Treaty.

The *Jahrhundertvertrag* is an agreement designed to guarantee a market for indigenous coal with the German electricity generators and could restrict intra-Community trade in either electricity or coal substitutes of German origin. The Commission is continuing its examination of the agreement with a view to limiting its restrictive effects on intra-Community trade as far as possible.

65.   The Commission also intervened in the privatization of the electricity industry in England and Wales, which is being carried out under the Electricity Act passed in 1989. The new structure aims to introduce a system of competition, based on the dismantling of the CEGB (Central Electricity Generating Board), responsible for electricity generation and transmission, and on the privatization of local distribution companies. Since 1 April 1990, the 12 area boards have been replaced by 12 Public Electricity Supply Companies (PES), which jointly own the National Grid Company. Three generating companies have been set up: two private (National Power and Power Gen) and one public (Nuclear Electric). As part of the reorganization, a large number of contractual agreements have been concluded between the various parts of the electricity industry. The Commission has been examining the compatibility of the agreements, notified in February 1990, with the Community competition rules and in particular with Articles 85 and 86 of the EEC Treaty.

The Commission has also been looking at the privatization of the electricity industry in Scotland under the Electricity Act 1989. The new system is based on the creation of two competing private-sector electricity companies from the two existing public-sector Boards. The nuclear power stations come under a separate company which remains in the public sector. The agreements linking the various parts of the electricity industry were notified to the Commission in 1990.

---

[1]   Nineteenth Competition Report, point 32.

66. The Commission drew up a Decision[1] prohibiting an agreement concluded by the electricity companies in the Netherlands preventing both the distribution companies and, indirectly, private industrial consumers from using imported electricity. The application of the agreement was liable to thwart the rights made available to private industrial consumers under the new law which entered into force on 8 December 1989. The new law allows electricity to be imported directly without having to go through the national electricity generation coordination company (SEP) and also allows exports by companies other than the generating companies.

The Decision rules that the agreement constitutes an infringement of Article 85(1) of the EEC Treaty in so far as it has the object or effect of impeding imports by private industrial consumers and exports outside the public supply area by the distribution companies and private industrial consumers, notably firms generating their own electricity.

67. In a working paper on security of supply, the internal energy market and energy policy, the Commission drew up a list of protective measures taken by Member States to ensure security of electricity supplies. It announced that it intended to establish a general framework for State aid and to examine additional measures designed to ensure security of supply to see whether they are compatible with Community law.

68. With regard to petroleum products, the year was marked by the sharp increases in prices as a result of events in the Gulf. The increases call for closer monitoring of the market so as to prevent as far as possible recourse to concerted practices by operators.

(d) Transport

Air transport[2]

69. Air transport was for a long time a sector in which airlines had little room for independent initiative. Their commercial strategies were often more a reflection of the rules applying, and the agreements entered into, than the constraints of the market.

With the adoption of an initial series of measures liberalizing air transport in December 1987,[3] the Community began a process of gradually relaxing the rules and regulations restricting airlines' business activities. Amongst other things, the measures enabled airlines to charge whatever fares they thought were commercially justified, and in

---

[1]   Decision adopted on 16 January 1991.
[2]   See also points 105 *et seq.* of this Report.
[3]   Seventeenth Competition Report, point 43.

particular to charge lower, more attractive fares. Airlines were able to respond with greater flexibility in matching capacity to developments in traffic, while the provisions relating to market access promoted the creation of new services and the opening up of new routes.

These measures were just a first step towards liberalization, and the Council gave a firm undertaking to pursue the process with the aim of creating a single market for air transport by 1 January 1993. A second stage was therefore embarked upon in 1990.

The new legislative provisions are backed up by effective implementation of the competition rules. The aim is to ensure that the new scope for airlines to pursue their own commercial strategies is not thwarted by restrictive agreements between airlines or by restrictive practices on the part of already established airlines designed to reduce such potential competition.

Consequently, the Commission is careful to ensure that airlines do not enter into fare agreements that would prevent real price competition. Similarly, the opportunities made available in terms of capacities and market access would be jeopardized through market-sharing agreements or through measures intended to shut out or eliminate new airlines from the market.

Lastly, the opening up of competition requires determined action to maintain a sufficiently competitive structure in the sector. The Commission will take action against the formation of any groups that would be liable to impede effective competition in the common market or in a substantial part thereof. The Commission will also make sure that new airlines are not restricted in their growth potential and competitive capacity.

Community policy aimed at liberalization and competition will not only allow the supply of air transport in the Community to be matched to demand, to the benefit of consumers, but it will also make a significant contribution to the creation of a dynamic and efficient industry, ready to compete with carriers from non-Community countries and to cope with a constantly evolving market.

Liberalization of air transport

70.   On 24 July, the Council adopted Regulations marking the second stage of the liberalization of air transport. [1] The second stage, which entered into force on 1 November, extends and develops the achievements of the initial stage. [2]

The Regulation on fares for scheduled air services sets out to introduce greater flexibility into the system for Community routes. It allows airlines to charge certain fares without

---

[1]   Council Regulations Nos 2342/90, 2343/90 and 2344/90, OJ L 217, 11.8.1990.
[2]   Seventeenth Competition Report, points 43 to 46.

prior approval; other fares may be charged once the authorities in only one of the Member States concerned have approved them. The elimination of fares which always require the approval of the authorities in the two Member States concerned is to be brought about by 1 January 1993. Lastly, the Regulation lays down criteria by which Member States should assess proposed fares, gives the Commission the power to suspend the application of excessively high or abnormally low fares and provides for the possibility of aligning fares for scheduled flights with the fares charged for non-scheduled flights where they offer equivalent conditions.

The Regulation on access for air carriers to scheduled intra-Community air service routes and on the sharing of passenger capacity between air carriers on scheduled air services between Member States provides for more liberal rules on multiple designation,[1] and on third, fourth and fifth freedoms.[2] It aims to phase out bilateral restrictions on capacity quotas, eliminating them totally when the internal market in air transport is completed.

Lastly, the Council extended the duration of the Regulation authorizing the Commission to adopt block exemptions in the period between 1 February 1991 and 31 December 1992. As the previous annual report stated,[3] the Commission considers that the Regulations satisfy a genuine need for legal certainty among air carriers and other market operators, while at the same time providing an incentive for them to abandon previous more restrictive agreements.

71.   On the basis of such authorization, the Commission adopted, on 5 December, three block exemption Regulations[4] extending beyond 31 January 1991 the block exemptions deriving from the first stage of liberalization.[5] The conditions imposed by the new Regulations are, in some respects, stricter than the previous conditions and make for greater competition in the sector.

The Regulation on commercial agreements between airlines introduces a number of new provisions enabling consumers and new market entrants to derive considerable benefits from a more competitive situation. The exemption for revenue-sharing agreements was withdrawn, since this form of collaboration between airlines has been abandoned in the Community in favour of less restrictive structures.[6] Joint planning and the coordination of capacities will be allowed to include connecting flights between different airlines. The coordination of fares will in future be allowed to include cargo rates; however, it will have to result in other airlines and consumers being able to benefit from interline

---

[1]   The acceptance by a Member State of several airlines from another Member State to operate air services between the two countries.
[2]   Services between the State in which an airline is registered and another Member State, and services between two States other than the State in which the airline is registered.
[3]   Nineteenth Competition Report, point 23.
[4]   OJ L 10, 15.1.1991.
[5]   Eighteenth Competition Report, point 28.
[6]   Reference to the text on joint operations.

agreements.[1] Lastly, agreements between airlines on slot allocation at busy airports will have to provide real scope for effective access by new entrants; if the measures taken by airlines pursuant to this condition are not sufficient to enable new entrants to draw up timetables enabling them to compete effectively with established carriers, the Commission might be obliged to withdraw block exemption and to impose appropriate conditions to allow access to the relevant airports.

The block exemption relating to computer reservation systems for air transport services is now aligned on the code of conduct for the use of such systems.[2]

As regards ground handling agreements, the Commission is maintaining the previous conditions, which ensure compliance with the competition rules in agreements between suppliers and airlines. However, it is concerned at the fact that such suppliers are limited in number at certain airports without any satisfactory justification. Situations where this is the case may be examined under Article 90 of the EEC Treaty.

Anti-competitive practices

72.   The Commission presented a proposal[3] amending Regulation No 3975/87 under which, by developing less formal consultation procedures with Member States, it would be able to speed up procedures in cases where anti-competitive practices were threatening the viability or the very existence of an air service operated by a competitor. The proposal is based on the concern that, in a liberalized market, new airlines should be able to play a growing role. However, new airlines are often highly vulnerable and generally have to compete with well-established, often dominant, airlines. Experience in the air transport sector shows that, unless the competent authorities react rapidly, anti-competitive practices can cause irreversible damage to the structure of competition in the sector.

Interline agreements

73.   The Commission looked at the question of how far the system of interlining is compatible with the competition rules.

Interlining is based essentially on an IATA agreement under which most of the world airlines have authorized the other signatories to sell their services. As a result, travel agents can offer passengers a single ticket providing for transportation by different

---

[1]   Reference to the text on interlining.
[2]   Council Regulation (EEC) No 2299/89, OJ L 220, 29.7.1989.
[3]   OJ C 155, 26.6.1990.

carriers (e.g. leaving on the airline issuing the ticket and returning on another airline serving the same route, or continuing to destinations not served by the issuing airline).

In addition, airlines recognize each other's authority to change a ticket so that passengers can change reservations, routings or airlines after the ticket has been issued. These changes would normally require the consent of the airline indicated on the ticket for the sector concerned ('endorsement'), but most airlines have agreed to waive this requirement in practice.

The interline system benefits airlines, travel agents and passengers, especially business travellers. It allows the issuing of travel documents for complex journeys and allows flexible use of such documents with minimal constraints.

74.   The agreements under which interline facilities are granted are to be regarded as technical cooperation agreements. Consequently, the Commission takes the view that they do not in themselves restrict competition and that they are covered by the exception for certain technical agreements provided for in Article 2 of Council Regulation No 3975/87. [1]

However, to the extent that such agreements result in airlines coordinating the level of their fares, they could create problems under the competition rules. In the block exemption, the Commission accepts that consultations on fares, by facilitating the methods for reimbursing and pro rata calculation between airlines, may contribute to the general acceptance of interline conditions. Consequently, the Commission accepts that airlines should be able to exchange information on their intentions regarding fares.

However, such consultations must result in the actual granting of interline facilities to any airline directly concerned, without going beyond this objective or leading to the elimination of price competition. Consequently, any airline participating in consultations on fares must authorize the other carriers providing the service in question to issue tickets for carriage on its intra-Community routes at its own fares. If the airline issuing the ticket is not authorized, under the relevant rules on fares, to charge the fare of the carrying airline, it can match the fare of this latter in accordance with Article 3(5) of Regulation No 2342/90 on fares. Thus, the airline issuing the ticket will be able to pursue an independent fares policy for the services which it operates on its own network and at the same time enjoy interline facilities enabling it to have access to the networks of other carriers.

75.   The question also arose of the circumstances in which a refusal to grant interline facilities could constitute an abuse of a dominant position. The possibility of having access to the network of a large number of airlines is a considerable advantage, not only

---

[1]   OJ L 374, 31.12.1987.

for the consumer, but also for other airlines which are often not able to operate a particular route or to provide the necessary capacity to meet demand. Furthermore, if interline tickets cannot be issued, this is often perceived, particularly by business travellers, as a handicap, which makes it difficult for the airline in question to market its tickets. If an airline in a dominant position refuses interline facilities to a competitor, particularly a new entrant on a route already operated by the dominant airline, such a refusal constitutes an obstacle to the development of competition and is liable to be covered by Article 86 of the EEC Treaty.

However, the Commission takes the view that, even in the case of airlines in a dominant position, there is no general obligation to grant interline facilities. An extensive network and frequent flights are assets which airlines are not necessarily obliged to share with competitors.

Furthermore, airlines must be encouraged to make use of the scope opened up by liberalization to develop their own network and increase the frequency of their own flights, without relying on their competitors. Similarly, the Commission accepts that sales under the interline system should be at the fare of the carrying airline, with a price supplement possibly being charged or the passenger being partially refunded.

Consequently, the Commission considers that any obligation to grant interline facilities must not necessarily extend beyond the period required to enable the relevant airline to establish itself on the route in question. A period of two years should generally be sufficient; however, a longer period could be appropriate if there are particular obstacles impeding the new entrant from obtaining frequencies and load factors comparable to those of airlines established on the relevant route. The obligation to grand interline facilities may extend beyond the route on which the service is operated and include other services operated by the dominant airline if access to such services is essential for penetrating the new market. This applies in particular to connecting routes if there is substantial demand for such routes in conjunction with the route on which the new entrant wishes to become established. Lastly, the obligation to grant interline facilities applies to any fare in respect of which the airline refused interlining needs to interline in order to compete effectively.

For a new airline to compete on a mainly tourist route, for instance, it may require interlining of APEX fares, whereas a primarily business route would require interlining only for standard unrestricted fares.

76.   On the basis of these considerations, the Commission took action in a number of cases under Article 86 to get national airlines to grant interline facilities to smaller airlines which had started services in parallel with the major airlines. Its action allowed agreements appropriate to the particular circumstances of each case to be concluded, to the satisfaction of the small airlines.

Regrouping of airlines

77.   The Commission followed closely restructuring operations in the European air transport sector. In two cases,[1] it initiated proceedings in order to prevent regroupings from taking place under conditions which did not ensure the maintenance of effective competition on the markets affected.

Sea transport[1]

Consortia

78.   On 18 June, the Commission presented to the Council a communication (COM(90) 260) on the possibility of granting a block exemption, under Article 85(3) of the EEC Treaty, for consortia agreements in liner shipping.

Such agreements, which emerged with the development of container services in sea transport at the beginning of the 1970s, take a wide variety of forms. They are joint service agreements concluded by various independent shipping lines seeking, through some form of cooperation, to ensure their profitability through rationalization and a sharing of the high investment costs associated with the operation of container services.

In the report, the Commission fulfils an undertaking given to the Council at the time of the adoption of Regulation No 4056/86. The report comes out in favour of the granting of a block exemption. It is accompanied by a proposal for a Council regulation authorizing the Commission to grant the block exemption, subject to certain conditions.

Having examined the consortia agreements available to it, the Commission draws conclusions in the report regarding the status of the consortia and the legal arrangements that should apply with a view to the granting of a block exemption.

The main conclusions of the report are as follows:

(a)   it does not appear possible for consortia to be regarded as mergers between the parties;

(b)   in principle, consortia agreements are not purely technical arrangements within the meaning of Article 2 of Regulation No 4056/86. They do not have as their sole object and effect the achievement of technical improvements or cooperation. The planned exemption cannot therefore be granted on the basis of the procedure provided for in Article 2(2);

(c)   consortia are not covered by the block exemption granted to liner conferences under Article 3 of Regulation No 4056/86. Consortia agreements differ from conferences

---

[1]   See point 105 *et seq.* of this Report.

in that they pursue different objectives. Their objective is rationalization and not the charging of the same rates for freight. Consortia agreements also involve more extended cooperation between participants. This gives rise to a number of restrictive arrangements which go beyond the scope of the block exemption granted to liner conferences;

(d) consortia offer multimodal transport services in approximately 40% of cases. Since Regulation No 4056/86 relates solely to maritime transport but consortia also supply land transport, the Commission's proposal cannot take the form of a simple amendment to Regulation No 4056/86, but must establish its own rules.

The Commission's decision to opt for the block exemption procedure is justified firstly by the large number of consortia agreements and also by the desire to allow shippers, as far as possible, scope to alter them in the light of market conditions and competition. Thus, the Commission will be able to adopt a flexible approach that will allow it to adapt its position to any fluctuations in the market.

However, so as to ensure that the conditions of Article 85(3) of the EEC Treaty are met, the Commission deems it necessary to couple the proposed block exemption with a number of conditions and requirements that would be established after further consultations with the industry and the Member States.

As a preliminary statement, the Commission considers that the guidelines relating to such conditions and requirements should be designed to:

(i)   ensure that a fair share of the benefits resulting from consortia could be passed on to shippers;

(ii)   ensure that competition in respect of a substantial portion of the total trade is not eliminated or unduly restricted, for instance by agreements between consortia operating in the same trade;

(iii) provide a maximum period of notice for withdrawal without penalty by a participant line;

(iv)   deal, in the case of multimodal transport services offered by consortia, with multilateral agreements with inland hauliers on through rates, and provide for the right of shippers to arrange their own inland haulage without any penalty being incurred;

(v)   ensure non-discrimination between shippers or ports;

(vi)   provide for the obligation to have proper consultations with shippers.

Eurocorde Agreements

79. The Commission published on 3 July 1990 a notice[1] concerning the Eurocorde Agreements between the two liner conferences in the Atlantic routes and their major independent competitors.

Following two complaints lodged by the European Shippers Councils (ESC) and the British Shippers Council, the parties to the agreements had notified them to the Commission, with a view to obtaining an individual exemption under Article 85(3) of the EEC Treaty.

It was envisaged that an exemption might be given, subject to various conditions and obligations. The most important ones concerned non-discrimination between countries or ports; the non-binding and voluntary nature of the agreements; consultations with transport users; requirements on transparency and information to be provided to the Commission; in multimodal operations, respect of shippers' choice concerning inland transport, without discrimination; and the prohibition of enlarging the geographic scope of the agreements.

The Commission is still considering the case having regard also to developments in the market subsequent to the publication of the notice.

West and Central Africa

80. The Commission sent four liner conferences operating between the Community and the west and central coast of Africa[2] statements of objections based on Articles 85 and 86 of the EEC Treaty and the relevant provisions of Council Regulation (EEC) No 4056/86. The liner conferences were able to present their comments at hearings held in autumn 1990.

As part of the same case, the Commission also sent a statement of objections to the Shipowners' Committees involved in cargo sharing between France and 11 West African countries.

Lastly, the Commission decided to impose an ECU 5 000 fine pursuant to Article 16(3) of Regulation (EEC) No 4056/86 on Secrétama — which is the body providing the secretariat for the abovementioned Shipowners' Committees — for having supplied incorrect information in response to a request sent to it.

---

[1]   OJ C 162, 3.7.1990.
[2]   Nineteenth Competition Report, point 28.

(e) Insurance

81.   On 18 December 1989, the Commission decided to present to the Council a proposal for a Regulation empowering the Commission to establish a block exemption for certain categories of agreements, decisions by associations of undertakings and concerted practices in the insurance sector.[1]

In 1990, the Economic and Social Committee was consulted, although this was not formally required, and adopted a favourable opinion on the proposal.[2] The European Parliament, consulted pursuant to Article 87 of the EEC Treaty, also adopted a favourable opinion, subject to a number of amendments.[3]

The Commission decided to incorporate a number of the amendments. It then presented an amended proposal to the Council.

(f) Audiovisual media

82.   In its communication to the Council and Parliament on audiovisual policy,[4] the Commission set out the broad lines of its policy on competition in the audiovisual sector. It pointed out that:

(a) undertakings in the audiovisual sector are subject to Articles 85, 86 and 90 of the EEC Treaty in the same way as undertakings in any other branch of industry;

(b) agreements that infringe the competition rules must not be allowed to undermine the Community's efforts to achieve a unified market;

(c) the difficult economic situation prevailing in the production sector and the cultural role which it plays justify a favourable attitude on the part of the Commission to cooperation between undertakings. However, the Commission must ensure a balance between the measures taken in the various Member States and the avoidance of discrimination against Community nationals;

(d) the granting of exclusive television rights is not in itself anti-competitive; however, agreements whose scope or duration are excessive or which impose additional restrictions on the parties may be covered by Article 85(1) of the EEC Treaty.

In broadcasting, in particular, the Commission is careful to ensure that markets remain open and that programme access is guaranteed to all operators, in accordance with the principle already established in the Decision of 15 December 1989.[5]

---

[1]   Nineteenth Competition Report, point 30.
[2]   OJ C 182, 23.7.1990.
[3]   OJ C 260, 15.10.1990.
[4]   COM(90) 78 final, 21.2.1990.
[5]   Film purchases by German television stations, OJ L 284, 3.10.1989.

However, the joint acquisition or distribution of television rights, which in principle are covered by Article 85(1) of the EEC Treaty, could be exempted if they allow rationalization, provided that they do not prevent market access for competitors.

It is in the light of these principles that the Commission is at present examining cases relating to the joint purchase of television rights, exclusive rights for sports events and restrictions on the broadcasting of football matches.

(g) Computer software

83.   On 13 December 1990, pursuant to Article 149(2) of the EEC Treaty, the Council adopted a common position on the amended Commission proposal for a Directive on the legal protection of computer programs.[1] The Commission had amended its initial proposal to take account of the amendments proposed by Parliament,[2] which it accepted on 17 October 1990.[3] Throughout 1990, the Commission departments examined the many comments sent to them by the sectors involved in the exploitation of programs so as to integrate them constructively into the legislative process.

The aim of the Directive is to ensure in the legislation of all the Member States an adequate level of protection for all computer programs and to eliminate any disparities that might affect the functioning of the common market. In accordance with the basic principle underlying copyright legislation, the protection provided by the Directive applies only to the expression of ideas or principles, including those which underlie the interfaces of the programmes, and not to the ideas or principles themselves.

The Commission's concern was to ensure that a fair balance was maintained between, on the one hand, the protection of the rights attaching to the program and, on the other, the safeguarding of an economic environment that could encourage competition and innovation on the market. A particularly important question was to determine the extent to which the decompiling of a program without the copyright holder's authorization would be possible. The solution adopted in the common position was that decompiling was permitted in so far as it proved necessary for the interoperability of a computer program created independently.

Decompilation is permitted to the extent necessary to ensure the interoperability of an independently created computer program. Such a program may connect to the program subject to decompilation. Alternatively it may compete with the decompiled program and in such cases will not normally connect to it. Article 6 does not however permit decompilation beyond what is necessary to achieve the interoperability of the

---

[1]   Nineteenth Competition Report, point 34.
[2]   Opinion of 11 July 1990.
[3]   OJ C 320, 20.12.1990.

independently created program. It cannot therefore be used to create a program reproducing parts of a decompiled program having no relevance to the interoperability of the independently created program.

The Commission will take careful account of any amendments proposed by Parliament on a second reading. The Directive is expected to be adopted by the Council in 1991.

(h) Review of the European Community beer market

84.   The Commission has completed the review of the Community beer market[1] which was initiated in March 1989. Its main conclusions are:

(i)   no general change is required to the Community rules which govern the tying arrangements between brewers and their outlets. These rules are set out in a block exemption regulation adopted by the Commission in 1983 (Regulation No 1984/83), which expires in 1997. However:

(ii)   the Commission will evaluate whether further measures are needed to take account of the United Kingdom market when newly introduced national measures have had time to take effect; currently 62% of all UK beer sales pass through the tied-house system;

(iii)   the Community rules concerning exclusive purchasing arrangements should not apply to small breweries: such agreements should be covered by national law;

(iv)   licensing agreements between major brewers will be examined by the Commission to see whether they are being used as vehicles for market sharing or control of imports.

Background to the review

85.   The review into the EC beer market was undertaken to see whether there were any appreciable competitive obstacles which might obstruct the opening of national markets in the run up to 1992 and whether new measures were needed to ensure that industry and consumers could benefit fully from the continuing liberalization of markets.

The Commission has undertaken a detailed examination of market conditions throughout the Community. Questionnaires were sent to a wide range of interested parties, including the relevant national and Community representative bodies and evidence was received from many undertakings in all Member States.

---

[1]   See point 395 of this Report.

The review shows the European beer market to be the most diverse in the world, with a high proportion of independent brewers in most Member States and a high level of consumer choice. Community exports account for 95% of total world trade in beer. Yet only 4% of all beer consumed in the EC has crossed a national border.

Conclusions

86.   Licensing agreements: the Commission has noted an increasing number of licensing agreements concluded between major brewers. Under these agreements, one brewery grants to another the exclusive right to brew and market its beers in the other's home country. The agreements are generally of long duration.

Many such agreements benefit consumers by enabling a small specialist brewer to make its product available outside its home market in the long term[1] or by acting as a stepping-stone for the full independent entry of a large multinational brewer into other geographic areas.[2] However, such agreements can also serve as vehicles for market sharing, enabling large breweries to control imports in order to ossify existing market structures and eliminate or reduce the risk of independent market entry by major competitors.

These agreements will be examined to see whether any of them have the effect of limiting competition and are therefore incompatible with the common market.

87.   Tying arrangements: special attention was given to tying arrangements in the EEC in the light of the differing and evolving structural characteristics in Member States. Following an analysis of the conditions on each market, the Commission has concluded that no change to the existing Community policy on such agreements, as set out in Commission Regulation No 1984/83, is required before the Regulation's expiry in 1997.

The tied-house system only exists in certain northern European markets: Belgium, the Federal Republic of Germany, France, Luxembourg, the Netherlands and the United Kingdom. In no country except the UK does more than 40% of total beer sales pass through tied outlets.

The beer markets in these countries may be characterized as static; total sales of beer are constant or declining and consumers are usually loyal to certain brands. The brewers contacted by the Commission tend to view these characteristics, rather than the effect of the tied-house system, as preventing penetration of new products into these markets.

Given these facts, there is not enough evidence to justify an amendment to Regulation No 1984/83 at this time. A possible exception to this is the United Kingdom, where some

---

[1]   See Whitbread-Moosehead, Commission Decision of 23 March 1990, OJ L 100, 20.4.1990.
[2]   See Carlsberg, Commission Decision of 12 July 1984, OJ L 207, 2.8.1984.

62% of all beer sales pass through the tied-house system. The resultant market foreclo-
sure is exacerbated by the restrictive licensing system which limits the number of new
retailers. However, the UK Government has recently adopted new measures to redress
this problem. These are now being implemented; only when they have taken effect can
the Commission decide whether further measures are needed.

88.   Small breweries: there is widespread confusion among small brewers as to whether
or not EC competition law is applicable to tying agreements concluded between them
and their retailers. This has given rise to litigation between resellers and small brewers
in relation to the validity of exclusive purchasing agreements[1] under EC competition
law.

In order to ensure that markets are not foreclosed by exclusive purchasing or tying
agreements it appears sufficient that the restrictions on tying should be confined to larger
brewers which account for the major proportion of total beer sales.

The application of Community competition law may therefore be limited to exclusive
purchasing arrangements entered into with brewers of a certain minimum size. Agreements concluded between a reseller and a brewer with an insignificant market share
would not normally restrict competition or affect trade to an appreciable extent and
would not therefore fall under Article 85(1) of the EEC Treaty. The *de minimis* rule
applies even when seen in the context of the existence of other parallel agreements
concluded by other brewers.

Such agreements should therefore be governed by national law; it is up to the Member
States to decide to what extent they accept such agreements by small brewers, for
instance to maintain or promote the large range of local, regional and speciality beers
presently available in many parts of the Community.

This conclusion is without prejudice to the judgment that the Court of Justice may make
on this point in the *Delimitis-Henninger Bräu* case.

In any event, where small brewers conclude such agreements, the Commission does not
intend to intervene. The application of Community rules to such undertakings would
place a disproportionate administrative burden upon them in relation to any possible
opening of the market.

The Commission is presently examining the level at which this *de minimis* rule should
apply and is contacting the relevant professional representative bodies to propose a
figure and invites their comments. Following this the Commission will consult the
Member States before issuing a notice.

---

[1]   The Court is presently considering this point in the *Delimitis-Henninger Bräu* case.

§ 5 —The Commission's powers

89.   The Commission took careful note of Parliament's comments on the powers which it enjoys under Regulation No 17/62. [1]

With more particular regard to the Commission's powers of investigation and its decision-making procedure, it was suggested that the Commission should, within its internal procedures, make a distinction between its investigatory, examinatory and decision-making functions regarding restrictive agreements and abuses of dominant positions.

The Commission noted this suggestion. However, a balance must be struck between respecting the rights of the defence of firms and the need for procedures to be effective. Bearing in mind these two objectives, the Commission considers that its practice is on the right lines.

At present, individual cases based on Articles 85 and 86 of the Treaty are examined under the responsibility of one of the three operational Directorates responsible for the sector in question. The draft decisions drawn up by these Directorates have to be forwarded for an opinion not only to the Directorate which, within DG IV, is responsible for coordination and for general competition policy but also to the Commission's Legal Service.

As regards respecting the rights of the defence, it should be borne in mind that the Commission has always allowed undertakings involved in proceedings the right of access to the file so as to allow them to present their arguments in full knowledge of the facts, before any decision having immediate effect is taken against them. This is consistent practice in the implementation of Articles 85 and 86 of the EEC Treaty[2] and was explicitly incorporated in the implementing Commission Regulation on merger control. [3]

Before any decision against firms is adopted, the firms also have the right to be heard orally and in writing. The objectivity and proper conduct of such hearings are ensured by the Hearing Officer, first appointed in 1982. [4] Furthermore, another Hearing Officer was appointed for the oral hearings required for the purposes of implementing the merger control Regulation. [5]

---

[1]   Nineteenth Competition Report, point 1.
[2]   See Eleventh Competition Report, points 22 and 25, and Eighteenth Competition Report, point 43.
[3]   Regulation (EEC) No 2367/90 of 25 July 1990.
[4]   Twelfth Competition Report, point 36.
[5]   OJ L 257, 21.9.1990; see this Report for developments regarding the implementation of Council Regulation No 4064/89 of 21 December 1989, point 147 *et seq.*

Lastly, draft decisions are presented to an Advisory Committee.[1] This is made up of representatives of the Member States with particular expertise in competition matters and is chaired by the Director within DG IV responsible for general competition policy and coordination. The Advisory Committee[1] delivers an opinion on the draft decision.

The Commission's internal procedures thus involve a high degree of control and balance in the various stages leading up to the final decision.

Lastly, the Commission's formal decisions are subject to judicial review at two levels, since the decisions of the Court of First Instance may be appealed against to the Court of Justice.[2]

---

[1]   Advisory Committee on Restrictive Practices and Dominant Positions established in accordance with Council Regulation No 17/62 of 6 February 1962 and Advisory Committee on Concentrations established in accordance with Council Regulation (EEC) No 4064/89 of 21 December 1989.

[2]   See the chapter in this Report dealing with the main decisions of the Court of Justice and the Court of First Instance, point 153 *et seq.*; see also Article 49 of the Rules of Procedure of the Court of Justice, 1990 version.

Chapter III

Main cases decided by the Community lawcourts

153. This Report covers a total of nine judgments. Seven were delivered in actions challenging a formal Commission decision which were brought by firms under Article 173 of the EEC Treaty. One was a preliminary ruling under Article 177 of the EEC Treaty, and one was in an infringement case under Article 169.

Five of these judgments were delivered by the Court of First Instance, to which original jurisdiction in competition matters has been transferred from the Court of Justice, and which entered on its duties on 1 November 1989.[1]

§ 1 — Definition of agreement; export ban

154. In *Sandoz* v *Commission*[2] the Court of Justice dismissed the main claims in an action brought by the Italian company Sandoz Prodotti Farmaceutici against the Commission Decision of 13 July 1987 in which the Commission had found that Sandoz had infringed Article 85(1) of the EEC Treaty;[3] the Court did reduce the amount of the fine imposed.

In the contested decision[4] the Commission had taken the view that a 'continuous commercial relationship set up and concretized by' a set of commercial practices in which the invoices sent by Sandoz to its customers bore the words 'not to be exported' was caught by the ban on restrictive agreements between undertakings laid down in Article 85(1) of the EEC Treaty. The object of such an agreement was anticompetitive, and it was not necessary to analyze its restrictive effects because it was by its nature liable to affect trade between Member States.

---

[1]   Council Decision 88/591/ECSC, EEC, Euratom of 24 October 1988 establishing a Court of First Instance of the European Communities, OJ C 215, 21.9.1989.
[2]   Case C-277/87.
[3]   OJ L 222, 10.8.1987.
[4]   Seventeenth Report on Competition Policy, point 62.

A — APPLICATION OF ARTICLES 85 AND 86 OF THE EEC TREATY

§ 1 — Horizontal agreements in the industrial and commercial areas

Soda ash[1]

92.   In a series of decisions sanctioning serious infringements of competition rules, Solvay was fined by the Commission a total of ECU 30 million and ICI a total of ECU 17 million.

The main Article 85 case involved a concerted practice of long standing by which Solvay and ICI divided the European market between them so that neither competed with the other. Solvay stayed out of the United Kingdom and in return ICI did not compete on the continent of Europe.

An important aspect of the case under Article 85 involved long-term 'market support' arrangements by which ICI obtained large tonnages from Solvay so as to continue to be able to supply its 'traditional' markets. In return Solvay did not itself enter those markets, which included the United Kingdom and Ireland. As a result of this collusion, each producer was dominant and able to control the market in its own allotted territory. The Commission took the view that the two undertakings bore an equal responsibility and fined each of them ECU 7 million for this part of the infringement.

In a separate decision[2] the Commission fined Solvay ECU 3 million and the German producer Chemische Fabrik Kalk (CFK) ECU 1 million for an unlawful agreement by which Solvay made up CFK's sales in the Federal Republic of Germany each year to 'guaranteed' minimum tonnage in return for CFK moderating its price policy.

The Commission's overall objective in these cases was to ensure the development of competition in a major industrial market which until now has not been noted for this phenomenon. At the same time as it prohibited and fined the collusive arrangements of the European producers, it refused an exemption under Article 85(3) of the EEC Treaty for Ansac (American Natural Soda Ash Corporation) the export cartel of the United States soda ash industry. Production costs of natural ash as found in the USA are considerably lower than those of synthetic ash and despite shipping costs natural ash can be sold in Europe at very competitive prices. Furthermore, since September 1990 imports of American natural ash are no longer restricted by anti-dumping measures.

---

[1]   See also point 113 of this Report.
[2]   Decision of 19 December 1990.

Shotton Paper Company

93. Shotton Paper Company plc, a leading British newsprint producer, concluded separate contracts with two wastepaper collectors and merchants, J. and J. Maybank Ltd and Davidsons Ltd, for the supply of wastepaper for use as feedstock at Shotton's new wastepaper conversion plant.

The new plant should enable Shotton to almost triple its present output of newsprint produced at an integrated woodpulp plant.

The new plant involved substantial investment in the technology used in treating printed wood-containing paper suitable for de-inking.

The purpose of the agreements is to give Shotton security of supply in wastepaper during the new plant's start-up period.

In adopting its position, the Commission made it clear that, while it can endorse the conclusion of supply agreements that are limited in time and do not impose too restrictive a link on the buyer or have the effect of closing off the market, it nevertheless keeps a careful eye on this type of agreement so as to ensure that suppliers are not tempted to conclude identical agreements with other large-scale users or to extend their effects to an undue extent.

The Commission noted that the agreements relate to significant tonnages and involve significant quantities for only three years. It also noted that there were many other collectors in the sector, which is not characterized by any substantial barriers to entry.

The parties requested negative clearance or, alternatively, individual exemption.

The arguments adduced in support of the application and the circumstances involved in the two cases were set out in a Commission notice[1] in which the Commission announced that it intended to adopt a favourable position.

Since no objections to the agreements were raised by interested third parties, the Directorate-General for Competition, in agreement with the parties, closed the file by sending comfort letters.

Alcatel Espace/ANT Nachrichtentechnik

94. The Commission granted a 10 year exemption, under Article 85(3) of the EEC Treaty, to the cooperation agreement on the research, development, production and marketing of certain electronic components for satellites, concluded between Alcatel

---

[1]   OJ C 106, 28.4.1990.

(France), the second largest world manufacturer of communication equipment and systems, and ANT, one of the leading companies in the Federal Republic of Germany in the field of telecommunications technology. However, the combined turnover of the two companies in the space satellite manufacturing sector is less than that of several other European manufacturers and much less than that of a number of non-European manufacturers. The market share of the parties to the agreement is less than 20% in the EEC.

The agreement establishes structures for cooperation between the parties that go beyond the object and scope of the block exemption Regulation on research and development agreements,[1] since the cooperation between the parties extends to include marketing of the products. The Commission noted that the joint research and development programme was likely to promote technical and economic progress. If the parties were to bear the efforts and risks involved independently, this would certainly not lead to results as rapid, efficient and economic as those envisaged. The level of individual R&D investment will remain the same for each party, which will lead to more efficient use of the expenditure and to the supply of higher quality equipment at lower costs.

In the particular field of satellites, the nature of demand means that the benefits of joint research and development and manufacturing can be obtained only if they are combined with some degree of joint marketing. Competition normally takes place by customers calling for tenders which are then submitted by consortia formed on a case-by-case basis. Consequently, it is not possible for the agreement in itself to enable the parties to eliminate competition in the common market in respect of a substantial part of the products in question.

Elopak/Metal Box — Odin

95.   The Commission decided that Article 85(1) of the EEC Treaty did not apply to the agreement setting up a joint venture (Odin) by Elopak and Metal Box. The joint venture is to carry out the research and development of a container with a carton base and a separate closure intended for the packaging of UHT processed foods. The joint venture will hold an exclusive licence to exploit anywhere in the world the intellectual property rights (patented and unpatented) of the two parent companies. The parent companies can obtain from Odin a non-exclusive licence (without the right to sub-license) for any improvement made by Odin, subject to certain conditions.

Negative clearance was granted because, when the agreement was concluded, the parent companies were not actual or potential competitors in the relevant product market. Both parent companies' experience and resources were necessary to develop the new product,

---

[1]   Regulation (EEC) No 418/85, OJ L 53, 22.2.1985.

which will be a combination of their respective technical and commercial know-how. Furthermore, the setting-up of the joint venture should not in principle prevent potential competitors from making use of similar possibilities. The provisions in the agreement relating to Odin's use of the parent companies' know-how and the requirement that it be kept secret are essential to avoid compromising or undermining Odin's purpose and existence. Lastly, the agreement did not contain any restriction of competition relating to price, quantity or territory.

Konsortium ECR

96.   The Commission decided that Article 85(1) of the EEC Treaty did not apply to the cooperation agreement concluded by AEG (Federal Republic of Germany), Alcatel (France) and Nokia (Finland). The agreement concerned the setting-up of the consortium 'ECR 900', which will jointly manufacture and market a pan-European digital cellular mobile telephone system, known as GSM (Groupe spécial mobile).

Cekacan

97.   The Commission granted a 10-year exemption, under Article 85(3) of the EEC Treaty, to a cooperation agreement concluded between the Swedish company Akerlund & Rausing and the German company Europa Carton AG. The agreement concerns the exploitation and marketing in certain Community and non-Community countries of a new method and new type of packaging known as Cekacan. The cooperation is based essentially on the setting-up of a new company, Ceka Europe, 74% of whose capital is to be held by A&R and 26% by ECA.

The setting-up of the new company seems to be limited to the initial stage of cooperation aimed at introducing and marketing Cekacan technology. The setting-up of Ceka Europe is liable to restrict competition because the agreement contains exclusivity clauses and exclusive supply clauses. Nevertheless, the agreement contributes to improving production and distribution and to promoting technical progress in the food-packaging sector. The cooperation between the two companies may be expected to lead to a faster increase in the number of customers. Consumers will receive a fair share of the resulting benefit, and the agreement will not afford the companies the possibility of eliminating competition in respect of a substantial part of the products in question, since the relevant market is the entire packaging market.

Irish timber importers association

98.   The Commission asked the Irish Hardwood and Panel Products Importers Association to remove from its rules a restrictive clause that was liable to restrict seriously the importation of timber and panel products into Ireland.

The clause encouraged members to buy through recognized timber agents and to support only those agents who in turn recognized the association.

The Commission took the view that the aim of the clause was to dissuade members of the association from dealing with sellers supplying non-members.

Given the very limited economic importance of the case and the fact that the clause was removed, the Commission took the view that it was not appropriate to adopt a formal decision, but it wishes to make clear that such practices, which are in direct contradiction with the competition rules laid down in the Treaty and the principles of the single market, are liable in other circumstances to be penalized.

Bayer/Hoechst

99.   The Commission did not raise any objections to the agreement concluded between Bayer AG and Hoechst AG on joint research, development and exploitation of a drug for the treatment of AIDS. The cooperation also related to the joint marketing of the drug. The Commission sent the two companies a comfort letter informing them that the agreement qualified for exemption under Article 85(3) of the EEC Treaty.

AIDS research requires long-term overlapping of research and marketing so as to promote medical progress while at the same time ensuring the protection of AIDS carriers.

KSB/Goulds/Lowara/ITT

100.   The Commission exempted two cooperation agreements to develop and produce the wet ends of a centrifugal pump. The extension of the cooperation, originally limited to KSB Aktiengesellschaft (Federal Republic of Germany) and Lowara SpA (Italy), to include two American firms, Goulds Inc. and ITT, not only created viable conditions for large-scale manufacture of the products, but also allowed them to be distributed at prices which were cheaper to the consumer. Without such cooperation, the development of the pumps up to the stage of mass production would never have been possible. For this reason, despite KSB's already strong position on the market, the Commission authorized the cooperation until 31 May 1993. In so doing, it accepted that the jointly

developed components would be made exclusively by Lowara for the partners in the cooperation agreement. The Commission stressed, however, that it would probably not be able to accept this form of joint exploitation of the results of research and development after this date if the exclusivity continued to be limited to the cooperation partners alone. This was to prevent structural changes which might occur to the disadvantage of competitors.

Bayer/Gist

101. The Commission sent a comfort letter in which it stated that the conditions for the application of Article 85(3) of the EEC Treaty remained fulfilled after the expiration of the initial period of exemption granted by decision in 1975[1] to the agreements concluded between Bayer (Federal Republic of Germany) and Gist-Brocades (Netherlands) relating to the manufacture and distribution of raw penicillin and 6-aminopenicillanic acid (6-APA). The object of the agreements is to secure the long-term supply of raw penicillin by Gist-Brocades to Bayer, to grant a non-exclusive licence enabling Bayer to use Gist-Brocades' chemical process technology for the production of 6-APA and to ensure the long-term supply of 6-APA by Bayer to Gist-Brocades.

---

[1]   Decision of 15 December 1975, OJ L 30, 5.2.1976.

§ 2 — Distribution agreements

EEIG Orphe

102.   This was the first case in which the Commission took a decision on the validity of an agreement on the setting-up of a European Economic Interest Grouping in relation to the competition rules laid down in the EEC Treaty.

The Commission sent a comfort letter giving its written agreement to the by-laws of the EEIG Orphe. Although the agreement contains some restrictions of competition, the Commission decided that it was eligible for exemption under Article 85(3) of the EEC Treaty.

The agreement brings together seven undertakings of average size, each from a different Member State, which specialize in the wholesale distribution of pharmaceutical and parapharmaceutical products in their respective countries. It provides that the members of the EEIG should give each other priority for commercial transactions. Joint purchasing is undertaken, a common trade mark has been created which will appear beside the trade mark of each member on the labelling and the wrapping of products distributed by the members, and a databank has been set up. The EEIG members are free to determine the prices and conditions of sale of their products, including those which they have obtained through the EEIG.

The EEIG members are small or medium-sized companies, most of them cooperatives. Thanks to the EEIG, they will be better placed in the European market, which is largely dominated by very large wholesale companies. This will allow diversification of distribution in this sector and will give consumers wider choice while maintaining prices at a reasonable level, thanks to joint purchasing through the central purchasing organization.

D'Ieteren

103.   The Commission confirmed that motor vehicle manufacturers could legitimately oppose the use within their network of motor oils whose quality did not meet the objective standards set by them.

VAG (Volkswagen AG) does not itself sell oils to the members of its network and confines itself to setting minimum quality requirements, and consequently it influences the type of oils sold to third parties. For this purpose, the manufacturer had sent out a circular requesting its network to comply with quality standards set in cooperation with lubricant manufacturers. The circular was technical and objective in character. It was intended to ensure uniform standards throughout the manufacturer's network. The standards set have the advantage of improving the performance, durability and environmental acceptability of the engine and of ensuring more economic fuel consumption. In addition, motor oil manufacturers can ask VAG for details of the standards so as to comply with them and can refer to this in their advertising. The Commission granted the negative clearance requested by D'Ieteren, since the circular did not contain any restriction of competition referred to in Article 85(1) of the Treaty.

In its decision, the Commission pointed out that the circular would in any case have been compatible with the block exemption Regulation No 123/85.

The Commission made it clear that objective and necessary quality standards set by means of agreement or circular no longer need to be notified.

§ 3 — Agreements in the service sector

Eurocheques

104.   The agreement establishing the Eurocheque system was granted exemption under Article 85(3) of the EEC Treaty in 1984. [1]

This exemption had expired, and Eurocheque requested renewal. During an initial stage of the procedure, the Commission informed Eurocheque that five aspects of the agreement appeared to contravene Community competition law. These were: the information given to customers issuing Eurocheques, the terms and conditions of the interbank commission, the rate of the interbank commission, the maximum clearing amount, and the way Eurocheques are accepted in the retail sector in France. The case is still under examination.

---

[1]   Decision of 10 December 1984, OJ L 35, 7.2.1985.

§ 4 — Agreements in the transport sector

Joint operations

105.   The six joint operation agreements between airlines on which the Commission had expressed serious doubts regarding the applicability of Article 85(3) of the EEC Treaty were terminated with effect from 31 October 1991 at the latest.

In addition, four new agreements are being examined. By the end of 1990, the Commission had expressed serious doubts on two of them.

Air France/Lufthansa

106.   Air France and Lufthansa concluded a cooperation agreement establishing a permanent structure for the regular exchange of information on the position of the airlines. The agreement also provided for closer cooperation between the airlines in certain technical and commercial activities.

The Commission took the view that, in a highly regulated market, traditionally in the hands of large airlines which are to a considerable extent shielded in practice from the effects of true price competition, the agreement could lead to the establishment of structures that would run counter to the development of healthy competition.

At the Commission's request, the parties abolished the Coordination Committee, which was composed of senior executives in charge of departments, and an organized exchange of executives having commercial responsibilities. The parties also undertook to notify the Commission of any new specific cooperation agreement.

Lufthansa/Air Europe

107.   The Commission intervened in a case concerning interline facilities, under which passengers of one airline are allowed to use their tickets on another airline, subject to certain conditions. Air Europe and Lufthansa will now be able to compete effectively on the London-Munich and London-Düsseldorf routes, while maintaining the advantages offered by interlining. The basic principle is that sufficient interlining should exist to allow a newcomer to compete on equal terms.[1]

---

[1]   See point 73 of this Report.

British Airways/Sabena/KLM

108.   The Commission also examined the agreement concluded on 13 December 1989 between British Airways, KLM and Sabena. The agreement provided for British Airways and KLM each to take a 20% shareholding in Sabena World Airlines (SWA), a subsidiary of Sabena.

The main purpose of the agreement was to establish a 'hub and spoke' system based on Brussels airport with a network of flights to up to 75 European towns and cities, and also to develop SWA's long-haul network through cooperation with British Airways and KLM.

The three airlines sent the Commission a request for negative clearance or, alternatively, exemption under the opposition procedure provided for in Article 5 of Regulation No 3975/87. Two other airlines, Trans European Airways (TEA) and British Midland, lodged complaints.

The Commission published a summary of the application in the *Official Journal of the European Communities*[1] in accordance with the provisions of Article 5 of Regulation No 3975/87. On 28 June 1990, the Commission notified the three airlines that it had serious doubts under Article 5 and at the same time sent them statements of objections. These recognized the potential benefits of the agreement both for the consumer and for technical and economic development. However, the Commission also pointed out a number of risks to competition: firstly, the reduction in competition between the parties, especially in view of the limited real scope for small airlines to compete on fair terms from Brussels airport, particularly on the London-Brussels route; secondly, the collaboration between Sabena and KLM, whose markets partly overlap; thirdly, the cooperation relating to long-haul routes, which was not clearly defined.

A memorandum was also sent to the United Kingdom Monopolies and Mergers Commission, which published it as an annex to its report on the case on 21 June 1990 (p. 72).

Discussions between the airlines and the Commission began in September 1990. Their aim was to seek a solution that would safeguard competition requirements without undermining the bases of the agreement.

The discussions were discontinued when, for economic and business reasons, the three airlines abandoned their project and terminated the agreement before 31 December 1990, as they had the right to do under the agreement.

---

[1]   OJ C 82, 31.3.1990.

Sea Containers/Stena Tiphook

109.   In August 1989, Sea Containers Ltd, the parent company of Sealink Ferries, lodged a complaint against Stena AB, a ferry company, and Tiphook PLC, a container leasing company, in respect of their public takeover bid for Sea Containers.

Sea Containers considered that the agreement between the two companies infringed Articles 85 and 86 of the EEC Treaty and it therefore asked the Commission to take interim measures to prevent the takeover bid.

In September 1989, the Commission replied to the complainant that its request did not contain sufficient substantiating evidence to justify interim measures and that, on the basis of its initial preliminary analysis, the agreement did not contravene the provisions of Articles 85 and 86 of the EEC Treaty.

The Commission arrived at this preliminary conclusion for the following reasons:

Article 85:

Stena AB and Tiphook PLC were not competing with each other in any market. The fact that they made a joint bid for Sea Containers did not in itself constitute a breach of Article 85.

Article 86:

(a) It was not apparent that Stena AB was in a dominant position in the market for the supply of ferry services between Scandinavia and the Federal Republic of Germany, as claimed by Sea Containers.

(b) Although it was arguable as to whether Sealink was in a dominant position in the market for the provision of ferry services between Ireland and the UK, and between the UK and continental Europe, it was not apparent that the addition of Stena's existing operators would strengthen any such dominance.

(c) Sealink's dominance in the market for the provision of port facilities was also arguable, and it was not apparent why Stena would be more likely than Sealink to abuse any such dominant position.

Sea Containers withdrew its complaint in February 1990. In October 1990, Stena notified an agreement which it had concluded with Sea Containers concerning the purchase of Sealink. The Commission is at present examining the notification.

§ 5 — Agreements relating to industrial property rights

Moosehead/Whitbread

110.   The Commission granted exemption under Article 85(3) to the agreement between Whitbread (United Kingdom) and Moosehead (Canada) granting Whitbread the exclusive right to brew and market Moosehead beer in the United Kingdom using the Moosehead trade mark.

In the United Kingdom, 81% of beer is sold in on-licensed premises, and 75% of all beer sold in the United Kingdom is in draught form. Brewers largely distribute their beer in the United Kingdom using their own lorries. No large-scale independent distribution facility therefore exists for beer in the United Kingdom. A total of 57% of all on-licensed premises in the United Kingdom are owned by brewers and 'tied' to them by an exclusive purchasing agreement. It is therefore very useful, and indeed essential, for a foreign brewer wishing to enter the United Kingdom market to gain the assistance of a large national brewer. Whitbread holds some 12% of United Kingdom retail sales of beer. Whitbread agreed to sell the contract product solely under the Moosehead trade mark. Moosehead granted Whitbread an exclusive licence to exploit the trade mark in respect of the product. It also agreed to provide Whitbread with all the appropriate know-how needed to make the product.

The Commission considered that the agreement was likely to contribute to the improvement of the production and distribution of Moosehead beer in the United Kingdom and to promote economic progress. Consumers would benefit from the agreement, since they would have a wider choice with the entry of the new beer in the market of the licensed territory.

The Commission also took account of measures to liberalize the beer market being implemented by the United Kingdom Government.

In addition, the Commission took the view that the clause in the licensing agreement preventing Whitbread from challenging either the ownership or the validity of the trade mark was not caught by Article 85(1) of the EEC Treaty.

As far as the ownership of the trade mark is concerned, the Commission considered that its use by any other party was in any case prohibited and that, consequently, competition was not affected.

As regards the validity of the trade mark, the Commission considered that, since the Moosehead trade mark was comparatively new in the licensed territory, its maintenance did not constitute an appreciable barrier to entry for any other company entering or competing in the beer market in the licensed territory. Accordingly, the Commission considered that the trade mark non-challenge clause, in so far as it concerned its validity, did not constitute an appreciable restriction of competition.

Lastly, the Commission took the view that Regulation No 556/89 on know-how licences did not apply in this instance. The provision in the agreement relating to the trade mark was not ancillary, since the principal interest of the parties lay in the exploitation of the trade mark rather than of the know-how. The parties viewed the Canadian origin of the product as crucial to the success of the marketing campaign to promote Moosehead beer.

Hershey/Herschi

111. The Commission sent a comfort letter clearing the agreements settling the litigation between Hershey Foods Corporation and Schiffers Onroerend Goed EBV over the right to use the 'Herschi' trade mark for certain food products. Hershey is a large US chocolate manufacturer which has used the 'Hershey' trade mark for a number of years in many countries throughout the world. Schiffers (a Dutch company producing soft drinks) uses the 'Herschi' trade mark on a number of its products. There was therefore a risk of confusion between the trade, marks.

To settle the litigation, Schiffers has assigned its Herschi trade mark to Hershey for valuable consideration, and Hershey has licensed Schiffers to use the Herschi trade mark on an exclusive basis for five years for a defined group of products.

Ford Motor Co. Ltd

112. Following a complaint filed in 1985 by UK independent panel manufacturers, Ford undertook to the Commission that it would reduce the period in which it could still claim registered design protection in respect of body panels in the United Kingdom. The total period of exclusivity will not exceed five years and may be shorter in some cases (three years).

The Commission considers that, while the interests of car manufacturers should not be damaged, it should be ensured that consumers are not dependent on a single producer.

The Commission has always attached importance to maintaining a competitive market for car parts, a policy reflected in the block exemption Regulation for motor vehicle distribution agreements.[1]

---

[1]   Regulation No 123/85, OJ L 15, 18.1.1985.

§ 6 — Abuse of a dominant position

Soda ash

113.   In addition to sanctioning the market-sharing arrangements in the soda ash sector under Article 85 of the EEC Treaty,[1] the Commission found that both Solvay and ICI had put into effect a system of exclusionary rebates contrary to Article 86 of the EEC Treaty.[2] These rebates were designed to induce, and in some cases oblige, customers to obtain the major part or even the whole of their requirements from the dominant producer. For this part of the case a fine of ECU 20 million, the largest fine for a single infringement of EEC competition rules, was imposed on Solvay, which dominates the soda ash market in continental western Europe. ICI, which has over 90% of the market in the United Kingdom and Ireland, was fined ECU 10 million.

The Commission already took action in 1980-82[3] to ensure that Solvay and ICI deleted from their supply agreements clauses requiring customers to purchase the totality of their requirements from the dominant producer.

Force of circumstance has required the glassmakers still to look to Solvay or ICI (as the case might be) for the bulk of their soda ash requirements. Most large customers however also sought a second source of supply, whether from non-EEC imports or from one of the smaller Community producers, as a counterbalance against the dominant producer. In order to minimize the competitive effect of such supplies, Solvay developed a 'two-tier' pricing structure by which the tonnage the customer would have bought from it in any event was charged at normal prices, but the remaining tonnage which the customer would normally have obtained from a second supplier was offered at a substantial (and secret) discount. It was made clear to customers that the 'special price' depended upon their buying most, if not all, their requirements from Solvay.

ICI introduced a system of secret 'top-slice' rebates in the United Kingdom similar to that of Solvay and which also had the object of excluding or minimizing purchases from a competitor. While such rebates cost the dominant supplier very little (being concentrated on a relatively small tonnage), alternative suppliers quoting for this marginal tonnage would have to go below their costs in order to obtain any business.

---

[1]   See point 92 of this Report.
[2]   Decision of 19 December 1990.
[3]   See Eleventh Competition Report, points 73 to 76.

Deutsche Lufthansa/Interflug

114. The Commission watched very closely the planned acquisition of a minority holding by the airline Deutsche Lufthansa in Interflug. Its concern was to ensure that this did not result in the reinforcement of a dominant position in air transport to and from the Federal Republic of Germany. In addition, the Commission was afraid that other investors might be deprived of the possibility of forming links with Interflug. Lastly, the Commission wished to ensure that essential facilities for all users of the airports concerned (air-traffic control, ground handling) would not be controlled by one company in a dominant position.

Memorandum to the railway companies

115. On 9 March 1990, the Commission sent a memorandum to the various national railway companies drawing their attention to the basic principles governing the implementation of the Community competition rules.

The first principle is that any public or private undertaking in a dominant position as a purchaser of goods or services is subject to obligations equivalent to those incumbent on an undertaking which is in a dominant position as a supplier of goods or services.

The second principle is that any undertaking in a dominant position whether as a purchaser or as a seller is under the obligation not to practise any discrimination between suppliers or between customers in the various Member States of the Community. This means that, save in exceptional circumstances, a rail transport undertaking in a dominant position may not set out to obtain the supply of goods or services exclusively from undertakings in its country or from its traditional suppliers.

Any natural person or undertaking suffering injury as a result of infringements of Article 86 of the EEC Treaty by an undertaking in a dominant position is justified in claiming damages in the national courts.

§ 7 — Mergers and concentrations[1]

Air France/Air Inter/UTA

116.   As was the case in March 1988, in connection with the merger between British Airways and British Caledonian, the Commission applied the Community competition rules to the mergers between Air France and Air Inter and UTA in January 1990. In both cases, the merger was finally approved by the Commission after the authorities and airlines in question had given substantial assurances ensuring market access for new airlines so as to allow genuine competition in the market-place to the benefit of consumers and airlines alike.

The agreement reached between the Commission, Air France and the French authorities provides for both substantial opportunities for competition and the setting-up of an independent sector separate from the new group and in competition with it. This independent sector is based on the existing companies which already have the know-how and adequate transport capacity. Air France will accordingly withdraw gradually from the company TAT, which is the fourth French scheduled airline.

The increase in competition will be reflected on a large number of important routes, both domestic and international, from French airports, with an independent French airline being entitled to compete with the Air France group on such routes.

On the French domestic network, the French authorities have given an undertaking that they will designate, in two stages, at least one other French airline not in the Air France group to serve eight routes accounting for more than half of domestic traffic.

In addition, on the Nice/Marseilles-Bastia/Ajaccio routes, Air France will freeze its capacity at current levels. Air France will also give up the Orly-Nice route, with priority being given to French companies not in the Air France group to take up these services. Air France will also, if necessary, surrender up to eight airport slots at intervals over the day from Charles de Gaulle airport.

Lastly, the French authorities will accede to requests for scheduled or non-scheduled air-traffic rights to and from the overseas departments submitted by airlines not in the Air France group and established in France.

With regard to international traffic, the French authorities have given an undertaking that they will designate at least one French airline not in the Air France group on intra- and extra-Community routes to and from France. However, the routes in question must exceed levels equivalent to the thresholds provided for in Article 6 of Council Regulation

---

[1]   See Nineteenth Competition Report, Annex.

No 2343/90 concerning market access and capacity sharing. This undertaking, which will be fulfilled in three stages, relates to 40 routes, to which must be added 10 on which Air France and UTA were already in competition before the formation of the group and where the route has been given up by one of the two airlines. The French authorities will also give priority to French airlines outside the group to operate routes not currently operated by the airlines within the group. Undertakings were also given on slot allocation.

As regards the airlines of the other Member States, the French authorities agreed to grant them air-traffic rights on any route with more than 100 000 passengers. However, this is subject to reciprocal arrangements with the other Member State concerned.

The French authorities will ensure that the airlines designated are entirely free as to the means by which they compete with the airlines belonging to the Air France group. Consequently no restrictions can be imposed on the choice of aircraft or the structure and level of fares nor can such restrictions be advanced as a possible reason for refusing to grant air-traffic rights.

The Commission will follow the implementation of these undertakings closely over a four-year period. For this purpose, reports will be submitted to it twice a year. The Commission also reserves the right to take any necessary measures should the undertakings not be complied with.

In view of the undertakings given, the Commission terminated the procedure which it had initiated on 16 February 1990 against Air France.

Metaleurop

117. The Commission decided not to take any action under Article 86 of the EEC Treaty on the transaction merging the non-ferrous metals activities of the French company Peñarroya SA and the German company Preussag AG. The two companies also set up a new entity known as Metaleurop SA. The commercial side of Metaleurop's operations is separate from the parent companies, as are its management bodies. The merger concerned the zinc and lead markets, on both of which the parent companies each held important positions. Although Metaleurop is the leading European producer, with around 20% of the zinc market and 29% of the lead market, the Commission found that sufficient competition would be maintained, given the presence of a large number of producers and the fact that consumers are able to obtain supplies outside the Community.

Neither party held a dominant position in the market for the products involved in the merger, thus excluding the application of the case-law of the Court of Justice in Continental Can in this instance. The Commission took the view that it was unlikely that the merger would weaken effective competition on the market. In addition, it held that the characteristics of price formation in the lead and zinc sectors made it highly unlikely that Metaleurop would have a decisive influence on the formation of prices.

Europcar/InterRent

118.   In a comfort letter sent following publication of a notice pursuant to Article 19(3) of Regulation No 17,[1] the Commission stated that the agreements notified by the Compagnie internationale des wagons-lits et du tourisme (France) and Volkswagen AG (Federal Republic of Germany) concerning the merger of their respective car rental subsidiaries Europcar and InterRent and providing for the organization of a joint network of affiliated companies or franchisees did not infringe Article 85(1) of the EEC Treaty.

Since the Compagnie des Wagons-Lits and Volkswagen were not competitors, the establishment of the joint arrangement did not restrict competition.

Nevertheless, two clauses in the agreement notified had been deemed unacceptable by the Commission under the competition rules. However, they were removed from the agreement after the Commission had informed the companies of its misgivings. The first of the two clauses provided for a system of preference in favour of Volkswagen in the purchase of new cars; the second provided for compulsory insurance brokerage by the parent companies in insuring Europcar and InterRent vehicles (Europcar and InterRent rank after Avis Europe and Hertz in terms of size in the car rental sector). Merged, the new group will probably be the largest in the Community. However, it will still be smaller than its two American competitors.

Enasa

119.   The agreement linking the German motor vehicle manufacturers MAN and Daimler Benz with the Spanish State holding company INI was notified to the Commission. The agreement provided for MAN to acquire a holding of some 60% and DB to acquire 20% in the capital of the industrial vehicles manufacturer Enasa (a company belonging to INI).

The Commission expressed reservations on this joint holding by two competitors in Enasa; the joint holding was liable to affect their future conduct and could not be accepted under the general principles of competition policy.

---

[1]   OJ C 300, 25.11.1988.

The Commission's position helped to persuade MAN and Daimler Benz to abandon their joint project. Enasa was later acquired by Iveco (Fiat group).

B — APPLICATION OF ARTICLES 65 AND 66 OF THE ECSC TREATY

120.   In 1990, as a result of the improved financial position of the steel industry, it became possible to apply Articles 65 and 66 of the ECSC Treaty with a view to strengthening competition. Over 100 cases were examined in that period, of which 75% related to iron and steel, 20% to coal and 5% to scrap metal.

Over one third of the mergers examined were approved by the Commission on the basis of Article 66(2) of the ECSC Treaty. One decision concerned an agreement prohibited under Article 65 of the ECSC Treaty. Most of the other transactions were exempted from authorization under Decision No 25/67/ECSC.

The operations examined under Article 66 of the ECSC Treaty can be broken down as follows: two thirds concerned the purchase of a majority shareholding or the acquisition of other firms, 14% the acquisition of a minority stake and 20% the setting-up of a joint venture or joint control of a firm.

121.   Between 1953, when the ECSC Treaty entered into force, and 1990, the High Authority, and subsequently the Commission, adopted some 450 decisions on the basis of Articles 65 and 66 of the ECSC Treaty. The following table shows the quantitative results of this policy:

Period	Number of decisions	Annual average decisions adopted
1953-59	21	3
1960-69	132	13.2
1970-79	166	16.6
1980-89	101	10.1
1990	33	33

As regards decisions taken in 1990 pursuant to Article 66, Table 1 shows the type of merger for each ECSC sector.

The ECSC Treaty in 1990 (Table 1)

122.   The Commission believes that, if competition policy is to become more consistent, despite the existence of two separate Treaties, the time has come to bring the ECSC competition rules as far into alignment as possible with those of the Rome Treaty.

TABLE 1

Decisions relating to Article 66 of the ECSC Treaty during 1990

	Coal		Steel		Scrap
	Production	Distribution	Production	Distribution	
Shareholding	BHP / Meekatharra	RAG / BP-Stromeyer Stinnes / Stromeyer	Usinor Sacilor / Allevard Thyssen / Otto Wolff Sollac / CBI ILVA / Zincor / Lavezzari British Steel / Klöckner	Ugine / SAIT Krupp / ESTA British Steel / Walkers Thyssen / ROS Stinnes / Schöder Usinor Sacilor / Merlin Hoesch / Gwent Usinor Sacilor / Beraud-Sudreau Thyssen / Austin Truman Ascometal / Carimi British Steel / Steel of Staffs	Sheerness / Mayer
Joint ventures		Anglo / Doherty / CHL	LME Sikel Mannesmann / GTS (Europipe) Acerinox / Armco	Arbed / Peine Salzgitter Usinor Sacilor / ASD Usinor Sacilor / Acier Rhenan	Hoesch / Kügelfischer Karle / Scholtz / Eisen Metall / Hoesch Usinor Sacilor / STE Monterelaise Rifinsider / RIVA

The application of Article 65 of the ECSC Treaty to agreements between enterprises could be based on the practice developed for Article 85 of the EEC Treaty, as regards both substantive law and rules of procedure.

This would not, however, exclude certain characteristics specific to Article 65 of the ECSC Treaty such as the possibility of authorizing specialization, joint-buying or joint-selling agreements. Furthermore, unlike Article 85 of the EEC Treaty, the application of Article 65 of the ECSC Treaty does not depend on whether trade between Member States is affected.

Mergers are subject to the rules set out in Article 66 of the ECSC Treaty and in the general ECSC implementing decisions, provided that at least one of the firms concerned is an ECSC undertaking within the meaning of Article 80 of the ECSC Treaty. Since the entry into force of Regulation No 4064/89/EEC on merger control on 21 September 1990, the Commission is considering harmonizing, as far as possible, the application of the competition rules laid down in the two Treaties, in particular where agreements or mergers involve both ECSC and EEC products. Harmonization can also be achieved by improving ECSC merger notification procedures and speeding up the adoption of decisions on mergers by the Commission.

§ 1 — Prohibited agreements and practices in the steel industry (Article 65 of the ECSC Treaty)

Agreement in the stainless steel industry

123.   By Decision 90/417/ECSC of 18 July 1990, [1] the Commission imposed fines on six major Community producers of stainless steel flat products for having, in the period 1986-88, engaged in concerted practices consisting in an agreement on a voluntary system of delivery limitation for cold-rolled stainless steel flat products.

The multilateral agreement restricted production and shared markets. It also, by restricting production levels and the freedom of producers to increase sales in the countries covered by the agreement, helped to keep prices higher than they would have been under normal conditions of competition.

124.   The Commission imposed a total of ECU 425 000 in fines on the firms involved.

125.   The fines imposed in this case were lower than in similar cartels in view of the fact that the industry had for a long time been protected from competition by the quota system. As the Commission pointed out in its document 'General steel objectives 1995', the restructuring of the steel industry is now over and, as the quota system has ended, the steel industry should operate in a free and competitive environment. The Commission will no longer tolerate any infringements of the competition rules laid down by the ECSC Treaty. All future ECSC cases will be fined on the same basis as EEC Treaty cases.

---

[1]   OJ L 220, 15.8.1990.

§ 2 — Merger authorizations in the coal industry (Article 66 of the ECSC Treaty)

BHP/Meekatharra

126.   The Commission authorized BHP-Utah International Exploration Inc., USA and Meekatharra (NI) Ltd, Northern Ireland, to set up a joint venture called Ballymoney Coal Venture. The common objective of the venture was to explore and develop brown coal reserves discovered in Northern Ireland. The rational exploitation of the reserves will lead to the construction of a large electricity generating station.

RAG/BP-Stromeyer

127.   The Commission authorized Ruhrkohle Aktiengesellschaft to acquire, through its subsidiary Ruhrkohle Handel GmbH, the domestic and craft solid fuel businesses from the subsidiaries of BP-Stromeyer GmbH, in Mülheim/Ruhr, Frankfurt/Main and Stuttgart.

Stinnes/Stromeyer

128.   Finally, Stinnes Intercarbon AG & Co. (VEBA Group) was authorized to acquire all the shares in Stromeyer GmbH. The two German companies distribute solid and liquid fuels throughout the common market.

§ 3 — Merger authorizations in the steel industry (Article 66 of the ECSC Treaty)

Usinor-Sacilor

129.   Usinor-Sacilor and its subsidiaries were authorized to carry out the following mergers:

(a) Ascometal took control of Allevard Industries (springs);

(b) Sollac acquired Société des forges de Basse-Indre and CMB steel (tinplate producer), followed by a 49% holding in Acier Rhenan, a French steel-slitting company;

(c) Ugine ACG SA acquired two Italian stainless steel distributors: SAIT and Castelli; and

(d) Usinor-Sacilor acquired Merlin SA and 35% of Beraud-Sudreau, two French distribution companies, and Carimi Srl in Italy; it also set up a steel service centre in the United Kingdom with ASD UK.

Thyssen

130.   Thyssen AG was authorized to acquire Otto Wolff, a coated products producer in the Federal Republic of Germany; its subsidiary Thyssen Handelsunion acquired Austin Truman Group Ltd, a steel products distributor in the United Kingdom, and also set up a joint distribution company in Spain with Francisco Ros Casares SA.

ILVA

131.   ILVA acquired an additional 30% of Zincor Italia and Lavezzari Lamiere Sud, of which it already held 35%. The companies manufacture electrogalvanized sheet.

British Steel plc

132.   British Steel plc was authorized to acquire some of the assets and liabilities of Mannstaedt-Werke, a branch of Klöckner Stahl GmbH, and all the equity of a number of German enterprises operating in similar fields to Klöckner Stahl Mannstaedt-Werke (production of heavy sections and merchant bars). British Steel was also authorized to acquire all the shares in C. Walkers & Sons (Holdings) Ltd, Blackburn. British Steel is a producer and distributor of steel products. Walkers is one of the largest steel stockholders and distributors in the United Kingdom.[1]

During its examination of this case, the Commission formally notified its position to the relevant national authorities: the Monopolies and Mergers Commission in the United Kingdom and the Fair Trade Commission in Ireland. Its position concerned, in the present case, the respective competences of the Commission and the Member States for the application of the EEC and ECSC Treaties. British Steel also acquired some of the assets and liabilities of Link 51, known as Steel of Staffs. The holdings relate to the production of cold-rolled narrow strip and equalized strip in the United Kingdom.

Krupp/Esta

133.   Krupp Stahl AG took a 50% stake in Esta GmbH, which processes, cuts and stamps special steels, and markets steel products in the Federal Republic of Germany.

Stinnes/Schöder

134.   Stinnes Stahlhandel GmbH acquired Baustahl Schöder GmbH. Both companies have steel sales centres in the Federal Republic of Germany.

Arbed/Peine Salzgitter

135.   A joint venture, AP-Steel UK Ltd, was set up by Trade-Arbed Participations Sarl (a subsidiary of Arbed SA) and Salzgitter Stahl GmbH (a subsidiary of Preussag Salzgitter AG). The new company will operate a steel products service centre in the United Kingdom.

Gwent Steel/Hoesch

136.   Hoesch AG, a steel producer, acquired an 86.5% majority holding in Gwent Steel, a steel products service centre in the United Kingdom.

---

[1]   Decision 90/234/CECA, OJ L 131, 23.5.1990.

LME: Usinor-Sacilor/Cockerill-Sambre/Arbed

137. Usinor-Sacilor (50%), Cockerill-Sambre (25%) and Arbed (25%) set up a joint venture in France, known as Laminés marchands européens (LME). The new company will organize the production and distribution of merchant bars manufactured by Société métallurgique de l'Escaut (Usinor-Sacilor), the Laminoirs du Ruau (Cockerill-Sambre) and Arbed's rolling mill 330 at Schifflange. Management contracts will enable LME to control all the operations of Société métallurgique de l'Escaut, Laminoirs du Ruau and rolling mill 330. As a result of this transaction, there will be a concentration between LME and each of its parent companies and between LME and the production units.

Sikel: Sidmar-Klöckner

138. Sidmar NV and Klöckner Stahl set up a new company, Sikel NV, in Gent, Belgium. The latter will operate an electrogalvanizing line on a cooperative basis with a capacity of 300 000 tonnes per annum, with Sidmar having two thirds of operating time and Klöckner Stahl one third.

Acerinox-Armco Europa

139. Acerinox SA and Armco Inc. USA set up a new joint venture to market and process in Europe ferritic stainless steel flat products used by the automobile industry for exhaust systems manufactured in Spain.

Europipe

140. Usinor-Sacilor and Mannesmann Röhrenwerke set up a new joint venture in the Federal Republic of Germany called Europipe, which will take over the manufacture and sale of large welded pipes formerly carried out by GTS Industrie and Bergrohr, part of the Usinor-Sacilor group, and by Mannesmann Röhrenwerke.

§ 4 — Merger authorizations in the scrap industry (Article 66 of the ECSC Treaty)

Monterelaise de Broyage

141.   A joint undertaking, the Société Monterelaise de Broyage, was set up by Aciéries de Montereau (30%), Compagnie française des ferrailles (20%), and by Etablissements Jean Robert SA, Etablissements Marchetto, Etablissements Vendrand and Etablissements Ternant, each with 12.5%. The new company will operate a scrap metal crusher in France.

Hoesch

142.   Hoesch Rohstoff GmbH was authorized to acquire all the shares in Schrott-Handelsgesellschaft mbH held by FAG Kügelfisher-Georg Schäfer KGaA. The Commission also authorized the creation by Hoesch Rohstoff GmbH, Eisen und Metall AG, CH. Scholz KG and Jürgen Karle of a joint venture in which each of the abovementioned companies will hold 25%. All the firms concerned are engaged in scrap trading in the Federal Republic of Germany.

Sheerness/Mayer

143.   Sheerness Steel Company plc was authorized to acquire a 75.1% stake in Mayer-Parry Recycling. Both enterprises plan to combine their ferrous and non-ferrous scrap recycling activities in the United Kingdom under the name of Mayer-Parry Recycling Ltd.

Rifinsider/Riva

144.   Riva Prodotti Siderurgici SpA acquired 50% of the shares in Rifinsider SpA, a scrap distributor owned by Ilva. As a result of this acquisition, Riva will improve its scrap supplies in Italy.

§ 5 — Complaints in the coal industry

Small mines, United Kingdom

145.   The Commission received a number of complaints in 1990 from several organizations representing small mines in the United Kingdom. The organizations, namely, the National Association of Licensed Opencast Operators, the Federation of Small Mines of Great Britain and the South Wales Small Mines Association considered in particular that they were the victims of discrimination as regards supplies of coal for the production of electricity. They also considered that the electricity generating companies were paying them lower prices than those obtained by the British Coal Corporation and that the provisions relating to authorization and charges which governed their activities were contrary to various articles of the ECSC and EEC Treaties.

The Commission informed the United Kingdom authorities that it had certain reservations concerning the provisions in question. Following its intervention, the Government of the United Kingdom made an offer to the complainants, on behalf of the electricity companies National Power and Power Gen, and the British Coal Corporation, which significantly improved the position of small mines. Although the offer was rejected, its conditions, relating to prices, a reduction in charges and sales volumes, were applied with retroactive effect from 1 April 1990.

The complainants and British Coal Corporation are still in dispute concerning the agreements under which British Coal authorizes the operation of small mines. The official complaints had still not been withdrawn by the end of the year.

§ 6 — ECSC inspections

146.   As in the past, a series of ECSC inspections was carried out on coal and steel productions subject to the levy (Articles 49 and 50 of the ECSC Treaty) and on steel prices (Article 60 of the ECSC Treaty).

A total of 71 checks were carried out on declared production by coal and steel undertakings and 33 checks on the application of pricing rules by steel undertakings.

Each of the checks was followed up by a report which was sent to the Directorates-General concerned (DG XVIII for Articles 49 and 50 and DG III for Article 60 of the ECSC Treaty).

On 20 February 1990, a fine of ECU 100 000 was imposed on an undertaking for failing to produce certain documents it was required to keep and make available to the Commission officials carrying out the levy checks.

C — MERGER CONTROL

Renault/Volvo

147. The Commission adopted its first decision under Regulation No 4064/89 on the control of concentrations between undertakings in the Renault/Volvo case. The case involved exchanges of shares and the setting-up of joint committees with decision-making powers, one for cars and the other for industrial vehicles.

The Commission decided that the transaction concerning cars had not reached the stage of a concentration within the meaning of Article 3 of the Regulation. It based its decision on the fact that the share swaps were limited to 25%, and that the parties could act independently in the event of disagreement within the joint committee for cars. As a result, the parties were not continuously subject to a single economic management in respect of their car activities.

As regards trucks, however, the parties exchanged 45% of their shares and decided permanently to merge their R&D, production and other truck, coach and bus operations. Their alliance in this sector created lasting and irreversible joint control in this sector. The Commission therefore considered that this operation constituted a concentration within the meaning of Article 3 of the merger control Regulation. As concerns this part of the operation, the Commission considered the merger compatible with the common market as the combined market shares held by Renault and Volvo in the Community barely exceeded 25%. Although the firms undoubtedly held larger shares of certain national markets in the Community, the existing and potential competition from several other major producers in a strong financial position and present on all the national markets would prevent Renault/Volvo alone from significantly determining prices and other conditions of competition on the national markets for industrial vehicles. As a result, the Commission considered that the alliance between Renault and Volvo would not create or strengthen a dominant position liable significantly to impede effective competition in the common market or in a substantial part of it.

As regards the part of the operation concerning cars which was not regarded as constituting a concentration, the Commission informed the parties by letter that there were no grounds for further action under Articles 85 or 86.

AG/AMEV

148. The Commission authorized Groupe AG, the leading Belgian insurance company, and AMEV, the third largest insurer in the Netherlands, to pool their activities and interests. Each company set up a sub-holding company to which they transferred all their shares in various subsidiaries.

AG and AMEV each took 50% of the new sub-holding companies which are managed jointly by the two parent companies. AG and AMEV now operate only as financial holding companies. The result is a new group subject to joint control and is therefore a merger within the meaning of Article 3(1)(b) of the merger control Regulation.

As regards the Community dimension of the case, it was necessary to decide whether the turnover of an insurance company with subsidiaries in the building sector should be calculated solely on the basis of gross premiums, or whether to include the turnover of the subsidiaries. If the activities of those subsidiaries were excluded, the total turnover of the AG and AMEV groups would not have reached the ECU 5 billion threshold. The Commission concluded that total turnover should not exclude the turnover of the building sector subsidiaries, as investments in the building sector were frequently linked to insurance activities. Article 5(3)(b) of the Regulation, which states that in the case of insurance undertakings the value of gross premiums should be used in place of turnover, is simply a special method for calculating turnover resulting from insurance activities. This provision does not exempt insurance companies from the general rules of Article 5. Therefore, Article 5(4) which provides for the adding together of the turnovers of all undertakings belonging to the same group also applies to insurance undertakings.

Both AG and AMEV hold leading positions on their respective national markets. In view of the fact, however, that each company is only a minor competitor on the national market of the other, the concentration does not have the effect of creating or strengthening a dominant position and is therefore compatible with the common market.

ICI/Tioxide

149.   The Commission also decided not to object to the acquisition by Imperial Chemical Industries (ICI) of the 50% stake held by Cookson in Tioxide Group plc, which it considered compatible with the common market under the merger control Regulation. ICI already owned 50% prior to the transaction; as a result it now holds the entire capital of Tioxide.

Tioxide is the second largest producer worldwide of titanium pigments (titanium dioxide), and the largest in Europe. In 1989, its sales accounted for over 30% of the Community market for titanium dioxide. Over 60% of its sales are used in the manufacture of paints.

ICI is one of the largest paint manufacturers in the world and the largest customer of Tioxide; the latter currently provides ICI with most of its titanium dioxide requirements for its European paint operations. In view of the extent of the vertical relationship, the markets for paints were regarded as the relevant markets and were also subjected to scrutiny.

ICI and Tioxide productions do not overlap and the transaction should not impede or restrict access to the markets concerned. In view of the facts of the case, the Commission considered that the acquisition of sole control by ICI did not create or strengthen a dominant position on any of the markets in question.

Under the terms of the transaction, a founding company took control of a joint venture previously run under joint control. The Commission considered that this was a concentration within the meaning of Article 3 of the Regulation because the acquisition of complete control changed the nature of the influence ICI had over Tioxide's decisions.

Arjomari-Prioux/Wiggins Teape Appleton

150.   Having examined the notifications submitted by the firms concerned, the Commission adopted a decision which concluded that the transaction did not fall within the scope of the Regulation as the worldwide turnover threshold laid down by the Regulation had not been reached.

The Commission considered that the two-stage transaction — transfer of the assets and liabilities of Arjomari-Prioux to one of its subsidiaries, followed by an exchange of all the shares in the latter for 39% of the shares in Wiggins Teape Appleton — constituted a concentration under Article 3 of the Regulation.

As a result of the transaction, Arjomari would be in a position to exercise decisive influence on Wiggins Teape, pursuant to Article 3 of Regulation (EEC) No 4064/89, the balance of the latter's capital being distributed among a large number of shareholders, none of whom would exercise significant influence.

On the other hand, the transaction did not have a Community dimension within the meaning of Article 5 of the Regulation since the aggregate turnover of the two enterprises concerned was less than ECU 5 billion, and the turnover of the parent company, Arjomari-Prioux, could not be taken into account.

The case allowed the Commission to define the method by which, in order to calculate thresholds, it would take account of enterprises with the power to appoint more than half the members of the management board of an enterprise affected by the concentration.

The question was to determine whether the principal shareholder in Arjomari-Prioux, St Louis, could be included in the calculation of turnover since it held only

45.19% of voting rights at the last general meeting of Arjomari shareholders. In the case in point, however, it was not shown that St Louis exercised the power referred to in Article 5(4)(b) of the Regulation to appoint over half the members of the management board of an enterprise. The Commission considered that this power existed not only if specifically provided for under a contract but also if an enterprise without an absolute majority in respect of voting rights in another enterprise was nevertheless able to secure a majority of votes at the general meeting in question.

Promodes/Dirsa

151.   Promodes, a French distributor, acquired through its Spanish subsidiary all the shares in the supermarket chain Dirsa, until then a subsidiary of the public undertaking Tabacalera.

The two firms concerned are engaged in the retail distribution of foodstuffs (fresh and dried products) and other goods (ironmongery, perfumes and cosmetics, toilet preparations). As the various groups of consumer products concerned amounted essentially to a service, the Commission did not distinguish between them; taken as a whole, they represent a distribution activity and as such should be assessed on an overall basis. On the other hand, the Commission distinguished between the supply of small specialized businesses, small neighbourhood shops (under 400 m²) and medium- and large-scale distribution areas offering a far greater assortment of products. In determining the geographical market, various factors pointed to the conclusion that retail distribution corresponds to local markets from the standpoint of homogeneous conditions of competition.

Although the transaction brought Promodes into the front rank of Spanish retail distributors, its share after the merger of all the local markets concerned did not give rise to serious doubts as to the creation or strengthening of a dominant position.

As to Promodes' vertical relations with its suppliers, the new group's purchases, taken as a whole, did not represent more than 15% of the turnover of each main supplier after the transaction.

The Commission therefore decided not to oppose the concentration and to consider it compatible with the common market.

Cargill/Unilever

152.   The Commission also ruled that the acquisition by Cargill plc (Cargill), a subsidiary of the American firm Cargill Inc., of United Agricultural Merchanting Ltd (UAM), a division of Unilever, was compatible with the common market.

Cargill and UAM both trade in agricultural products in the United Kingdom, including the purchase of cereals, oilseeds and seed legumes from farmers, and the sale to the latter of seeds, animal feedingstuffs, fertilizers and agricultural chemicals.

The Commission examined the horizontal and vertical effects of the merger on the markets concerned.

In its analysis, despite the local nature of the activity concerned but with no evidence of any segmentation into separate markets with sufficiently different competitive conditions, the Commission left open the question of whether the relevant geographical market was local, regional or national. It noted that, even taking the narrowest definition, i.e. the territories in which each distributor party to the contract provided its services to farmers, the concentration did not have the effect of creating or strengthening a dominant position through the combining of the shares held by the parties in the product markets concerned. Among the reasons for this is the fact that the merger does not result in market shares exceeding 26% on the markets concerned, barriers to entry are very low and there is little structural concentration.

As regards the vertical effects of the merger, the Commission considered that the advantages accruing to Cargill in terms of access to the UK market for cereals and oilseed would not be an obstacle to effective competition on downstream markets.

Chapter II

Main decisions and measures taken by the Commission

90.   In 1990, the Commission adopted 15 decisions on substantive matters under Articles 85 and 86 of the EEC Treaty. The nine decisions taken on the basis of Article 85 of the EEC Treaty are broken down as follows: four exemption decisions under Article 85(3), three negative clearances, one prohibition decision without any fine and one prohibition decision accompanied by fines. There were three decisions formally rejecting complaints.

In addition, 158 procedures were terminated by the sending of comfort letters, including three following publication of notices pursuant to Article 19(3) of Regulation No 17.[1] The procedures concern notifications which did not result in a formal decision: the undertakings concerned being satisfied with a written statement of position from the Directorate-General for Competition on the conformity of their agreement with Article 85(1) or (3).

A further 710 cases were settled either because the agreements were no longer in force, their impact was too slight to warrant further consideration, the complaints had become inapplicable or the file had been closed without any further action being taken.

The Commission also adopted 33 decisions under Articles 65 and 66 of the ECSC Treaty.

91.   On 31 December 1990, there were 2 734 cases pending (as against 3 239 on 31 December 1989), of which 2 145 were applications or notifications (201 submitted in 1990), 345 were complaints from firms (97 made in 1990) and 244 were proceedings initiated by the Commission on its own initiative (77 commenced in 1990).

---

[1]   Council Regulation No 17 of 6 February 1962, OJ 13, 21.2.1962.

The Court upheld this analysis.

(a) Definition of agreement within the meaning of Article 85(1) of the EEC Treaty

155.   The principal interest of the judgment lies in the Court's reasoning on the applicant's main argument, which was that the inclusion of the words 'not to be exported' on the invoices sent to customers was a purely unilateral act, so that there was no unity of purpose between Sandoz and its customers which might constitute an agreement within the meaning of Article 85(1) of the EEC Treaty.

The Court held that the invoices 'did not constitute unilateral conduct but, on the contrary, formed part of the general commercial relations which the undertaking maintained with its customers'. Sandoz's customers had acquiesced in the restriction.

The judgment follows precedent in holding that where the conduct of an undertaking forms part of a contractual relationship with dealers it may be caught by Article 85(1) of the EEC Treaty if the dealers are found to have accepted it, tacitly or expressly.[1] In this case the Court observed that the customers had placed fresh orders and had repeatedly settled invoices bearing the words 'not to be exported' without protest; this amounted on their part to 'tacit acquiescence in the clauses stipulated on the invoice and in the kind of commercial relationship on which the business relationship between Sandoz and its customers was based'. The approval initially given to customers by Sandoz rested on the tacit acceptance by the customers of Sandoz's conduct towards them.

(b) An export ban is by its nature covered by Article 85(1) of the EEC Treaty

156.   The Court pointed out[2] that for the purpose of applying Article 85(1), there was no need to take account of the concrete effects of an agreement once it appeared that it had as its object the prevention, restriction or distortion of competition in the common market.

Therefore the absence in the contested decision of any analysis of the effects of the agreement on competition did not constitute a defect which would be grounds for annulling the decision.

---

[1]   Case C-107/82 *AEG.*
[2]   Joined Cases 56 and 58/64 *Consten* and *Grundig* v *Commission* (1966) ECR 299, p. 342.

(c) An export ban is a serious infringement of the EEC Treaty rules, and justifies a fine

157. The Court nevertheless stated that it was necessary, in determining the amount of fines, to take account of all the factors likely to affect assessment of the seriousness of the infringement; as an extenuating circumstance it noted that the company had changed its conduct by dropping the contested words as soon as the Commission asked it to do so. The Court accordingly reduced the fine imposed from ECU 800 000 to 500 000.

§ 2 — Absolute territorial protection clauses

158.   In Tipp-Ex[1] the Court of Justice upheld in its entirety the Commission Decision of 10 August 1987,[2] which found that agreements concluded and practices engaged in by the applicant and its distributors were contrary to Article 85(1) of the EEC Treaty because they established a system of absolute territorial protection. The Court also upheld the fine imposed by the Commission.

The judgment follows precedent in refusing to accept the applicant's argument that it was not aware that it might be infringing the ban in Article 85 of the EEC Treaty. It was sufficient, the Court said, that an offender 'could not have failed to be aware that the purpose of the conduct involved was to restrict competition'.

In the circumstances of the case the Court said that the fact that legal advice which the firm had obtained was wrong was not sufficient to exonerate it from blame.

---

[1]   Case C-279/87.
[2]   OJ L 222, 10.8.1987; Seventeenth Competition Report, point 61.

§ 3 — Application of Article 86 to agreements covered by a block exemption under Article 85(3) of the EEC Treaty

159.   In Tetra Pak, its first judgment in a competition case, the Court of First Instance had to determine the question whether Article 86 could be applied to behaviour which was covered by a block exemption under Article 85(3) of the EEC Treaty.[1]

In a Decision adopted on 26 July 1988[2] the Commission found that Tetra Pak, the largest manufacturer of cartons for liquid foods in the Community, had abused its dominant position by acquiring an exclusive licence for a new process for sterilizing long-life milk cartons. Tetra Pak acquired the exclusive licence when it took over a competitor and thus deprived another competitor, Elopak, of the possibility of using the new technology.

The licence was within the scope of the block exemption Regulation for patent licensing agreements,[3] but it enabled Tetra Pak to abuse its dominant position by strengthening its dominant position and making it more difficult for new competitors to enter the market. The Commission took the view that it was also entitled to withdraw the benefit of the block exemption under Article 9 of the Regulation.

Tetra Pak sought the annulment of the Commission Decision, relying on one ground only: an agreement which qualified for a block exemption under Article 85(3) of the EEC Treaty, it said, could not at the same time be prohibited by Article 86 so long as the Commission had not withdrawn the benefit of the exemption. In other words Article 86 of the EEC Treaty was inapplicable to an agreement which was exempted under Article 85(3).

The Court upheld the Commission's view, and dismissed Tetra Pak's application, holding that the grant of exemption, under Article 85(3) of the EEC Treaty, whether to an individual agreement or to a category of agreements, could not render inapplicable the prohibition set out in Article 86 of the EEC Treaty.

There are three important points which deserve special mention.

(a) Relationship between Articles 85 end 86 of the EEC Treaty clarified

160.   The relationship between Articles 85 and 86 of the EEC Treaty was clarified in certain respects by the judgment, which expressly accepted that the applicability of

---

[1]   Case T-51/89 *Tetra Pak Rausing* v *Commission*.
[2]   OJ L 272, 4.10.1988; Eighteenth Competition Report, point 72.
[3]   Commission Regulation (EEC) No 2349/84 of 23 July 1984 on the application of Article 85(3) of the EEC Treaty to certain categories of patent licensing agreements, OJ L 219, 16.8.1984; corrigendum OJ L 113, 26.4.1985.

Article 85 to an agreement did not rule out the application of Article 86 of the EEC Treaty. It had already been established in other judgments that there were situations where the Commission was free to apply both Articles,[1] and three cases currently pending before the Court of First Instance raise the same question in more general terms.[2]

The two provisions, the Court now said, were complementary: they pursued the same general objective, namely ensuring that competition in the common market was not distorted (Article 3(f) of the EEC Treaty), but were legally independent, as Article 85 dealt with agreements between undertakings while Article 86 of the EEC Treaty related to unilateral action by one or more undertakings.

(b) Scope of Article 86 of the EEC Treaty

161.   The Court was at pains to make it clear that mere acquisition of an exclusive licence by a company holding a dominant position did not by itself constitute an abuse within the meaning of Article 86 of the EEC Treaty. In applying Article 86 account had to be taken of the circumstances surrounding the acquisition, and in particular its effects on the structure of competition on the market concerned. The Commission had been right not to challenge the exclusive licence itself, but to apply Article 86 of the EEC Treaty specifically to the anticompetitive effect of Tetra Pak's acquisition of the licence (ground 23).

(c) A block exemption does not have to be withdrawn for a finding that Article 86 of the EEC Treaty has been infringed

162.   The Court said that for Article 86 to apply it was not necessary that an individual or block exemption be withdrawn first, as Tetra Pak had argued. 'If the Commission were required in every case to take a decision withdrawing exemption before applying Article 86 of the EEC Treaty, this would be tantamount, in view of the non-retroactive nature of the withdrawal of exemption, to accepting that an exemption under Article 85(3) of the EEC Treaty operated in reality as a concurrent exemption from the prohibition of abuse of a dominant position'. But an abuse of a dominant position could never be exempted.

---

[1]   Case 85/76 *Hoffman-La Roche*; Case 66/86 *Ahmed Saeed*; Nineteenth Competition Report, points 90 to 93.

[2]   Cases T-68/89 *SIV*, T-77/89 *Fabbrica Pisana* and T-78/89 *Vernante Pennitalia* (flat glass); the actions are directed against a Commission decision finding that the applicants had abused a 'collective dominant position'. A hearing is to take place at the end of May 1991.

§ 4 — Procedure: complaints

163.   The judgment of the Court of First Instance in Automec is of interest for two reasons. Firstly, it sums up and clarifies the administrative procedure to be followed where the Commission rejects a complaint lodged under Article 3 of Council Regulation No 17.[1]

It also clarifies the proper form of the preliminary observations which the Commission departments generally send to an applicant before embarking on an analysis of the substance of the case.[2]

(a) Procedure where a complaint is rejected

164.   A complainant has no right to demand that the Commission take a formal decision finding that an infringement has or has not taken place. But the complainant is entitled to be told the reasons why the Commission does not propose to act on his complaint.[3]

In line with the Commission's own administrative practice the Court distinguished three stages in the procedure leading to the rejection of a complaint.

(i)   At the first stage, which the Court referred to as the 'communication of preliminary observations', the Commission assembled the information necessary to determine what action to take. There might for example be an informal exchange of views and information between the Commission and the complainant, intended to clarify the points of fact and law to which the complaint related and to give the complainant the opportunity of enlarging upon his allegations if necessary in the light of initial comments from the Commission departments.

(ii) The second stage corresponded to the notice to be given under Article 6 of Commission Regulation No 99/63/EEC.[4] This was something like a statement of objections in reverse, in that the Commission here gave a full explanation of the reasons why it could not act. This provision was essential in order to safeguard the rights of complainants, who had to be given the information they needed in order to be able to protect their interests.

(iii) At the third stage the Commission considered any further comments submitted by the complainant. This stage could end with a final decision. The Court of Justice

---

[1]   OJ 13, 21.2.1962; OJ 58, 10.7.1962; OJ 162, 7.11.1963; OJ L 285, 29.12.1971.
[2]   Case T-64/89 *Automec* v *Commission*.
[3]   Case 125/78 *GEMA* v *Commission*; Ninth Competition Report, points 30 to 32.
[4]   OJ 127, 20.8.1963.

had several times accepted that the Commission was entitled to take a final decision rejecting the complaint and closing the case. Only this final decision could be the subject of proceedings before the Court of First Instance. [1]

The Court of First Instance was careful to distinguish the two later stages of the procedure from the communication of preliminary observations, which ought not to appear to be a final refusal to act on an application for a finding that an infringement had taken place.

(b) The 'communication of preliminary observations' is a preparatory legal act which cannot infringe a complainant's rights

165.   The letter from the Commission departments fell within the first stage of the investigation of the complaint, and was in the nature of a preparatory act which by definition could not affect the applicant's rights. Proceedings brought against such a preparatory act had therefore to be dismissed as inadmissible, because that act was not an act or decision within the terms of Article 173 of the EEC Treaty.

The Court accordingly considered what the proper form of such a communication would be. The assessment put forward in it had to be provisional.

The parts of the letter sent in this case which briefly drew the applicant's attention to the absence of any information which might suggest that the distribution system was incompatible with Community law did not show that a final assessment had already been made.

In any event the letter contained no express statement saying that the complaint had been rejected and that the case was to be closed, unlike the decisions the Commission had adopted on other complaints.   .

The case shows that where a firm has lodged a complaint with the Commission under Article 3(2)(b) of Regulation No 17, the explanations given to it by the Commission departments must be complete.

The Court held that the Commission's reaction to the applicant's complaint in this case was ambiguous, and could have given rise to doubts as to its legal nature. The applicant had been left 'in a position of legal uncertainty as to whether the Commission's document constituted a decision'.

In future, therefore, the Commission departments will take particular care to avoid wordings which might be thought ambiguous and which might give a complainant the impression that his complaint had been definitively rejected.

---

[1]   Case 210/81 *Demo-Studio Schmidt* v *Commission*.

Letters stating the Commission's preliminary observations will be drafted so as to make it clear that they represent only an initial Commission reaction on the basis of the information in the Commission's possession. Complainants will in any event always be asked to submit any further comments within a reasonable time, failing which the case may be considered closed.

§ 5 — Legal character of certain letters sent by the Commission

166.   In its *Omni-Partijen Akkoord* judgments[1] the Court of First Instance accepted the Commission's view that a letter to the Dutch Government from the Member of the Commission with special responsibility for competition policy, which was purely factual in nature, produced no legal effects and consequently was not an act against which proceedings could be brought under Article 173 of the EEC Treaty.

The judgment also pointed out that the letter was not founded on a legal basis which would authorize the Commission to take a decision binding a Member State. The letter, which was addressed to a Member State, was therefore merely an opinion which had no legal effect. As the Commission had argued in its submissions to the Court, neither Article 85 of the EEC Treaty nor Regulation No 17 give the Commission power to take decisions binding on Member States. Article 3(1) of Regulation No 17 empowered the Commission to require undertakings or associations of undertakings to bring infringements of Community law committed by them to an end, but it did not authorize the Commission to require a Member State to take particular measures in its domestic law.

---

[1]   Case T-113/89 *Nefarma* v *Commission*; Case T-114/89 *Vereniging Nederlandse Ziekenfondsen and Others* v *Commission*; Case T-116/89 *Prodifarma and Others* v *Commission*.

§ 6 — Copyright management

167.   In Cholay[1] the Court of Justice confirmed its findings in earlier cases, in response to a request for a preliminary ruling referred by the Paris Court of Appeal. It held that a supplementary mechanical-reproduction fee collected by a national performing-rights society in addition to the royalties for the performing rights was compatible with Articles 30 and 36 of the EEC Treaty even where such an additional fee was not provided for in the Member State in which the same recordings had been lawfully marketed.

---

[1]   Case C-270/86 *Cholay and Another* v *SACEM*.

§ 7 — State monopolies

168.   In Case C-347/88 *Commission* v *Greece*[1] the Court of Justice held that by adopting a law and the measures for its implementation which maintained in effect the State's importing and marketing rights for petroleum products imported from other Member States, subjected the distribution companies' annual procurement programmes to the approval of the Greek authorities, and established a system of marketing quotas, Greece had failed to fulfil its obligations under Articles 30, 34 and 37(1) of the EEC Treaty.

The Court did not rule on the substance of the Commission's objections to certain aspects of the rules on maximum consumer prices, because the Commission had failed to observe the procedural requirements.

The Court also rejected the Commission's objections to the State's exclusive right to import crude oil. Although Article 30 of the EEC Treaty prohibits all quantitative restrictions on imports and all measures having equivalent effect between Member States, which includes all trading rules enacted by Member States which are capable of hindering trade within the Community, directly or indirectly, actually or potentially, the Court pointed out that, independently of any provision conferring an import monopoly on the State, the fact that the State had a refining monopoly allowed it to control both the volume of imports of crude oil for refining purposes and the conditions under which they were carried out. In other words, the fact that such imports were exclusively carried out by the State or under its control was inherent in the existence of a national refining monopoly. Consequently, the legislative provisions conferring on the State a monopoly of the importation of crude oil for refining purposes merely confirmed the existence of a privilege which could not be dissociated from the national refining monopoly.

Under those circumstances, the lawfulness in Community law of the Greek State's monopoly of the importation of crude oil could be challenged only if the lawfulness in Community law of the national refining monopoly was also contested. However, the Commission had expressly indicated that it did not contest the national refining monopoly.

The Court accordingly dismissed the claims relating to the State's rights in respect of the import of crude oil.

---

[1]   Case C-347/88, Judgment of 13 December 1990.

Part Three

Competition policy and government assistance to enterprises

Chapter I

State aid

§ 1 — General policy problems and developments

Overall thrust of policy

169. Since the beginning of the common market, competition policy has been an important instrument in stimulating economic growth and integrating the economies of the different Member States. State aid policy has always played a key role in this respect because without adequate Community control State aid could constitute a barrier to the construction of the common market. Now with the moves towards completing the internal market the role of competition as the main stimulus to economic change is becoming even more important. Competition is bound to intensify as the internal market nears completion because barriers to, and therefore costs of, trade between Member States are being systematically reduced as a result of Community action. Consequently, hitherto partially protected national markets will become increasingly accessible to more competitors in other Member States. If Member States use aid to defend companies or industries coming under pressure from this increased competition, or grant aid to counteract the effect of assistance given in other Member States, competition will be distorted and there is a danger that industrial structures will become ossified. Furthermore, unless undistorted competition is allowed to restructure Community industry, very little of the macroeconomic gains which according to forecasts should result from the completion of the internal market (e.g. a 5% increase in national income, or the creation of two million jobs) will in fact be realized. Competition is the main vehicle for securing these advantages, and competition-distorting aid measures threaten the very rationale of the internal market. Consequently, a reinforced State aid policy is not only vital to the successful completion of the internal market but a necessary prerequisite if the projected gains from such integration are to be realized.

In assessing State aid the Commission will be even more vigilant than in the past in order to ensure that aid measures are approved only if they both promote recognized Community objectives and do not frustrate the move towards the internal market. In this respect the Commission has in mind particularly the goal of cohesion which permits aid for the promotion of peripheral and poorer regions of the Community. A stricter policy in the richer regions will increase the aid differentials in favour of less-advantaged regions and thereby contribute to cohesion. This policy of tightening discipline in richer regions where aid can have a greater distorting effect will be focused not just on regional aid in these regions but also on other general or industry schemes whose impact is felt primarily in such richer regions. Such a reinforced State aid policy will act as a complement to the Community's structural Funds.

Transparency

170.   The reinforced aid discipline described above implies a need for increased transparency in the Commission's knowledge of aid schemes currently in operation in Member States and their real economic impact. It also necessitates a better understanding by Member States of the operation of this policy. The Commission has already started this policy of increased transparency. In 1988 it published its first survey on State aids[1] which analyzed the volume, trends, form and objectives of aid measures in 1981-86. This information has now been updated for 1987-88 in the second survey, which includes Spain and Portugal for the first time.[2] The volume of aid identified in this survey confirms the threat aid measures pose to the internal market. It is intended that the survey will be updated regularly.

These surveys also provide important background material for a review of the Commission's general policy in key areas. As an essential part of this review the Commission has decided to hold regular (usually at least twice-yearly) multilateral meetings with aid experts from all Member States. These meetings normally discuss proposals outlining general policy or aid codes in key areas before they are adopted by the Commission. This allows experts from Member States to give their views at an early stage of policy formulation and enables the Commission's staff to explain the necessity for the proposed action at the same early stage. This two-way flow of information greatly helps transparency on both sides.

In previous years the Commission has held such meetings on an *ad hoc* basis to discuss the general policy implications of the results of the first survey on State aids[3] and for the standardization of notifications of aid measures and of annual reports by Member States on the operation of approved aid schemes.[4] During 1990 the experts discussed

---

[1]   See point 162 of the Eighteenth Competition Report.
[2]   See point 188 of this Report for details.
[3]   Eighteenth Competition Report, points 162 and 163.
[4]   Nineteenth Competition Report, point 126. It is expected that final proposals on this topic will be produced in the course of 1991.

proposals from the Commission departments on two topics: aid to public enterprises, and rescue operations and the treatment of enterprises in difficulties. There will be further consultation with these experts and within the Commission during 1991 before any final proposals are made. A series of multilateral meetings with experts is also envisaged for 1991 to discuss other key policy areas.

Likewise with improved transparency in mind, a discussion was held in the Industry Council in October 1990 between the Ministers for Industry of the Member States and the Commissioner responsible for competition matters, Sir Leon Brittan. The meeting considered the effects of the rules of competition on industrial policy and the follow-up to the surveys on State aids. The discussion was initiated by the proposal from certain Member States that the Council should play a greater role in policy formulation for State aids and in particular that the Commission should propose a Regulation under Article 94 to the Council with the aim of making aid policy more transparent. However, this view was rejected by the majority of Member States, who felt that the Commission's proposals for increasing transparency and legal certainty for Member States were sufficient. As part of its programme to increase transparency, the Commission offered to:

(a) hold twice-yearly meetings with experts from Member States;

(b) publish a collection of the existing rules of competition, setting out State aid procedures, general policy guidelines, aid codes and regulations, and judgments of the Court of Justice in the field;

(c) present its annual Competition Report to the Industry Council as a basis for a general discussion.

The programme to implement this offer is already under way. The Commission has already started to hold regular multilateral meetings.[1] It has also published this year a collection of policy guidelines, aid codes and regulations on State aids[2] which will be followed by a further volume to include Court decisions and administrative rules. It is intended that these collections of State aid rules will be regularly updated. Also with transparency in mind, the Commission publishes a summary of all cases dealt with in the monthly Bulletin of the European Communities and issues press releases in the more important cases. This is in addition to the publication of all final decisions in the Official Journal (L series), and to the notice given in the Official Journal (C series) of all cases in which Article 93(2) proceedings are initiated.

---

[1]   See point 5 of this Report.
[2]   Competition law in the European Communities, Volume II: Rules applicable to State aids.

Review of aid schemes under Article 93(1) of the EEC Treaty[1]

171.   One of the conclusions drawn at a multilateral meeting with experts from the Member States held in 1989 was that the Commission needed to exercise the powers given to it by Article 93(1) of the EEC Treaty to review existing aid schemes in the Member States more systematically. Article 93(1) of the EEC Treaty provides for such reviews to be undertaken, in cooperation with Member States, following which the Commission may propose any appropriate measures required by the progressive development of the common market. If the Member State concerned does not agree to take the measures proposed, the Commission is empowered to use the Article 93(2) procedure of the EEC Treaty to impose whatever changes or reductions it considers necessary, or indeed to require the ending of a scheme as a whole.

The review of existing schemes is necessary because many of them were approved years ago at a time when the economic circumstances were different, for example during the recession of the second half of the 1970s and early 1980s, and when the Community market was more fragmented than is the case today. It may be, therefore, that the authorization given by the Commission at the time is no longer justified.

This general review had to begin by considering the schemes most likely to distort competition and trade in the Community. First and foremost among these are general investment aid schemes,[2] that is to say schemes which are not directed at a specific industry or region and do not pursue a specific Community objective, so that they do not qualify for exemption under Article 92(3)(a) or (c) of the EEC Treaty. In practice such schemes are used as a general investment incentive, available on a wide scale, or, when they are used more selectively, are simply a means of helping individual firms on an *ad hoc* basis.

Such assistance has repercussions contrary to economic and social cohesion and to Community regional development policy. Not only does it reduce the cost of investment by the recipient firms by comparison with their competitors in other Member States; it also attracts to the Member State concerned mobile investment which might have located elsewhere in the Community. In addition, a general aid scheme in one Member State can neutralize the attraction of regional aid available in other Member States and in the same Member State's own development areas.

For these reasons, and in view of the fact that as the single market is established the negative effects of aid of this kind on competition and trade within the Community will be accentuated, the Commission must take an increasingly strict line towards such schemes.

---

[1]   Nineteenth Competition Report, point 120.
[2]   Nineteenth Competition Report, point 121.

Unnotified aid

172. The Treaty requires all aid to be notified to the Commission at the proposal stage, in order to allow it to determine whether the aid is compatible with the common market. Where aid schemes are not so notified they enter into force without this prior examination of their compatibility, and thus represent a threat to the single market. The Commission has repeatedly expressed its concern[1] at the delays which have arisen in the scrutiny of unnotified aid and has recognized that examination of these measures needed to be accelerated. In the *Boussac* case, the Court of Justice had occasion to consider the entire range of questions relating to unnotified aid measures.[2] The conclusions the Commission has drawn for the handling of such cases are as follows.

When such a measure comes to the Commission's notice it will first ask the Member State for full information on the aid involved. If the Member State does not reply, or if its reply is unsatisfactory, the Commission may take:

(a) a provisional decision requiring the Member State to suspend the operation of the aid scheme, or payment of the illicit aid, and to inform the Commission of the manner of its compliance with the decision within 15 days;

(b) a decision initiating proceedings under Article 93(2) of the EEC Treaty and giving the Member State one month's notice to submit its comments and all information relevant to an assessment of the compatibility of the aid with the common market.

If a Member State should fail to supply the information requested in the time allowed despite the opening of proceedings, the Commission may take a final decision under Article 93(2) of the EEC Treaty, on the basis of the information in its possession, finding that the aid is incompatible with the common market. The decision will require that aid already paid over unlawfully be recovered, in accordance with the domestic law of the Member State concerned, including its rules on the charging of interest on debts owed to the government, such interest normally being payable from the date on which the unlawful aid was paid over.

If the Member State does not comply with the decisions, whether a provisional decision or the negative final decision, the Commission may refer the matter directly to the Court of Justice under the second subparagraph of Article 93(2) of the EEC Treaty, and apply for interim measures if necessary.

---

[1]   OJ C 252, 30.9.1980; OJ C 318, 24.11.1983.
[2]   Case 301/87, Part Three, Chapter IV of this Report.

State aid and German unification

173. At the beginning of 1990, when the process of German unification was at an early stage, the Commission defined its general approach to State aid in that context. It said that while State aid was clearly needed in order to help the adaptation and restructuring of the East German economy the distortion of competition to which such aid might lead could not be overlooked. The Community rules on State aid should be applied from the outset, in order to maintain a balance between the needs of the former German Democratic Republic as it underwent the necessary economic changes and the avoidance of distortions of competition.

Even in the period before monetary union between the two Germanys, the Commission agreed with the Federal German authorities that they would keep it informed of all measures taken to develop the economy of the East. If these measures constituted State aid, or contained an aid element, the Commission would determine whether they were compatible with Article 92 of the EEC Treaty. The Commission would seek to ensure that all such measures were in line with Community objectives and did not unduly distort competition.

174. Thus, in May, the Commission raised no objection to the extension of the ERP (European Recovery Programme) Fund to the territory of the German Democratic Republic. The Federal authorities had made provision for interest subsidies on loans for investment totalling about ECU 3 billion (DM 6 billion) for the period 1990-93, ECU 0.6 billion (DM 1.2 billion) of this figure being for 1990. In June the Commission approved 11 more measures taken by the Federal and regional (*Länder*) authorities to promote the conversion of the economy of the German Democratic Republic. Three further measures were accepted in July, one being an increase in the volume of ERP loans for 1990 from ECU 0.6 billion (DM 1.2 billion) to ECU 3 billion (DM 6 billion).

175. The Staatsvertrag entered into force with the introduction of monetary union on 1 July. Article 14 provided for coordination between the governments of the Federal Republic and of the German Democratic Republic regarding certain structural measures proposed by the German Democratic Republic, and Article 28 provided for financial assistance from the Federal budget to offset budget deficits in the German Democratic Republic. Inasmuch as these articles led to the provision of assistance in the German Democratic Republic which could be granted only with the consent of the Federal authorities and which was to be financed directly or indirectly by the Federal budget, the Commission took the view that these measures, too, had to be assessed under Articles 92 and 93 of the EEC Treaty.

176. Since political union on 3 October, the existing rules on State aid which are part of the established law of the Community, the *acquis communautaire*, have been fully applicable throughout the united Germany.

177. Only two legislative changes were needed in the State aid field, in relation to shipbuilding and the steel industry. On shipbuilding, the Council accepted the Commission's proposal that the existing Community legislation, the sixth Directive, could apply to East Germany as far as restructuring aid was concerned (investment aid, aid for closures, and aid for research and development). For operating aid, however, a special clause was inserted, similar to that applying to Spain and Portugal, to allow a higher rate of assistance to be granted in the former GDR than was permitted for other Community yards until the expiry of the sixth Directive at the end of 1990. This exemption clause was not included in the seventh Directive, which was adopted by the Council on 21 December 1990 and is to apply from 1 January 1991 to 31 December 1993.[1] However, it was recorded in the minutes of the Council meeting that 'the Council and the Commission acknowledge that the particular problems of the shipbuilding industry in the territories of the former German Democratic Republic may, during a transitional period, require aid support which cannot be covered under the provisions of the Directive. It is, however, evident that at this stage it is not possible with any certainty to ascertain the aid requirement necessary in order to adapt the shipbuilding industry in that part of the territory to operate at the same level of competitiveness as yards in the remainder of the Community'. The Council and the Commission stated that they are 'willing to reconsider a request from the German Government for a transitional arrangement ... as soon as transparency on the above questions has been provided'.

The steel industry in the former German Democratic Republic will need to be restructured to a considerable extent in order to ensure its viability and to integrate it into the common market. Acting under Article 95 of the ECSC Treaty, after consulting the Consultative Committee and with the assent of the Council, the Commission authorized the Federal Republic of Germany to grant aid for investment in the steel industry, provided the investment was intended to make the industry competitive without increasing production capacity.

178. On the question of State aid granted in the areas of the Federal Republic bordering on the former German Democratic Republic and in West Berlin, the Commission has taken the view that, since political union, there is no longer any economic justification for continuing to subsidize these areas. It has welcomed the Federal authorities' stated intention of completely doing away with such aid. Initial talks with the Federal authorities regarding the ending of this aid have focused on the question of transitional periods and the reduction of regional aid in the territory of the former Federal Republic from 1 January 1991 onward; the principle of such a reduction was agreed in 1987.

179. In November the Commission approved a package of 15 measures planned by the Federal authorities and the *Länder* in the territory of the former German Democratic

---

[1]   OJ L 380, 31.12.1990.

Republic. These measures included:

(a) a further increase in the ERP budget (now ECU 3.75 billion for 1990 and ECU 3 billion for 1991);

(b) the extension to the former German Democratic Republic of aid schemes generally available throughout the rest of Germany;

(c) aid for consultancy help, particularly for small businesses;

(d) investment guarantees given by the *Länder* of Hesse and Bavaria;

(e) limited and declining investment grants to be available in the former German Democratic Republic, from 1 July 1990, with an aid intensity of 12% until 30 June 1991 and 8% until 30 June 1992;

(f) extension of the existing joint Federal/*Länder* Regional Development Programme (*Gemeinschaftsaufgabe*) to the entire territory of the former German Democratic Republic; this measure, which was approved on a provisional basis until 31 March 1991, allows aid of up to 23% of investment costs, with up to 10 percentage points extra if this assistance is combined with aid under other, non-regional schemes.

Export aid

180.   The Commission continued work on compiling an inventory of schemes in the Member States aimed at assisting exports to non-Community countries. It has asked several Member States whose initial contributions were inadequate for further information. It should be possible to complete the inventory in the course of 1991.

Shipbuilding

181.   The sixth Directive on aid to shipbuilding, Council Directive 87/167/EEC of 26 January 1987,[1] expired on 31 December 1990. On a proposal from the Commission and with Parliament's approval the Council on 21 December adopted a seventh Directive, which essentially continues the strategy followed hitherto.

182.   The seventh Directive is to apply for three years, from 1 January 1991 to 31 December 1993. The main changes are a limitation of aid for ship conversions to the maximum rate applying to small vessels, a tightening up of the rules designed to avoid undue concentrations of shipbuilding orders, and alterations to the monitoring proce-

---

[1]   OJ L 69, 12.3.1987.

dure. The transitional period in which operating aid may be granted in Spain has also been extended until 31 December 1991, and Article 5 is not to apply to Greece for the same period, so that operating aid which is not contract-related may be considered compatible with the common market even if it exceeds the common ceiling, while a restructuring programme is carried out. Lastly, the difficulties in the shipbuilding industry in the former German Democratic Republic will be looked at as soon as more accurate information is available on the future structure of the industry and on the current order book.

183.   After consulting the Member States the Commission set the ceiling of production aid under the new Directive at 13% for 1991. For small vessels the ceiling is 9%.

Steel

184.   The Commission approved the conclusions of the study of Member States' reports on aid disbursed in 1988 to parts of the steel industry not covered by the ECSC Treaty, in accordance with the framework for aid to these sectors.[1] The study has been forwarded to the Member States, with a request to those who have not yet supplied the reports called for by that code to comply with their obligations.

Electricity contracts at preferential rates offered by EdF

France

185.   Since the decision of the Commission in the *Pechiney* case in 1988,[2] the French authorities have informed the Commission of all cases in which EdF is to offer consumers preferential rates for electricity; the arrangement is to last for the limited period in which EdF has spare nuclear generating capacity.

186.   The Commission examined two contracts under which EdF was to supply electricity to Usinor-Sacilor for a new unit to produce manganese alloys at Dunkirk and to Exxon Chemicals for investment at Notre-Dame-de-Gravenchon. In both cases the Commission decided that the contracts did not include any State aid element and were in line with what a private investor would do under normal market conditions.

---

[1]   OJ C 320, 13.12.1988.
[2]   Nineteenth Competition Report, point 168.

Overall activity in the State aid field (Table 2)

187.   The 1990 figures given in Table 2 below show that the number of notifications increased substantially by comparison to the preceding years and to 1989 in particular. The figures include a growing number of notifications under the simplified procedure for notifying schemes of minor importance. [1] The Commission raised the ceilings for this procedure by an average of 50% as compared with the preceding arrangements, leading to a sharp rise in the number of notifications qualifying.

The minor schemes procedure accounted for 35 cases. The number of notifications also increased as a result of cofinancing of Community measures in several fields suitable for joint funding, such as Eureka and regional policy, where Member States were careful to make a full notification of the accompanying national aid which is a condition of the Community funding.

In 105 cases where aid measures had not been notified at the proposal stage the Commission decided either to raise no objection or to initiate proceedings under Article 93(2) of the EEC Treaty.

---

[1]   OJ C 40, 20.2.1990.

TABLE 2

Activity in the control of State aid (excluding aid to agriculture, fisheries and transport)

| Year | Number of plans notified | Action taken by the Commission[1] | | | Plans notified and later withdrawn by Member States |
		Raise no objection	Initiate the procedure in Article 93(2) EEC or Article 8(3) of Decision 2320/81/ECSC	Terminate the procedure in Article 93(2) EEC or Article 8(3) of Decision 2320/81/ECSC[2]	Final decision under Article 93(2) EEC or Article 8(3) of Decision 2320/81/ECSC[3]	
1981	92 (of which steel −16)	79 (of which steel −11)	30 (of which steel −9)	19 (of which steel −4)	14	—
1982	200 (of which steel −81)	104 (of which steel −25)	86 (of which steel −56)	30 (of which steel −13)	13 (of which steel −1)	—
1983	174 (of which steel −4)	101 (of which steel −18)[4]	55	18	21 (of which steel −9)	9
1984	162 (of which steel −10)	201 (of which steel −66)[4]	58 (of which steel −1)	34	21[5]	6
1985	133 (of which steel −7)	102 (of which steel −21)[4]	38 (of which steel −1)	31	7	11
1986	124	98	47	26	10	5
1987	326	205	27	32	10	1
1988	375	311	31	32	13	—
1989	296	254	37	27	16	7
1990	429	352	33	24	12	2

NB: The figures in the first column do not total with those of the next four columns on accounts of carry-overs from one year to the next and because of the fact that if the procedure in Article 93(2) EEC or Article 8(3) of Decision 2320/81/ECSC is initiated, the Commission has to take two decisions, first to open the procedure and then a final decision terminating it.

[1] For details see the Annex to this Report. Steel here includes both EEC and ECSC steel products, and because of the tranche system the number of procedural steps taken exceeds the number of notifications.

[2] In most cases after amendments negotiated during the proceedings to remove those aspects which at the outset made the proposal incompatible with the common market.

[3] Published in the Official Journal.

[4] Including tranches of aid released under decisions of 29 June 1983.

[5] Excludes the 'conditional' decision on French investment aids (see Fourteenth Competition Report, point 253).

§ 2 — Second survey on State aids in the Community and follow-up

188.   To improve transparency and to provide material for a thorough review of the consistency of aid policy in the run-up to the single market, the Commission published a second survey on State aids in the European Community.[1] The survey outlines the level of spending on State aid in each Member State, and updates the information in the first survey[2] to include 1987 and 1988 and figures for Spain and Portugal.

Although the survey shows that there has been some reduction in the level of State aid as a percentage of GDP, the figures are still relatively high in several Member States. Such high aid levels pose a serious threat to the completion of the single market.

189.   Like the first, the second survey covers assistance to enterprises in agriculture, fisheries, railways and inland waterway transport, the coal industry and manufacturing, that is to say both measures within the scope of Article 92 of the EEC Treaty and others that are not necessarily so. Total assistance to these industries in the Twelve amounted to ECU 82.3 billion on average for the period 1987-88 (ECU 76.2 billion in the Ten), compared with ECU 85.2 billion in the Ten in the period 1981-86 (all figures at 1987 prices). As a percentage of GDP the figure fell from 2.8% (1981-86) to 2.2% (1987-88). A fall was also noted in all the individual Member States except in the Federal Republic of Germany and the Netherlands. The fall was substantial in the United Kingdom and Ireland. Aid to manufacturing industry, which accounted for 41% of total assistance (as compared with 13% for agriculture, 31% for railways and 16% for the coal industry) is discussed in detail in the survey.

190.   As a percentage of value added, aid to manufacturing (not including steel and shipbuilding) in the Twelve amounted to 3.8% in the period 1987-88, as compared with 4.0% in 1981-86. Four Member States had aid levels above the Community average: Greece (16.4%), Portugal (8.1%), Italy (6.5%) and Ireland (6.2%), while three Member States were below the average: Denmark (1.6%), the United Kingdom (2.5%) and the Federal Republic of Germany (2.7%). The other Member States were somewhere around the average, at between 3.5 and 4.6%. Among the four major economies there was a widening gap between Italy on the one hand and France, the Federal Republic of Germany, and the United Kingdom on the other, with the total volume of aid in Italy reaching about twice the level in the other three. On this indicator (percentage of value added), only Italy, Ireland, the Netherlands and Denmark had shown an appreciable fall in aid levels by comparison with the preceding period. These results belie the widespread belief that the rise in the level of State aid in the early 1980s was a temporary

---

[1]   EN ISBN 92-826-0386-5.
[2]   EN ISBN 92-825-9535-8; Eighteenth Competition Report, points 162 and 163.

phenomenon due to restructuring in various industries following the second oil-price crisis.

191.   The survey also shows that the objectives of the aid granted (for example, research and development, regional aid, small businesses) and the forms used (grants, low interest loans, guarantees) vary considerably from one Member State to another. The persistence of a high overall level of aid and wide disparities between the Member States mean that a periodic reassessment of aid policies must be undertaken.

192.   The survey data will be updated regularly and will provide a basis for monitoring State aid policy as the single market programme is completed.

§ 3 — State aid for research and development

General policy developments

193.   The Member States notified 53 cases of aid for R&D totalling ECU 2 222.8 million, of which ECU 1 370.8 million was budgeted for 1990. This latter figure gives only a very incomplete picture of the aid to R&D received by European businesses in 1990: further assistance was provided under multiannual programmes that had been approved previously, while R&D aid also forms an integral part — how big a part may not be ascertainable in advance — of schemes serving other specific purposes, such as regional development, improvement of the environment, or energy saving, where the encouragement of research activities is just one of the types of activity provided for.

Cases notified in 1990 included 26 schemes, only 12 of which were new, the other 14 being extensions or amendments of schemes the Commission had already considered. The other 27 notifications concerned major awards of aid under existing schemes, the majority of which, as in previous years, were for Eureka projects.

The Commission continued to base its assessments on the criteria laid down in the Community framework for State aids for research and development, which was adopted in 1986.[1] The Commission embarked on a review of the policy it had followed in the more than 200 decisions taken under that code, in preparation for a revision of the code in 1991. The revision will also have to take account of the outcome of the negotiations going on in GATT.

A study of the State aid aspects of R&D contracts which was announced in the framework (paragraph 9.2) has been completed, and the main results are summarized in the last chapter of this Report.[2]

194.   The main decisions taken in 1990 are summarized by country below.

Belgium

195.   In February the Commission approved under Article 92(3)(c) of the EEC Treaty the new rules of the prototypes scheme. In September 1988 the Commission had proposed to the Belgian Government as 'appropriate measures' under Article 93(1) of the EEC Treaty to reduce the maximum aid intensities available for basic research to 50% and for applied research or development to 25% in the event of success and 40% in the event of failure.

---

[1]   OJ C 83, 11.4.1986.
[2]   Point 386 of this Report.

The Belgian authorities agreed to apply the new rules subject to the possibility of granting exceptional financing in certain cases of 10 percentage points higher than the rates laid down, which the Commission accepted. The intensity may be increased in this way if the recipient is an independent enterprise with less than 200 employees and a turnover of less than ECU 15 million, if the assisted project accounts for more than half of the business's annual expenditure on R&D, or if the project is expressly linked to a current Community programme.

196.   In July the Commission decided to initiate proceedings under Article 93(2) of the EEC Treaty in respect of a draft order of the Flemish Executive concerning the Fund for the Promotion of Industrial Research in Flanders (FIOV), which set out the rules the Flemish Region proposed to apply to aid for basic industrial research, formerly granted by the Institute for the Promotion of Scientific Research in Industry and Agriculture (Irsia/Inwonl), and aid for prototypes. The intensities proposed of up to 80% for basic industrial research and 60% for development were unacceptable by the criteria of the framework; also the Commission felt that transparency and dissemination of results were less well provided for under the new scheme than under the old one operated by Irsia/Inwonl. The new Fund had ECU 58 million available for commitment in 1990.

Federal Republic of Germany

197.   In June the Commission terminated proceedings initiated under Article 93(2) of the EEC Treaty in respect of a section of the transport research (Verkehrsforschung) aid scheme. The subprogramme concerned consisted of the 'Transrapid' magnetic levitation train and the ICE (Intercity Experimental) and ICE-M (M for *Mehrstromsystem* or multi-current system) high-speed trains.

The German authorities proposed a budget of ECU 248.7 million of this research. In the course of the proceedings it became clear that the funds were to be spent on both basic research and applied research.

Under the R&D aid code the Commission could not accept the initial proposals, and following the Commission's observations the Federal Government reduced the budget to ECU 194.5 million. The aid intensity for the Transrapid project, which had been 75%, was reduced to 35%. Intensities of 36% for the ICE train and 21.7% for the ICE-M were approved. The Commission took a positive final decision under Article 93(3)(c).

198.   In October the Commission decided under Article 92(3)(c) of the EEC Treaty not to raise any objection to the German research network scheme (Deutsches Forschungsnetz — DFN).

This R&D programme is aimed at providing a data-communication network allowing the exchange of graphical information between research institutes and others. For 1990-93 it has a budget of ECU 52 million, to be spent on fundamental research and basic industrial research; the maximum aid intensity is 50% both for projects undertaken by firms on their own or in collaboration with universities or research centres.

199. Also in October, the Commission approved under Article 92(3)(c) of the EEC Treaty a scheme to support the development of high-definition television. The provisions of the scheme are the same as for the DFN research network already described; it has a budget of ECU 41.8 million for the years 1990-93 to carry out aspects of research into high-definition television which are not covered by the Eureka HDTV project.

200. In March the Commission decided to grant exemption under Article 92(3)(c) of the EEC Treaty for a research programme to promote information technology. The basic information technology scheme (Basistechnologien der Informationstechnik) operates in the same way as the DFN to promote such techniques as parallel processing, artificial intelligence, photonics and industrial optics. A budget of ECU 303 million has been allocated for R&D carried out by public institutions and industry in the period 1990-93.

201. In October the Commission granted exemption under Article 92(3)(b) of the EEC Treaty for an extension of the German contribution to Eureka project EU-147, digital audio broadcasting. This measure is to provide ECU 16.1 million for basic research by industry, which would be financed at a rate of 50%, and fundamental research carried out by public research institutes, which would be financed at a rate of 100%.

202. At the same time the Commission decided to approve aid for German participation in Eureka project EU-95 on high-definition television. The German funding towards the project would amount to ECU 24 million, with the aid covering up to 100% of costs for public institutions and 50% for industry.

The Commission regarded the project to be of common European interest.

203. In September the Commission also granted exemption under Article 92(3)(b) of the EEC Treaty for assistance to the German participants in the Jessi project (Joint European sub-micron silicon initiative).

The Jessi project is the fifth Eureka project which the Commission has classed as 'an important project of common European interest', after HDTV, DAB, ESF and Eprom. The budget available until 1993 to the German participants in the project, including universities and research centres, amounts to ECU 223.3 million.

France

204. In July the Commission granted exemption under Article 92(3)(c) of the EEC Treaty for the research tax credit (crédit d'impôt recherche) scheme, which offers tax incentives covering all stages of research. The scheme had been authorized previously but had been amended in two major respects, concerning the calculation of the tax credit and the provision for firms that had not yet benefited under the scheme: these will be entitled to a tax credit on the increase in their research expenditure over the whole period 1990-92.

The extra cost of these amendments, which will be met for the first time out of the 1991 budget, is about ECU 94 million; this brings the estimated cost of the scheme to ECU 325 million.

205. In October the Commission authorized fresh funding for the Research and Technology Fund (FRT) for 1990. The objective of the scheme continues to be to develop and coordinate concerted research activity, in accordance with national priorities laid down each year in the annual Finance Act; but there were major changes in the scheme in 1990.

There is no longer any provision for financing applied research under the scheme, so that it will now assist only basic research carried out by industry. Some ECU 230 million was made available in 1990 in the form of direct grants for basic industrial research.

206. In July the Commission decided not to raise any objection to French government assistance for designing a new generation of high-speed trains, the 'TGV of the future'. A total of ECU 25 million is to be provided over the period 1990-94 in grants to firms (mainly GEC-Alsthom) taking part in the programme. The research will be looking mainly at the use of new materials and the development of a new engine.

The bulk of the assistance will go to applied research, but ECU 8 million is for basic research. The intensity will be limited to a gross grant equivalent (gge) of 50% for basic research and 25% for applied research, with a possibility of the latter rate being increased by 10 points if there is international cooperation. The approval decision was based on Article 92(3)(c).

207. In October the Commission granted exemption under Article 92(3)(c) of the EEC Treaty for the 'PUMA procedure'. This new French scheme is to apply specifically in the field of advanced materials, and is targeted mainly at firms with fewer than 500 employees. It will have a budget of ECU 10 million in 1990 and will finance research at all stages. Feasibility studies will qualify for grants of up to ECU 33 000 and 50% gge. Repayable loans will be available for R&D proper; these may amount to 50% of the cost of the project, but not more than ECU 280 000. Depending on whether or not the loans are repaid the intensity varies between 16.8% and 40% gge.

208.   In December the Commission raised no objection to aid for a new research project to develop a fuel-efficient, low-polluting car, for which the French authorities propose to provide assistance of ECU 70 million over eight years. The project, although to be financed under schemes already approved by the Commission, was notified because of its being in the motor industry, which is covered by a Community aid code,[1] and because the cost of the programme exceeded ECU 20 million.

The aid would go essentially to PSA and Renault, with intensities of 50% gge for basic research and 25% gge for applied research.

Italy

209.   In April the Commission authorized fresh financing for the Special Applied Research Fund for 1990. The rules of this scheme, which provides grants and low-interest loans to Italian firms engaging in research activities, remained unchanged, except that the annual budget was reduced to ECU 387 million from the ECU 500 million of 1989.

210.   Over the year the Commission also approved national aid for the participation of Italian firms in 13 Eureka projects. In all cases the assistance was cleared under Article 92(3)(c) of the EEC Treaty.

Netherlands

211.   In September the Commission approved a new Dutch scheme called VEDI, which had a budget of ECU 4.7 million for 1990 and was to encourage pilot and demonstration projects to promote the use of electronic data-interchange technology in businesses. Those taking part in network projects could obtain grants covering up to 25% of technological development costs.

212.   In addition, several extensions of existing schemes were approved. They included the Instir scheme for encouraging innovation, which covers 30% of researchers' salary costs and has a budget of ECU 82 million for 1990-91, the TOK scheme for the development of technology, which had a budget of ECU 61 million for 1990, the PBTS scheme for the stimulation of business-oriented technology, with a budget of ECU 54 million in 1990, the BTIP scheme for international research and Eureka in particular, with a budget of ECU 11.8 million, and a scheme for collaborative industrial research with a budget of ECU 4.3 million in 1990.

---

[1]   Point 249 of this Report.

213.   In May the Commission applied the exception of Article 92(3)(b) of the EEC Treaty to assistance totalling ECU 23.6 million granted to Philips in 1989 for its participation in the Eureka HDTV and Jessi projects.

Portugal

214.   In January the Commission approved new rules for the grant of aid by the National Council for Scientific and Technological Research (JNICT).

The Commission had previously proposed 'appropriate measures' to the Portuguese Government in order to increase the transparency in the rules governing the grant of aid by the JNICT. As a result, the Portuguese authorities came forward with draft regulations laying down intensity ceilings of 65% for basic industrial research and 50% for applied research and development, the latter rate being reached only if the project failed. The Commission took account of the regional aspect to allow a level of assistance higher than what would otherwise be permitted. The budget available to the JNICT for 1990 was ECU 10 million, only part of which was to go to businesses.

§ 4 — Aid to industries with specific structural or related problems

Aid to the coal industry (Tables 3 and 4)

215.   The Commission continued to scrutinize aid to the coal industry under the terms of the Decision establishing Community rules for aid to this industry.[1] Such aid that Member States proposed to give to their industry was authorized whenever it conformed to the general objectives and criteria set out in the Decision.

The Commission approved aid notified for 1990 by Belgium[2] and France.[3]

On 14 February the Commission authorized aid in Germany under the scheme to compensate electricity generators for using Community coal.[4] The decision covered an additional amount for 1988 and the total aid for 1989 which was, however, maximized at the previous year's level.

At the same time the Commission authorized aid under the same scheme for 1990[4] sufficient to meet current expenditure for that year.

On 28 February[5] the Commission authorized aid to the German coal industry in respect of 1989 under a number of other schemes and on 6 February 1991[3] cleared a further package of aid for 1990 and additional payments for 1989.

Additional financial assistance for the Spanish industry for 1987 and 1988 under the Ofico scheme to compensate electricity generators for coal purchases was approved by the Commission on 20 December 1989.[5]

At the same time, although authorizing aid under the compensation scheme for 1989, the Commission asked the Spanish Government to come forward with a plan for reducing the compensation payments and for restructuring, modernizing and rationalizing the Spanish coal industry.

On 25 July[3] the Commission approved a compensation payment for 1990 at the same level as that authorized for 1989.

---

[1]   OJ L 177, 1.7.1986.
[2]   OJ L 133, 24.5.1990.
[3]   Not yet published.
[4]   OJ L 346, 11.12.1990.
[5]   OJ L 105, 25.4.1990.

Aid to the Spanish industry for 1988, 1989 and 1990 under other schemes was also cleared on 25 July.[1]

The 1990 aid to cover the operating losses of the firms Hunosa, Minas de Figaredo and Minero Siderurgica de Ponferrada (in respect of the Camocha mine) was pegged at the 1989 level.

The Commission also asked the Spanish Government to provide a plan for reducing aid to cover such losses as part of the wider restructuring plan.

On 20 June[1] the Commission authorized the aid which Portugal was proposing to grant its coal industry for 1989. In the decision, the Commission asked the Portuguese Government to submit a corporate plan for the aided firm.

For the United Kingdom coal industry, the Commission on 28 March[2] and 1 August 1990[3] cleared aid in respect of the financial years 1987/88, 1988/89 and 1989/90. In the March decision it authorized only part of the aid pending further information on the British Coal Corporation's business strategy. After this information had been supplied the Commission was able to authorize the rest of the aid on 1 August.

In both the decisions on the UK aid, the Commission noted that the UK Government intended not to grant any further aid to its coal industry until the expiry of the current aid code under Decision No 2064/86/ECSC, except in respect of the costs of redundancies and other social costs of restructuring, rationalization and modernization of the industry.

Aid to shipbuilding

Application of Article 4(5) of the sixth Directive where there is competition between Community yards

216.   In May the Commission decided to set a ceiling of 5.88% of the contract price on aid in a case where Community yards were competing for the contract to build two ferries for De Danske Statsbaner; this would enable a Dutch yard to compete and thus keep the order in the Community.

217.   In four other cases, the Commission, having found that none of the governments concerned planned to grant aid for the contracts in question, did not need to apply Article 4(5).

---

[1]   OJ L 5, 8.1.1991.
[2]   OJ L 346, 11.12.1990.
[3]   Not yet published.

Application of Article 4(7) of the sixth Directive (aid for building vessels supplied under development assistance programmes)

218.   In September the Commission approved aid for the construction by the German yard Schlömer Werft of three fishing vessels for Guinea-Bissau. The aid consists of a 90% loan over 10 years at an interest rate of 2.9% (grant equivalent of 28.4%).

Belgium

219.   In July the Commission issued a negative decision concerning the financing terms offered to two shipowners for the construction of two refrigerator vessels and one LPG carrier with a capacity of 34 000 m³. Since the conditions amounted to a grant equivalent of 35%, when the ceiling on aid laid down by the Commission for 1989 was 26%, the Belgian Government was required to review the financing terms so as to bring the grant equivalent within the ceiling. The Belgian Government has appealed the decision in the Court of Justice.

220.   At the same time, the Commission initiated proceedings under Article 92(2) of the EEC Treaty against nine other shipbuilding contracts in various Belgian yards which had been granted similar terms to those offered in connection with the above three vessels.

Denmark

221.   In August the Commission gave its approval under Article 3 of the sixth Directive for special tax concessions granted to shareholders in ship-owning partnerships (skibsan-partsvirksomheder) under Tax Law No 388 of 7 June 1989. The grant equivalent of the tax concessions assuming a 25% shareholding was around 5.4%.

Federal Republic of Germany (not including former GDR)

222.   In August the Commission took a final negative decision on two guarantees granted by the German authorities, in respect of which proceedings had been initiated under Article 93(2) of the EEC Treaty in December 1989. The guarantees covered 90 and 95% respectively of DM 1.8 million and DM 20.7 million loans for recapitalizing the bankrupt Schiffswerft Germersheim. The Commission's decision required the German Government to recover the 10% aid element in the guarantees.

223.   In September the Commission decided to close the Article 93(2) proceedings with regard to four financial transactions connected with the setting up of Bremer Werftenverbund. First, the Commission found that the sale by Hibeg of 600 750 shares in Seebeckwerft to Bremer Vulkan did not involve any aid.

On the other hand, aid was involved in the provision of a guarantee by Hibeg covering the purchase of 1.43 million new shares out of the 1.48 million issued on the stock exchange at a price of DM 90 per share. The aid element was quantified at DM 13.9 million.

The third transaction, consisting of Hibeg's purchase in 1988 of shares in ships of Bremer Vulkan and Seebeckwerft at their respective book values, was also considered to contain an aid element worth DM 44.7 million (17.6%).

The fourth transaction concerned the provision of a guarantee of DM 128.2 million by the *Land* of Bremen for the restructuring of Bremer Werftenverbund. The Commission regarded this as consistent with the restructuring plan for coastal shipyards approved in 1987.

The aid involved in the second and third transactions was not found to exceed the aid ceiling in force in 1987 and 1988 when added to the production aid granted to the consortium.

224.   Also in September the Commission opened Article 93(2) proceedings against investment aid of DM 3.4 million for Flensburger Schiffbau Gesellschaft, since the investment would increase the yard's capacity and did not therefore satisfy the requirements of Article 6 of Directive 87/167/EEC.

Greece

225.   On 20 June the Commission initiated Article 93(2) proceedings against shipbuilding aid granted to Neorion Shipyards of Syros. The assistance included: in 1987, an export subsidy of ECU 6 500 and conversion of ECU 4.75 million of debt into equity and, in 1988, a guarantee issued by the Greek Government on a loan of ECU 9.95 million. The Commission regarded both cases as operating aid, of an intensity clearly above the ceiling laid down for 1987 and 1988.

226.   The Commission also requested information on a number of laws relating to shipbuilding.

France

227.   In August the Commission took a decision requiring the French Government to recover the closure aid which it had been authorized to grant to the La Ciotat shipyard under Article 7 of the sixth Directive. The Conseil Général des Bouches-du-Rhône had sold the site of the shipyard to the company Lexmar France which was planning to resume the construction of large ships there, although this was against the conditions on which closure aid is granted (closure must be irreversible).

The French Government responded by taking legal action to overturn the Conseil Général's action, on the ground of non-compliance with the Commission's decision.

Lexmar France, which was maintaining the site, however, became insolvent and filed a petition for bankruptcy on 15 December.

Ireland

228.   In November the Commission authorized aid for the purchase of the Damen Shipyard from Verolme Cork Dockyard, which had been closed in November 1984.

The aid was authorized pursuant to Article 6(2) of the sixth Directive, which allows investment aid to be granted for the opening of a new shipyard in a Member State which otherwise would have no shipbuilding facilities or for investments in a Member State's only existing yard, where the yard in question had a minimal impact on the Community market. This shipyard would be the only one in the Irish republic.

Italy

229.   On 20 June the Commission terminated the Article 93(2) proceedings initiated in May 1989 against Law No 234/89 on shipbuilding aid and against the aid granted to cover the losses of Fincantieri in 1987 and 1988. In view of changes made in the application of the Law, commitments given by the Italian Government and the clarifications provided about Fincantieri's losses, the Commission decided that the Law and the loss compensation payments could now be considered compatible with the sixth Directive.

Netherlands

230.   On 10 October the Commission opened the Article 93(2) proceedings with regard to the rescheduling of a loan granted in 1978 by the Dutch national investment bank

(NIB), in which the Dutch State has a majority shareholding, to Van der Giessen de Noord (GN). The rescheduling took place in August 1989.

The rescheduling involved the writing off of a HFL 46.7 million loan, repayment of which to the NIB was subject to various conditions. In return, the NIB would receive over a 10 year period part of the yard's profits, half of which will be returned in the form of a further subordinated loan. The Commission regarded the rescheduling as rescue aid within the meaning of Article 5(1) of the sixth Directive, the total amount of which could exceed the ceiling on shipbuilding aid.

Portugal

231.   On 13 December the Commission approved aid measures in connection with the restructuring of the Setenave shipyard in Portugal. The measures included aid of ESC 83 650 million to cover losses, contract-related production aid of ESC 8 885 million and restructuring aid of ESC 5 603 million. Since the restructuring plan was systematic and specific, was aimed at an irreversible reduction of the yard's capacity to 7 000 cgt/year, and would enable the yard to operate competitively from 1991 with aid being progressively reduced, the Commission considered that all the requirements of Article 9(3) of the sixth Directive were satisfied.

Aid to the steel industry

Belgium

232.   In July the Commission decided not to raise any objection to an injection of capital by the Belgian authorities in ALZ in connection with investment in a third annealing and pickling line at its Genk plant. It concluded that the transaction was in line with the behaviour of a private investor operating under normal market economy conditions and that therefore no aid was involved.

233.   In July the Commission closed the Article 93(2) proceedings initiated in December 1988 against the acquisition in 1986 by Société Liégeoise de Financement (SLF) of five subsidiaries of Tubemeuse and the sale in 1988 of Tubemeuse and Tubemeuse-OCTG assets to Soconord. The Commission found that SLF had subsequently resold the companies for the price it paid in 1986 and that the second sale had been made by public competitive tender in which the purchaser had been the highest bidder. It therefore concluded that the transactions did not involve aid within the meaning of Article 92(1) of the EEC Treaty.

The Commission decided not to take any further action on another transaction in the same case, the sale by Tubemeuse of 51% of Tubemeuse-OCTG, its tube-finishing subsidiary, to the Liège investment corporation. The Commission took the view that this transaction, which had been decided by the Belgian authorities in May 1986, had been made possible only by State aid, in particular through a guarantee provided by the Wallonia Region. It concluded, however, that this aid had already been covered by its decision of 4 February 1987[1] on Tubemeuse and that the matter could be regarded as closed.

Spain

234.   In June the Commission regarded as compatible with the orderly functioning of the common market for the purposes of Article 4(1) of Decision No 322/89/ECSC two awards of closure aid by the Spanish Government to the steel firms José María Aristrain and Esteban Orbegozo. The aid of ECU 19.1 million would cover part of the redundancy payments to workers dismissed or retired early as a result of the closure of some of the firms' less economic plants.

235.   In July the Commission opened proceedings under Article 6(4) of Decision No 322/89/ECSC against proposed aid for Extremeña de Laminados. The firm was to be awarded a grant of about ECU 1.4 million (PTA 182 million), covering 30% of the cost of an investment project. The Commission terminated the procedure in October after the Spanish Government had decided to withdraw the project.

236.   In December the Commission decided not to object to aid proposed for Acerinox and therefore closed the proceedings under Article 6(4) of Decision No 322/89/ECSC which it had initiated on 28 February 1990. The firm was to receive grants of approximately ECU 571 000 (PTA 73 million).

The aid was considered compatible with the common market, under Article 3 of Decision No 322/89/ECSC, because the purpose was to bring the firm's plant into line with new statutory environmental standards and the aid intensity did not exceed the 15% ceiling.

Italy

237.   In April the Commission decided to terminate the procedure initiated in July 1988 pursuant to Article 93(2) against the Italian Government's injection of ECU 92 million (LIT 143 billion) of new capital in the tube producer Dalmine, a subsidiary of the

---

[1]   Seventeenth Report on Competition Policy, point 203.

publicly-owned Ilva group (formerly Finsider). The Italian Government had agreed to reduce its share of the capital increase to an amount such that the public and private shareholders would contribute equally to it in proportion to their original shareholdings and had put forward additional measures for restructuring the company to restore its viability and ensure a satisfactory return for investors. Also, throughout the period, Dalmine's share price had held up well. The Commission therefore took the view that the transaction was in line with what a private investor would do under normal market economy conditions and did not involve aid.

238.   In April the Commission authorized the Italian Government to pay the first instalment of aid to Ilva, the publicly-owned Italian steel producer that had taken over the viable parts of Finsider, which is now being wound up. The aid amounted to ECU 1 975 million (LIT 2 989 billion) and will serve to reduce the debts accumulated by Finsider.

The authorization covered about two thirds of the aid of ECU 3 330 million (LIT 5 170 billion) approved under the general restructuring programme adopted in December 1988[1] and amended one year later[2] to take account of the delayed closure of certain plants. The approval was made to subject to certain conditions, notably the progress of Ilva's restructuring plans and compliance with the legal conditions imposed in connection with the setting up of Ilva. The Commission found that the conditions had been met, since, for instance, Ilva had been formally constituted and certain closures had already taken place within the agreed time-limit. The Commission also found that Ilva's debt service charges did not exceed 5.5% of its turnover, as required by the decision adopted by the Commission in 1988.

239.   In July the Commission took a final negative decision on two awards of aid in the form of subsidized loans and grants to Italian steelmakers. In one case ECU 550 000 (LIT 835 million) was to be provided to the Tirreno steelworks for energy-saving investment and in the other ECU 1.074 million (LIT 1 632 million) was to be granted to Siderpotenza for environmental protection investment.

The Commission found that these aids did not qualify for any of the exemptions listed in Decision No 322/89/ECSC.[3]

240.   In July the Commission adopted a final negative decision on a subsidized loan of ECU 3.9 million (LIT 6 billion) granted in December 1987 to the Bolzano steelworks by the autonomous province of Bolzano. The purpose of the investment was to convert the plant for the production of high value-added special steels. The Commission found

---

[1]   OJ L 86, 31.3.1989.
[2]   OJ L 61, 10.3.1990.
[3]   Commission Decision of 1 February 1989 establishing Community rules for aid to the steel industry (steel aids code, OJ L 38, 10.2.1989).

that the aid could not qualify for any of the exemptions listed in Decision No 3484/85/ECSC[1] (aids code applicable from 1 January 1986 to 31 December 1988), the only operative decision in this case.

241.   Also in July the Commission examined a proposal to provide ECU 1.07 million (LIT 1.62 billion) of aid to the same steelworks submitted by the Italian Government pursuant to Article 6 of Decision No 322/89/ECSC.[2] The Commission decided not to object to the aid for environmental protection which satisfied the tests of Article 3. However, the other aid proposed for energy saving, improvements in health and safety standards, innovation and quality improvements, did not qualify for exemption. The Commission therefore opened proceedings under Article 6(4) with regard to that aid.

242.   In July the Commission terminated the Article 93(2) proceedings initiated in October 1989 against aid which was supposed to be granted for the installation of a drop-forging press at Foggia. It had emerged from information belatedly supplied by the Italian authorities that they had not granted the aid nor were they planning to do so.

243.   In November the Commission initiated proceedings under Article 6(4) of Decision No 322/89/ECSC against ECU 1.2 million (LIT 1 796 billion) of assistance paid to Ferriere Acciaierie Sarde pursuant to a Sardinian law on promoting the use of scrap collected on the island. The aid did not satisfy the requirements of the steel aids code under Decision No 3484/85/ECSC concerning the grant of environmental protection aid, and the Italian authorities had not taken steps to reclaim the aid despite the Commission's requests to do so.

Luxembourg

244.   In January the Commission approved the grant of aid under the Economic Expansion Law of 14 May 1986 for research and development forming part of the Luxembourg steel industry's R&D programme for 1989.

In July 1989 it had already approved aid under the same scheme for the 1986, 1987 and 1988[3] R&D programmes. The eligible costs of 64 projects were estimated at ECU 16.5 million (LFR 702 million). The aid was provided in two parts, an outright capital grant of 15% gross, subject to a ceiling of ECU 2.5 million (LFR 106 million), and a loan, repayable if the projects prove successful, of 10% gross, subject to a ceiling of ECU 1.7 million (LFR 70.5 million).

---

[1]   OJ L 340, 18.12.1985.
[2]   OJ L 38, 10.2.1989.
[3]   Nineteenth Report on Competition Policy, point 159.

In addition to this direct aid, the public corporation Société nationale de crédit et d'investissement granted a loan of approximately ECU 2.1 million (LFR 90 million), for the programme, repayable over five years at 5%.

Portugal

245.   In April the Commission decided not to object to an aid scheme for restructuring the Portuguese foundry industry. As part of the specific programme for the development of Portuguese industry (Pedip) introduced by Council Regulation (EEC) No 2053/88 of 24 June 1988, the scheme seeks to promote the restructuring of Portuguese foundries so as to increase the competitiveness and ensure the long-term viability of the most efficient firms in the industry. The Commission also found that the aid would not significantly increase production capacity.

Aid to the synthetic fibres industry

Federal Republic of Germany

246.   In December the Commission took a negative decision on aid provided by the Federal Government and the *Land* of Bavaria to Rheinhold KG, Selbitz (Bavaria) for investment to increase polyamide and polypropylene yarn capacity. The aid — a grant of DM 344 000 (10% of the investment) and a subsidized loan of DM 1 800 000 — was notified to the Commission in accordance with the rules on aid to the synthetic fibre and yarn sector industry that were introduced in 1977 and have since been renewed every two years, most recently until July 1991.

The Commission's decision requires that the aid contained in the subsidized loan, which was granted to the recipient illegally in spring 1989, before notification, should be repaid. The German Government is required to reclaim the aid immediately, either by asking for the loan to be repaid or by charging the rate of interest on loans granted by the Kreditanstalt für Wiederaufbau (M_1 and M_2 programmes). Interest is to be charged for any delay in repayment. The proposed grant was also considered incompatible with the common market under Article 92(a) and was to be cancelled.

§ 5 — Investment, sectoral and horizontal aid

General investment aid

Review of existing aid schemes

247.   In the first series of general investment schemes aid which it had selected for review under Article 93(1) of the EEC Treaty,[1] the Commission in July proposed 'appropriate measures' to the Member States concerned. As a result, two States agreed to abolish the schemes in question: from 1 January 1991, the Netherlands stopped granting investment aid outside of assisted areas under a budget line entitled 'Strengthening economic structures' (Versterking economische structuur), while in Belgium the Economic Expansion Law 1959 will no longer be applied after the end of June 1991 for granting general investment aid. In two other cases — Section 8 of the Industrial Development Act (United Kingdom) and the Innovation Fund (Italy) — the governments' replies are still being studied. In October, a second round of reviews, involving nine schemes in seven countries, was begun with requests for information sent to the Member States concerned. A third round is under preparation.

Spain

248.   In May, the Commission approved the allocation of PTA 8 473 million of new funds for 1990 to an aid scheme to support industrial investment operated by the Regional Government of the Basque country. The Commission based its decision on the serious industrial decline of the area and the need to attract alternative employment. The aid scheme had already been approved by the Commission on two previous occasions, in 1988 and 1989.

Sectoral aid

Motor industry

249.   In December 1988, the Commission decided to introduce a framework for State aid to the motor industry, for a two-year period starting on 1 January 1989.[2] It proposed the framework under Article 93(1) and asked the Member States to accept the new rules.

---

[1]   See point 188 of this Report.
[2]   OJ C 123, 18.5.1989.

The Federal Republic of Germany and Spain refused, whilst the other 10 Member States agreed in the first half of 1989 to abide by the framework. In July 1989, therefore, the Commission initiated proceedings against Spain and the Federal Republic of Germany in respect of existing State aid schemes that could be used to support the motor industry. [1]

Early in 1990, the Spanish authorities informed the Commission that they had decided to apply the framework in Spain from 1 January 1990. The Commission therefore decided to close the proceedings against Spain. [2]

Faced with the German authorities' refusal to accept the framework, the Commission decided in February 1990 to terminate the procedure against the Federal Republic of Germany with the adoption of a negative decision. [3] The decision required the Federal Republic of Germany from 1 May 1990 to notify the Commission in advance of all aid covered by the framework. Any aid granted before that date would be regarded as covered by the German law on legitimate expectations and not be challenged; aid granted subsequently without prior notification would be illegal and could be subject to recovery. However, the Commission accepted the German authorities' proposal that all aid granted under the *Berlin Förderungsgesetz* to car manufacturers in West Berlin would not be subject to the prior notification requirement. The decision in the German case placed German car manufacturers on the same footing as those in other Member States and reaffirmed the Commission's intention to keep aid in this sector under close scrutiny.

However, the consequence was that the Community framework only became applicable throughout the Community in May 1990.

250.   In December 1990, the Commission reviewed the utility and scope of the framework. The limited experience acquired by then in applying the framework had confirmed the strategic importance which many Member States attached to their motor industry and their concern to attract new projects or promote existing projects in their less-developed regions. The risk of a bidding up of aid levels offered to attract new investment was greater than ever.

With 1990 apparently marking the end of several years of steady growth in demand for passenger cars, during which many manufacturers had started to expand capacity in the Community, there was clearly an increased risk of overcapacity. Demand in the Community is set to fall slightly in 1990 and 1991, before resuming a medium-term growth rate of some 1% a year, according to some forecasts. The most severe problems are possible in commercial vehicles. The uncertain outlook for the industry overall calls for even greater vigilance in the control of State aids.

---

[1]   Nineteenth Competition Report, point 127.
[2]   OJ C 281, 7.11.1989.
[3]   OJ L 188, 20.7.1990.

The Community motor vehicle industry will face major challenges in the coming years, both domestically and worldwide. The Commission had already indicated that the framework was a key element of its policy for completing the integration of the Community car market. It is essential to provide stable and fair conditions of competition, since this is the best guarantee of a car industry that is capable of improving its competitiveness on world markets.

251.   On the basis of these considerations, the Commission decided to extend the framework on State aid to the motor vehicle industry. The only change that has been made is to extend the prior notification requirement to West Berlin, which was previously excluded, and to the territory of the former German Democratic Republic now forming part of the Federal Republic. [1] After two years, the framework will be reviewed by the Commission. If amendments are found necessary — or even repeal of the framework — the Commission will take the appropriate steps after consulting the Member States.

Motor vehicles and related industries — individual cases

Application of the framework

252.   The following decisions were taken by the Commission under the framework on State aid to the motor vehicle industry.

Belgium

253.   In April the Commission initiated the Article 93(2) procedure in respect of a proposal by the Brussels regional authorities to grant aid for six investment projects to be carried out by Volkswagen Bruxelles SA. The projects, in various sections of an assembly plant, were all concerned with the start up of production of a second model. Total investment costs would be ECU 33 million (BFR 1 409 million), the aid being granted under the 1959 Economic Expansion Law in the form of a grant of ECU 2.7 million (BFR 112.7 million) and a five-year exemption from property tax. The Commission considered that there was insufficient evidence of the need for aid for general investment of this nature and that there were no grounds for deeming it compatible with the criteria laid down in the Community framework.

In November the Commission decided not to authorize the proposed aid, except that for parts of the investment projects that were genuinely innovatory — namely, aid of

---

[1]   Article 1(3) of the Commission Decision of 21.2.1990, published in OJ L 188, 20.7.1990, is no longer applicable from 1 January 1991.

BFR 12 million or 8% of estimated investment of BFR 150 million — plus a corresponding portion of the five-year exemption from property tax. The Commission had made a detailed technical analysis of six parts of the projects claimed as innovatory, and had concluded that only three could be regarded as innovation from a Community standpoint and were thus eligible for aid under the framework.

The Commission rejected the Belgian authorities' argument that all the planned aid was justified to alleviate the particular difficulties of the Forest plant due to its location in the Brussels conurbation. The project was found to be essentially a normal investment aimed at modernizing the plant and increasing its operational flexibility. In addition, the Brussels area did not meet the requirements for assisted area status under the Community rules.

France

254.   In December the Commission approved a French proposal to grant aid of ECU 27 million (FF 190 million) to Saab-Scania for building a new heavy truck manufacturing plant at Angers. The aid represented 9.8% of the total estimated cost of the project, which was FF 1 928 million. A previous notification for the same project (then estimated to cost FF 1 782 million) involving regional aid of FF 276 million plus tax exemptions had been withdrawn.

The Angers project comprises the fitting out of an assembly plant with a capacity of 12 000 trucks of over 16 tonnes (1991-92) and the construction and fitting out of a cab plant with a capacity of 12 000 units (1992-93) and an engine plant with a capacity of 25 000 units (1993-94).

The aid was to be for the last two plants, and comprised a regional grant from the State of FF 152 million under the regional planning grants (PAT) scheme, a grant of FF 30 million towards construction costs from the local authority and a five-year exemption from local business tax worth FF 8 million.

In its examination of the aid proposal, the Commission took account of the valuable contribution the project would make to solving the structural problems of the region, in particular the high unemployment. As required by the framework, the Commission also analyzed the possible adverse effects the aid could have on the industry as a whole. It took particular account of the problems of declining demand and overcapacity in the Community heavy trucks industry. However, demand is expected to rise in 1993. In view of this, the Commission considered that a concentration of the aid on the later stages of the project would reduce its distorting effect on competition and avoid exacerbating the industry's current difficulties. It would also reduce the nominal intensity of the aid from 9.85% to around 8.5% in 1990 prices (7% net), or half the regional aid level of 17% authorized for the Angers area. In the opinion of the Commission, such an aid level was sufficient to compensate for the structural disadvantages of the site and so allow the project to be undertaken in the assisted area.

Luxembourg

255.   In July the Commission approved an ECU 7 million (LFR 292 million) grant provided by Luxembourg to General Motors for the setting up of a new R&D centre at Bascharage. The aid, awarded under a regional aid scheme (Economic Expansion Law of 14 May 1986) approved in 1985, covered 15% of the LFR 1 950 million investment cost. It satisfied the criteria for regional aid, since General Motors had chosen this disadvantaged area from among several possible sites. It was concluded that the aid would not have adverse effects on the industry sufficient to outweigh the regional benefits as the project involved a transfer of technology to which all European manufacturers would have access.

Portugal

256.   In May, the Commission cleared aid that the Portuguese Government planned to grant to the electronic automotive components manufacturer Delco Remy, a subsidiary of General Motors, under a regional aid scheme (Sistema de incentivos de base regional) approved in 1988. The aid of ECU 16.8 million (ESC 2 911 million), or 39% of the investment costs, was considered likely to have a considerable impact on the economic development of this part of Portugal without adversely affecting the sector at Community level.

United Kingdom

257.   In July the Commission opened Article 93(2) proceedings in order to examine a plan by Derbyshire County Council to grant indirect aid to Toyota Motor through the asking price for development land at Burnaston, which is a non-assisted area. The Commission was satisfied that central government had not granted any aid to Toyota, but wanted to look closely at whether the local authorities had provided indirect aid, which was also subject to the State aid rules. In the Commission's opinion, the County Council had sold a 280-acre site to Toyota at less than its market value. The site had been valued by the District Valuer, an independent public official employed by the Inland Revenue, and sold to Toyota for less than the valuation. The Commission also decided to investigate the sale by the County Council to Toyota of an adjoining piece of land to determine whether this part of the sale also comprised an aid element.

Decisions not covered by the Community framework

258.   The following decisions taken by the Commission in 1990 were not covered by the aid framework as the Member States concerned were complying with decisions adopted before the framework entered into force on 1 January 1989.

France

259.   In November 1989 the Commission determined[1] that its Decision of 29 March 1988[2] on aid granted to the Renault group had not been implemented correctly in that the French Government had failed to comply with two essential conditions imposed by the Commission. The Commission gave the French Government three months from the date of service of the Decision to comply with its terms and inform the Commission of the measures taken. After receiving further information from the French authorities, the Commission re-examined the case to determine to what extent the two conditions had been met.

On 22 May 1990 the Commission reached the following compromise with the French Government:

(a) In view of the change in Renault's status under a law passed in May 1990 and the fact that approximately half of the commitments concerning capacity cuts had been fulfilled, the amount of aid that had to be recovered would be reduced from FF 12 billion to 6 billion, of which FF 3.5 billion would be repaid immediately to the French Treasury and FF 2.5 billion would be re-entered in Renault's accounts as long-term debt-bearing interest in accordance with the original refinancing plan.

(b) The French Government would not inject any capital into Renault before the end of 1990.

The approval of the other FF 6 billion was regarded by the Commission as fully subject to conditions 2 and 4 in Article 1 of its Decision of 29 March 1988.

United Kingdom

260.   In July 1990, the Commission, having investigated further advantages provided to British Aerospace when it took over the Rover Group that were not covered by its conditional decision of 1988[3] and having reviewed the decision in the light of the further information obtained about the deal, decided that the UK authorities had granted

---

[1]   Nineteenth Competition Report, point 187.
[2]   OJ L 220, 11.8.1988; Eighteenth Competition Report, point 227.
[3]   OJ L 25, 28.1.1989; Eighteenth Competition Report, point 233.

UKL 44.4 million of illegal aid to British Aerospace and asked them to recover it. The Commission found that the following items constituted illegal aid on top of that authorized by its 1988 decision, in that they had not been notified to the Commission prior to its decision:

(i) UKL 9.5 million paid to British Aerospace to cover part of its expenditure in acquiring shares in the Rover Group held by minority shareholders;

(ii) UKL 1.5 million paid to the Rover Group to cover expenditure incurred by the sale;

(iii) UKL 33.4 million, representing the financial benefit to British Aerospace resulting from the decision of the United Kingdom authorities to defer from 12 July 1988 to 30 March 1990 payment of the UKL 150 million purchase price.

The Commission also investigated a number of other advantages promised by the UK Government in letters accompanying the final sales contract but not communicated to the Commission at the time. It called upon the UK authorities to restore the situation to the terms of the sale announced at the time. As regards the valuation of Rover at the time of the sale in 1988, the Commission concluded from opinions and analyses obtained from various sources that all the valuations were fairly similar and that UKL 150 million was a reasonable price in view of Rover's position at the time and the restrictive conditions imposed. It therefore concluded that there were no grounds for reversing its original decision.

The UK Government announced that it accepted the Commission's decision. However, British Aerospace has appealed to the Court of Justice.

Chemicals

Belgium

261. In July, the Commission initiated the procedure under Article 93(2) of the EEC Treaty[1] against a proposal notified by the Belgian Government to grant aid of ECU 2.78 million (BFR 118.58 million) to Solvay SA and Solvic SA for the automation of several production lines and the development and use of new technologies. The firms specialize in the production of chlorine, caustic soda, hydrogen and polyvinyl chloride. On the basis of the information in its possession, the Commission considered that the proposed aid was not compatible with the common market pursuant to Article 92 of the EEC Treaty.

---

[1]   OJ C 280, 8.11.1990.

Pharmaceutical products

Belgium

262.   In July the Commission closed the Article 93(2) proceedings[1] commenced in October 1989[2] against aid notified by the Belgian Government for a pharmaceutical manufacturer. The government proposed to provide aid of ECU 5.7 million (BFR 243.75 million) and to grant an exemption from property tax for five years to SmithKline Biologicals SA for investment in expanding R&D work on new-generation vaccines developed with the assistance of genetic engineering techniques and the industrial application of results obtained. During the proceedings, the Belgian authorities provided further information showing that the project involving new technologies was innovatory and high-risk. It therefore decided that exemption could be granted under Article 92(2)(c) of the EEC Treaty.

Paper and wood

Federal Republic of Germany

263.   In October the Commission initiated the Article 93(2) proceedings against plans to grant investment aid to Nefab (plywood processing) and Chukyo (manufacture of heat-sensitive paper) at Hückelhoven in North Rhine-Westphalia. The Commission considered that the aids of ECU 420 000 (DM 850 000) and ECU 310 000 (DM 630 000) did not qualify for exemption under Article 92(3) of the EEC Treaty and that they might therefore be incompatible with the common market.

France

264.   In January the Commission approved an aid scheme to promote research in the paper and forestry sectors that would run over the period 1990-94. The scheme was to be financed by levies on pulp, paper and paperboard produced in France. The proceeds of the levy, of around ECU 10 million (FF 70 million) a year, would be used to finance research by the Centre technique du papier, the recovery of waste paper and measures to promote forestry and research work by the Association forêt cellulose. In its decision the Commission took particular account of the fact that the collective activities being assisted were far from the market-place, the levy did not favour either national

---

[1]   OJ C 229, 14.9.1990.
[2]   OJ C 5, 10.1.1990.

production or exports to other Member States, and the levy would no longer be charged on products from other Member States.

The same considerations led the Commission in September to approve an aid scheme that was to run over the period 1991-95 to assist the Comité de développement des industries françaises de l'ameublement, financed by a levy on sales of wooden furniture by French manufacturers. The revenue from the tax would also be around ECU 10 million (FF 70 million).

Italy

265.   In February the Commission proposed 'appropriate measures' to the Italian Government under Article 93(1) of the EEC Treaty concerning aid granted to the paper, pulp and forestry industries. The aid was financed by a levy on pulp and paper. The Commission decided that the levy could no longer be regarded as compatible with the common market because it was charged on imports from other Member States but exports to other Member States were exempt. As the Italian Government failed to implement the measures proposed in July, the Commission opened proceedings under Article 93(2) of the EEC Treaty against the scheme.

Glass and related products

France

266.   In July, the Commission decided to open Article 93(2) proceedings against unnotified aid of ECU 5 million (FF 32 million) granted to Saint-Gobain for investment.[1] The company had apparently received the aid to set up a new float glass production unit at Salaise-sur-Sanne (Isère). The French Government having failed to reply to requests for information from the Commission, the latter considered that the aid was liable to distort competition and affect trade in a vulnerable industry and that it did not qualify for any of the exemptions provided for in Article 92 of the EEC Treaty.

Italy

267.   In July the Commission decided that aid of ECU 11 million (LIT 17.3 billion) provided in 1986, without prior notification to the Commission, to Industrie Ottiche Riunite (IOR), a manufacturer of contact lenses and spectacles, was incompatible with

---

[1]   OJ C 274, 31.10.1990.

the common market. The Commission had opened the procedure in November 1988.[1] In its decision, the Commission found that the government had written off IOR's losses of LIT 17.3 billion before privatizing the firm. No further aid had been paid on privatization. The Commission decided that the aid distorted competition and affected trade within the meaning of Article 92(1) of the EEC Treaty and that it did not qualify for exemption under that article. Although the aid was illegal, the Commission decided not to require its recovery in view of the time that had elapsed since it had been informed about the aid.

Cement and related products

Greece

268.   In May, the Commission decided that aid to the Greek cement manufacturer Halkis was incompatible with the common market and should therefore be withdrawn. However, lack of cooperation by the Greek Government meant that the Commission was unable to quantify the exact amount that should be recovered.

Article 93(2) proceedings had been initiated in April 1989.[2] In its final negative decision, the Commission held that the aid in the form of an accumulation of debt to State-owned enterprises distorted competition and affected trade within the meaning of Article 92(1) and that none of the exemptions provided for in Article 92 of the EEC Treaty applied.

France

269.   In November the Commission authorized aid over the period 1991-95 for collective research in the concrete and earthenware products sector. The aid programme is financed by levies on domestic sales and exports, but not on foreign products marketed in France. The levy yields some ECU 9 million (FF 60 million). In taking its decision, the Commission considered that the collective activities assisted were far from the market and that the levy did not subsidize national production or exports to other Member States.

---

[1]   See Eighteenth Competition Report, point 237.
[2]   Nineteenth Competition Report, point 181.

Textiles

Spain

270.   In July the Commission opened Article 93(2) proceedings against the injection of PTA 7 100 million of new capital between 1986 and 1989 into the textile manufacturer Hytasa by Patrimonio del Estado. Hytasa had later been sold to the private sector for a token sum of PTA 100 million. The company is one of Spain's leading textile manufacturers with factories at Seville in Andalusia, and was formerly State-owned through the Patrimonio del Estado, an organization controlled by the Spanish Treasury.

The markets for Hytasa's products in the EC are highly competitive on account of the stagnation in demand and the increasing pressure from imports from non-EC countries. Consequently, prices are depressed and much production capacity remains unused.

In these circumstances, the Commission took the view that the capital injections included elements of State aid and affected trade between Member States, with the result that they were incompatible with the common market under Article 92 of the EEC Treaty.

In July the Commission initiated the Article 93(2) procedure against all the injections of capital made by the Spanish Government into the publicly-owned firm Intelhorce between 1986 and 1989 (a total of PTA 7 820 million) and the further capital injection of PTA 5 859 million made when the company was sold to Benorbe and Benservice. The Commission also wanted to investigate the price paid by the buyers — PTA 12 000 million — which appeared unduly low compared with the commercial value of the business after the capital injections.

The Commission considered that in view of Intelhorce's poor performance in recent years private investors would not have provided the capital, so that the government's action involved aid. Cotton fibres and woven fabrics, the firm's principal products, were a sector where competition was intense, which was reflected in very low prices and low capacity operating rates. Consequently, any aid granted to the undertaking was likely to affect trade and to distort or threaten to distort competition for the purposes of Article 92(1), in a case where none of the possible exemptions provided for in Article 92 of the EEC Treaty applied.

Portugal

271.   In November the Commission authorized under Article 92(3)(c) of the EEC Treaty an extension until the end of 1991 of the current scheme of aid to the Portuguese wool textile industry introduced by Law 381/88 of 15 June 1988.[1] The extension did not entail an increase in the budget originally allocated to the scheme (ESC 4 billion).

In arriving at its decision, the Commission took account of the fact that the extension would enable the Portuguese authorities to carry out the planned restructuring measures fully without producing any trade-distorting effects other than those foreseen when the scheme was authorized by the Commission.

Footwear

Spain

272.   In July the Commission opened proceedings under Article 93(2) of the EEC Treaty against injections of ECU 21 million (PTA 2.7 billion) of capital made by the Patrimonio del Estado in 1986 and 1987 into the firm Imepiel. The firm later was privatized at a token price of PTA 100 million. Imepiel (formerly Segarra) is the leading Spanish footwear manufacturer, with factories in the Uxo valley (Castellon-Valencia), and was formerly owned by the State through the Patrimonio del Estado, an organization controlled by the Spanish Treasury. The Commission had already investigated other capital injections to Imepiel in 1987 and 1988.[2]

The Community footwear market is highly competitive with steadily increasing import penetration from the developing and newly industrialized countries.

The industry is extremely fragmented, the average manufacturer being only about a sixtieth of the size of Imepiel. In these circumstances, the Commission considered that the Spanish Government's measures were likely to contain elements of State aid and affect trade between Member States, and therefore appeared to be incompatible with the common market under Article 92 of the EEC Treaty.

France

273.   In December the Commission authorized an extension for a further five years of the levy scheme whose proceeds are used to finance aid to the Centre Technique Cuir, Chaussure, Maroquinerie and to the Comité interprofessionnel de développement économique des industries du cuir, de la maroquinerie et de la chaussure.

The collective nature of the two centres' activities, the low rates of the levy, and the fact that all imports from Community countries are exempt while French exports to other

---

[1]   Eighteenth Competition Report, point 225.
[2]   Seventeenth Competition Report, point 222.

Member States are subject to the levy led the Commission to conclude that the extension qualified for exemption under Article 92(3)(c) of the EEC Treaty.

Clocks and watches

France

274.   In November the Commission decided to authorize the renewal, for the period 1991-95, of the French levy scheme in the clock and watch industry whose proceeds go to finance the operating expenditure of the specialized technical centres, CPDH and Cetehor. The rate of the levy will be determined annually by ministerial decree, with a ceiling of 0.80% of the value of the transactions. The centres carry out collective activities and programmes of common interest to the industry in the fields of technical research, market research, participation in trade fairs and exhibitions and promotion of quality.

The Commission checked that the scheme satisfied the conditions of compatibility with the common market that had been established in a large number of previous decisions on levy schemes, i.e. basically that they did not subsidize individual firms, were not charged on imports and did not assist exports to other Member States. The clock and watch industry scheme did not aid individual firms since the activities performed by the centres were of collective benefit. The levy was refunded on imports from other Member States and the scheme did not involve direct aid for exports.

Heavy electrical plant

Spain

275.   In July the Commission initiated the Article 93(2) procedure against the grant of aid by the Spanish authorities to rescue a group of private manufacturers of heavy electrical equipment consisting of the companies Cenemesa, Conelec and Cademesa. The Commission took the view that the following measures could contain aid elements: the assistance of ECU 115 to 229 million (PTA 15 to 30 billion) to finance a major reduction in the companies' workforces, the write off of PTA 35 910 million of debts owed to public bodies and possible aid elements in the terms on which the companies' assets were sold to the Swedish-Swiss heavy engineering group Asea Brown Boveri (ABB), including the price, tax advantages, and a commitment to place future public contracts with the companies.

The Commission had the impression that the measures were designed to assist the sale of the companies to ABB. On a preliminary analysis it believed that the aid was probably incompatible with the common market as it was likely to distort competition and affect trading conditions and none of the derogations provided for in the Treaty appeared to be applicable, according to the information currently available.

Non-ferrous metals and ores

Greece

276.   In December the Commission terminated the Article 93(2) proceedings that had been opened against assistance of approximately ECU 131 million (DR 20 420 million) from the Greek Business Reconstruction Organization (ORE) to the mining company Fimisco. The assistance had been provided under Law 1386/83, which empowers the government to grant aid to Greek industry, in an attempt to turn the company round by restoring its finances and introducing the necessary restructuring measures.

In view, in particular, of the Greek Government's commitment to reduce significantly employment in the company so as to set it on the road to permanent recovery with a view to possible eventual privatization, the Commission took the view that the aid involved in the operation would contribute to the development of mining activity and would not affect Community trade to an extent contrary to the common interest.

Italy

277.   In February the Commission terminated the Article 93(2) proceedings it had initiated against certain aid in the new Italian five-year plan for mining policy. The Commission had opened the proceedings because certain of the rules of the scheme and the amount of aid available for environmental protection, continued operation and attracting alternative enterprises were not, at first sight, compatible with the common market.

The Commission took its decision after the Italian Government had undertaken:

(a) to limit environmental aid to a grant of 15% of the total cost of restoration of the land. The 20% rate could be maintained in the Mezzogiorno;

(b) to keep operating aid to the minimum needed for restructuring mines so that they became viable or were definitively closed by the end of 1992;

(c) to submit a restructuring plan, notified to the Commission in advance, for each mine receiving assistance;

(d) to limit grants for replacement activities to 50% of the cost of the total investment in the Mezzogiorno and 25% in the rest of Italy, provided that, in the latter case, the recipient firms employed less than 51 workers;

(e) to reduce the budget for this last purpose to LIT 215 billion.

The Commission considered that the amended Italian plan accorded with the Council Resolution of 28 July 1989 and with its own policy for the mining industry.

278.   In June the Commission decided not to object to a scheme of aid introduced by Sicily concerning mineral deposits in quarries. The total budget for 1989-92 was approximately ECU 9.2 million (LIT 14 billion). The object of the scheme was to solve the problem of tipping quarry waste with the help of local authorities and to encourage its use as inert filling material. The aid was intended for very small firms which by this means were able to restore the landscape spoilt by the quarries. Given that the market for the materials was almost entirely local, that the danger of intra-Community competition being affected was remote, and that the aim of restoring the land accorded with the Community's environmental policy, the Commission granted an exemption for the scheme under Article 92(3)(c) of the EEC Treaty.

Sports goods

Belgium

279.   In December the Commission decided not to object to a capital injection of ECU 2.36 million (BFR 100 million) and a participatory loan of ECU 2.36 million (BFR 100 million) from the Wallonia Region to Donnay, a company in which the Region is a minority shareholder. As the majority shareholder was also putting money into the company, the Commission concluded that the action of the Wallonian authority was that of a private investor so that the measure did not involve aid.

Manure

Netherlands

280.   In December, the Commission terminated the procedure under Article 93(2) of the EEC Treaty procedure which it had initiated in June[1] against a scheme of aid for the construction of manure-treatment plants.

During the proceedings, the Dutch Government had altered its proposal and provided clarification of certain points. It had also introduced the 'polluter pays' principle into

---

[1]   OJ C 229, 14.9.1990.

the scheme by financing half of the aid budget of ECU 110 million (HFL 256 million) from a levy on excess manure produced in the Netherlands. It had also withdrawn the supplementary operating aid originally proposed.

In view of the amendments, the Commission decided that the scheme could qualify for exemption under Article 92(3)(c) of the EEC Treaty. However, it made clear that it would not be sympathetic towards any further aid if the treatment plants proved not to be viable.

Employment aid

In line with past practice[1] the Commission continued to take a generally favourable attitude to aid schemes for promoting employment where they were designed not just to keep workers in employment but to encourage firms to take on new workers, and especially to create additional jobs for particular categories of workers who have special difficulty in finding employment, and where the aid is not confined to particular industries or firms.

In this policy the Commission takes into consideration the need to encourage the special effort made by firms recruiting such workers. The scrutiny of the rules of such schemes leads the Commission in most cases to the conclusion that the aid is not likely to alter the conditions of intra-Community trade to an extent contrary to the common interest.

Federal Republic of Germany

281.   In April the Commission authorized a major employment-promotion programme for the long-term unemployed, which will be in operation until the end of 1991 with a budget of ECU 739 million.

282.   Under the programme, an employer taking on a long-term unemployed person on a permanent contract would be entitled for one year to a monthly indemnity amounting to 40 to 80% of the employee's wage, the actual rate depending on how long that person has been unemployed. In addition, grants would be offered to promoters organizing training for workers unemployed for at least two years who have particular difficulty in finding jobs. Since the aid for taking on new staff was granted automatically and was not targeted at particular sectors, regions or categories of firm, the Commission decided that it would not fall within the scope of Article 92(1).

---

[1]   Seventh Competition Report, point 223 et seq.; Nineteenth Competition Report, point 197.

Spain

283.   During 1990 the Commission authorized the introduction of several employment and training aid programmes in Spain, both countrywide and in most of the regions.

The employment aid offered by the various programmes was essentially of two types: grants for job-creation, and aid for job-creating investment. Support was also provided for technical assistance to the self-employed and to cooperatives.

The job-creation grants, ranging from PTA 250 000 to 900 000 (PTA 1 200 000 in the Basque Country), were available to employers taking on young people or long-term unemployed and for workers in these categories going into business themselves as self-employed or as members of cooperatives (and co-ownerships (SALs)).

The investment aid was available to the self-employed and to cooperatives (or SALs) and businesses set up under local employment initiatives (ILEs). It usually took the form of a subsidized loan (occasionally a grant) and in most cases was subject to a limit related to the number of jobs concerned.

Aid for environmental protection

284.   The Commission continued to apply the general criteria set out in the Community framework on State aid for the environment[1] which, while endorsing the goal of consistent application of the 'polluter pays' principle, allows certain exceptions. Accordingly, aid not exceeding 15% of investment required for firms to bring their plant into line with new environmental standards is deemed compatible with the common market under the exemption provided for in Article 92(3)(b) of the EEC Treaty.

In addition, the Commission is prepared to apply the exception of Article 92(3)(c) to aid for specific purposes, such as to assist existing firms to undertake research and development on the environment or to adopt environmental protection measures beyond what is statutorily required.

Spain

285.   In September the Commission approved a draft government programme to create an industrial, energy and environmental technology base. The programme provided for grants covering between 15 and 50% of the cost of investment, depending on the various types of project eligible.

---

[1]   Sixteenth Competition Report, point 259.

A budget of ECU 23.8 million (PTA 3 000 million) was allocated for 1990, with the budgets for 1991, 1992, 1993 and 1994 to be determined later.

286.   In December the Commission approved an aid scheme introduced by the regional government of Catalonia to prevent industrial atmospheric pollution. The grants were in line with the criteria set out in the Community framework. The budget allocated for 1990 was PTA 240 million.

France

287.   In March the Commission closed the Article 93(2) proceedings initiated on 28 June 1989[1] in respect of a French aid scheme introduced by the Agence sur la qualité de l'air (air-quality agency — AQA) for investment in a desulphurization plant. The aid is provided in the form of grants of up to 50% of investment costs.

The French Government had announced that it was discontinuing the aid and had notified a new AQA scheme for innovative investment in a non-productive plant that involved the first industrial application of a new technology. The Commission gave its approval for the new scheme, which offered aid of varying intensity up to a maximum of 50% gross for investment that would, for example, reduce pollution beyond the statutory requirements. The Commission took the view that such measures encouraged industry to make an additional effort to reach the highest possible standards, even going further than those currently in force in the Community.

Netherlands

288.   In July, the Commission approved tax incentives for the purchase of buses and lorries that complied with stricter standards for noise and exhaust emissions. The budget for the period 1990-93 was ECU 104.8 million (HFL 204 million).

The investigation showed that all the major European manufacturers were capable of making trucks and buses that met the standards. Also, the tax relief covered only part of the additional costs of such vehicles. The Commission cleared the scheme, having concluded that the measure did not involve State aid falling within Article 92(1).

---

[1]   Nineteenth Competition Report, point 198.

Aid in the energy sector[1]

Federal Republic of Germany

289. In March, the Commission investigated an unnotified Bavarian scheme to assist new technologies contributing to more efficient energy use. The annual budget was ECU 3.6 million (DM 8 million), and the rate of aid varied from 30 to 50% depending on the project.

In view of the modest budget and the fact that the rates of aid were generally lower than the abovementioned maxima and, moreover, mainly benefited small and medium-sized firms, the programme was exempted under Article 92(3)(c). The Commission asked the German authorities to take the necessary steps to ensure in future that State aid programmes were notified to the Commission.

290. In September the Commission approved a scheme in North Rhine-Westphalia to encourage the extension of district heating and the use of combined heat and power systems. The budget for 1990 was ECU 10.8 million (DM 22 million) and the rate of aid 35%. The recipients of the aid are industrial firms.

In view of the limited impact the scheme would have on trade between Member States and competition and its contribution to the Community's and the environment policies, the Commission did not raise any objection to the programme, applying the exemption provided for in Article 92(3)(c) of the EEC Treaty.

291. In December, the Commission approved a German law setting a minimum price for electricity generated from renewable energy sources (windmills, hydroelectric, solar and biomass). The rate of aid varied from 28 to 48% depending on the renewable energy source involved.

The impact of the measure on trade between Member States and on competition would be slight. Also, the law was in line with Council Recommendation 88/611/EEC of 8 November 1988.[2] The Commission therefore decided not to raise any objection to this law.

Netherlands

292. In July the Commission approved a Dutch scheme offering investment grants for energy conservation in existing buildings. The programme promoted better insulation

---

[1]   See also points 215 *et seq.* concerning aid to the coal industry.
[2]   OJ L 335, 7.12.1988.

and improved installation techniques. The aid was subject to a ceiling of 30% of the investment cost in the case of apartments and houses and 20% of costs in the case of offices and factories. The total funding available for 1990 was ECU 56 million (HFL 130 million) and it was to be used mainly to promote energy conservation in houses and apartments.

The programme was found to be consistent with the Community's energy policy objectives. Furthermore, it was established that any impact on competition and trade would be indirect and that it was not discriminatory. The Commission approved it under Article 92(3)(c) of the EEC Treaty.

United Kingdom

293. In connection with the reorganization of the electricity supply industry in the United Kingdom and the privatization of most of it, the Commission on 30 March approved a package of aid that the UK Government wished to provide to the nuclear sector of the industry which was remaining in public ownership. The Commission decision authorized a levy charged on the price of electricity generated from fossil fuels (the 'fossil fuel levy'), which is mainly intended to cover the extra cost of nuclear electricity for which the newly formed private electricity distribution companies in England and Wales will be obliged to contract with the nuclear company. This 'non-fossil fuel obligation' will cover 8 500 MW of nuclear capacity and a smaller quantity (initially 500 MW) of electricity generated from renewable energy sources, which will represent a total of some 17% of overall electricity demand in the United Kingdom. The rate of the levy, which the Commission authorized for eight years, would initially be 10.5%, but should come down to about 5.5% by 1998. Its average proceeds are estimated at some ECU 1.55 billion (UKL 1.15 billion) a year.

The Commission also authorized an ECU 3.38 billion (UKL 2.5 billion) government guarantee to cover possible increases in the cost of storage and reprocessing of nuclear fuel, the treatment, storage or disposal of radioactive waste and the decommissioning of existing nuclear power stations at the end of their life. In addition the Commission approved the writing off of ECU 1.9 billion (UKL 1.4 billion) of debt accumulated by the Scottish nuclear industry.

In authorizing the aid, the Commission accepted the case for keeping nuclear power stations operating until the end of their useful life, given the low marginal cost of the electricity they produce, and the nuclear sector's contribution to the security and diversity of energy supplies.

Aid to improve the general business environment

294.   In addition to the reductions in the overall volume of spending on aid observable in some Member States, the Commission also saw it as a positive trend that countries are tending to allocate aid budgets to schemes that are both less harmful to competition and more likely to strengthen the general efficiency and competitiveness of the Community economy. In the forefront of such aid schemes are programmes to improve the general business environment, particularly for small and medium-sized businesses, through the use of specialized consultants, training, the dissemination of advanced technology and the improvement of production and management methods. The favourable view the Commission takes of such aid is in line with similar action undertaken at Community level. [1]

Denmark

295.   In December the Commission approved a package of aid schemes that will be in operation in Denmark from 1991 onwards following the reform of Danish trade and industry support under Law No 394 of 13 June 1990. The new schemes are characterized by the almost total abandonment of aid for individual firms in favour of general measures aimed at creating a climate more conducive to improvements in competitiveness and technological change. They include schemes to encourage technical cooperation between small and medium-sized enterprises, training and consultancy help, R&D cooperation, and the dissemination and transfer of advanced technology. Total expenditure on trade and industry support is set to fall by half between 1990 and 1992, continuing a trend which already in 1988 marked out Denmark as the country with the lowest total aid spending in the Community. [2]

Spain

296.   In July the Commission decided not to object to the implementation of a number of schemes proposed by the Spanish Government that offered aid to improve the quality standards achieved by Spanish industry. Firms carrying out projects in the areas of dissemination, training, diagnosis and technical assistance and improvement of quality control systems were eligible for grants of up to 50% (gross) of the cost of the projects. The budget for 1990 was PTA 1 430 million.

---

[1]   See Council Decision of 28 July 1989, OJ L 239, 16.8.1989.
[2]   See Second Report on State aids in the European Community.

297.   A similar scheme aimed at the technological modernization of industry in Andalusia was approved by the Commission in September. The scheme, with a 1990 budget of PTA 454 million, offered grants of up to 20% of the investment cost to small businesses undertaking projects to improve their quality assurance systems.

298.   The Commission authorized several schemes to improve firms' marketing and distribution facilities.

Thus, in April, it approved schemes in Andalusia and Castilla-La-Mancha[1] to improve, set up or pool shared facilities, produce trade catalogues, and assist representation at trade fairs or on trade missions.

Aid to small and medium-sized businesses

Spain

299.   In 1990 the Commission approved a number of aid schemes for small and medium-sized firms in Spanish regions. Two such schemes were introduced by the regional governments of the Canary Islands and Madrid which the Commission approved in April and May. These offered an interest subsidy of four percentage points on loans contracted by small businesses investing in the region. The budgets for the schemes in 1990 were PTA 500 million and 1 100 million respectively.

The Commission also approved several schemes[2] to assist craft businesses in consolidating and developing the production of certain specialist food products. The generally low-budget schemes award grants for modernizing workshops and training craftworkers.

Italy

300.   In July the Commission approved a scheme to improve craft businesses in Sardinia. The scheme had a total budget for 1989 of approximately ECU 25 million (LIT 37 billion). The maximum grant to a craft business was about ECU 46 000 (LIT 70 million), with an estimated intensity of 18.9% net grant equivalent and cumulation with other regional aids possible up to 33.2%. The Commission, which has always encouraged national and regional schemes to assist craft businesses and promote cooperation and partnership, especially in the more disadvantaged parts of the Community, decided that the scheme qualified for exemption under Article 92(3)(c).

---

[1]   Asturias, Catalonia and Extremadura set up similar schemes with the Commission also approved in 1990.
[2]   Andalusia, Asturias and Catalonia introduced such schemes in 1990.

United Kingdom

301. The Commission approved a large number of aid schemes operated by local or regional authorities. Most were reserved for small and medium-sized enterprises, had a low aid intensity or aid level and a small budget.

Aid to tourism

Spain

302. The Commission gave its approval for a number of aid schemes to promote tourism in Spanish[1] and Italian regions.[2] The schemes were aimed at encouraging investment in the construction, modernization or improvement of all types of tourist facilities (hotels, restaurants, camp sites, rural accommodation, leisure and sports facilities, etc.).

The Commission maintained a favourable approach to such schemes, provided they were reasonable and — as is usually the case — involved small-scale tourism projects that are unlikely to affect the tourist trade in the Community to an extent contrary to the common interest. In one case,[3] the Commission approved a tourism aid programme with a very high budget (LIT 203 billion) because of the serious damage suffered by the industry as a result of the algae problem in the Adriatic in 1989.

Italy

303. In July the Commission authorized an aid scheme for the hotel and tourism trades in Sardinia. The scheme had a budget of ECU 16.1 million (LIT 24 billion) and an aid intensity of 14.78%. The Commission granted an exemption under Article 92(3)(c), having concluded that the aid would help develop the tourist trade without adversely affecting trading conditions to an extent contrary to the common interest.

---

[1] Andalusia, Asturias, Castilla-Leon, Extremadura, La Rioja, Pais Vasco and Valencia.
[2] Marches, Liguria and Piedmont.
[3] Italian Law 424/89: Adriatic coast (Friuli-Venezia, Giulia Veneto, Emilia-Romagna, Marches, Abruzzo, Molise).

Tax measures

France

304.   The Commission investigated various kinds of financial assistance allegedly granted to the Pari Mutuel Urbain in France. The examination proved complex in view of the peculiarities of the system for betting on horse-races which is linked to issues of public order and morality. According to the Commission's analysis, however, significant amounts of aid had been granted to Pari Mutuel Urbain and, in December, the Commission decided to initiate the procedure under Article 93(2) of the EEC Treaty with respect to this aid.

Italy

305.   On 25 July the Commission decided that certain tax concessions provided for in Bill No 4 230 of 4 October 1989 were incompatible with the common market pursuant to Article 92(1) of the EEC Treaty. The Commission confirmed in its decision that only concessions that applied throughout the tax system and were available automatically and without any exercise of discretion in the economy as a whole constituted general measures not covered by Article 92(1). It found that the tax relief provided for in the Bill was not a general measure but appeared to be intended exclusively for certain recipients, in particular Montedison in connection with the merger leading to the creation of Enimont. The Commission based its conclusions on the fact that the measures were limited to a very short period of time, involved restrictions as to the size of the firm to which assets were transferred and finally allowed the Italian Government a wide discretion. The Commission found that the tax provisions would have entitled Montedison to a tax exemption of LIT 774 billion, strengthening its financial position. Furthermore, Montedison was in the chemical industry where there was considerable intra-Community trade and fierce competition.

There was therefore a serious risk of distortion of competition. During the proceedings, the Italian Government did not contest the Commission's findings, but stated that a general law on tax provisions applicable to reorganizations of industrial production structures was to be presented to Parliament.

§ 6 — Regional aid

306. The Commission continued to keep regional aid schemes in the Member States under review pursuant to Article 93(1) of the EEC Treaty. It completed its general review of French regional aid started in 1989 and began detailed examinations of regional aid in Italy, Belgium and the Federal Republic of Germany, in cooperation with the relevant national authorities. In the case of the Federal Republic of Germany, the examination took account of the changes resulting from unification.

In addition, the Commission continued to ensure that all aid schemes cofinanced by the structural Funds had been approved under the competition rules. As in the previous year, this involved the Commission examining schemes operated at all levels of government in the Member States.

It paid close attention to the principle of economic and social cohesion in its monitoring of schemes.

The Commission also began a detailed review of the interface between Community policy on national regional aid and assistance provided by the structural Funds. It will, if appropriate, take any measures necessary to improve the coherence between these two aspects of Community action.

Belgium

307. In May and September, the Commission approved the new rules for implementing the Economic Expansion Law of 30 December 1970 in the Walloon and Flemish regions respectively. This law is the basis of the Belgian system of regional aid. The Commission took the view that the new rules, which did not alter either the aid ceilings or the development areas previously approved, significantly increased the transparency of the system. However, it made clear in each case that the changes in the rules amounted to amendments to an existing scheme which required prior notification in accordance with Article 93(3) of the EEC Treaty.

308. In May, the Commission approved an investment aid scheme for small and medium-sized businesses setting up in the areas of Wallonia covered by the Community Resider programme or designated as Objective 2 areas under the reformed structural Funds. Decisions to award aid were to be based on the Economic Expansion Law of 30 December 1970. However, simplified criteria for calculating the amount of aid would be applied. The system was to be 50% cofinanced by the ERDF under operational programmes to be approved by the Commission.

The Commission approved the scheme because it applied only in assisted areas approved by the Commission for the Economic Expansion Law, it kept within the authorized aid ceilings and only small and medium-sized businesses (employing fewer than 250 persons and having a turnover of less than ECU 20 million) were eligible.

Federal Republic of Germany

309.   In July a start was made, in cooperation with the German authorities under Article 93(1) of the Treaty, on a comprehensive review of all national regional aid in the Federal Republic of Germany, including aid for Berlin and the former Zonal Border Area. The review is in line with the Commission's policy of re-examining existing aid already approved by it. The aim is to examine the compatibility of existing aid measures with the common market in the light of the structural changes that have taken place since the Commission's previous decisions, notably German unification. In accordance with Article 93(1) of the EEC Treaty, the Commission will propose any appropriate measures required by such changes.

310.   In July the Commission prohibited a scheme that had been illegally introduced under which the Hamburg authorities granted investment subsidies to dissuade firms from moving from the city. The Commission's decision required the German authorities to repeal the programme and to recover aid totalling ECU 13 million (DM 27.3 million) granted to 31 firms between 1986 and 1988.

The Commission took the view that the scheme was incompatible with the common market because regional aid was not justified in Hamburg as the economic and employment situation was relatively good. Consequently, the granting of investment aid in Hamburg, a non-assisted area, would reduce the effectiveness of aid granted in regions in which the Commission has recognized the need to offset structural disadvantages. The Commission could find no justification for the aid granted by the city of Hamburg.

311.   In July the Commission approved aid granted under the special programme for Bremen, forming part of the Joint Federal Government/*Länder* Regional Development Programme (Gemeinschaftsaufgabe), to an investment project by Daimler-Benz AG in Bremen. The special programme for Bremen requires awards to be notified if they involve investment of more than ECU 6 million.

312.   Also in July the Commission approved an aid scheme in Bavaria providing for the granting of subsidized loans to certain small and medium-sized businesses.

313.   In September the Commission approved the 19th general plan of the Joint Federal Government/*Länder* Regional Development Programme (Gemeinschaftsaufgabe). The

19th general plan extended the 18th plan for the year 1990. The Commission's approval of the current assisted area map in Germany expired on 31 December 1990.

314.   In September, the Commission approved the renewal for 1991 of a programme in Baden-Württemberg to assist a number of its rural areas.

315.   In October the Commission initiated the Article 93(2) procedure in respect of two aid awards with an intensity of 15% which the *Land* of North Rhine-Westphalia intended to make to firms setting up in the district of Heinsberg, an area covered by an aid scheme allowing a maximum aid intensity of 7.5%.

Greece

316.   In December the Commission decided to approve the new Greek regional aid scheme provided for in part A of Law 1892/90, which amended Law 1262/82. The forms of aid provided for under the new scheme are the same as previously, namely grants, interest subsidies, tax relief and accelerated depreciation. The country is divided into five development areas, A, B, C, D and Thrace. Area A is not in principle eligible for regional aid, and the lowest levels of aid are available in area B and highest in Thrace.

The Commission was able to adopt its decision since the whole of Greece is classified as eligible for regional aid under Article 92(3)(a) and since the maximum intensity of the aid had been reduced compared with the most recent amendment to Law 1262/82 approved by the Commission in July 1990.

Spain

317.   In February the Commission authorized an aid scheme in Andalusia for firms setting up in the Malaga Technology Park in Andalusia. The aid consisted of grants, interest subsidies, preferential availability of official loans, and training aid, which in total could not exceed 50% of the approved investment and which when combined with other aid could not exceed 50% net grant equivalent (NGE). The Commission's decision was based in particular on the bad economic and employment situation in the region.

318.   In July the Commission opened Article 93(2) proceedings against plans to offer aid under the national regional aid scheme with an intensity of up to 45% NGE in Sierra Norte in the Madrid area. The Commission's decision was based on the fact that aid of this level was generally reserved for Article 92(3)(a) regions and the Madrid area was not such a region and that the economic and employment situation in the area did not justify the authorization of aid up to this level under Article 92(3)(c).

The Commission however authorized the granting of aid under the national regional aid scheme with an intensity of up to 45% NGE in the lateral and central mining areas in the Asturias region up to 1 June 1993. The Commission's decision was influenced by the rise in structural unemployment in the Asturias region and the restructuring of the mining industry in the region.

319.   In November the Commission opened Article 93(2) proceedings against investment aid granted by the autonomous government of Catalonia in areas which did not appear to be eligible for regional aid or in cases where the location, the investment and the aid intensity were not stipulated. The Commission also opened proceedings in respect of certain budget appropriations in the Catalonia region that might be used to finance aid that had not been notified to the Commission and might prove incompatible with the common market.

The Commission authorized other aid granted by the autonomous government of Catalonia between 1986 and 1990, in view of the characteristics and limited scale of the aid.

France

320.   In December the Commission proposed to the French authorities appropriate measures under Article 93(1) in relation to French regional aid schemes.

The proposals, which follow on from the review begun in 1989,[1] are as follows.

Reduction in the territorial coverage of French assisted areas
(Regional planning grant scheme — Prime d'aménagement du territoire (PAT))

Taking account of the changes, in terms of relative economic performance and unemployment level, that had taken place in the French regions since 1984 (when the Commission last took a decision on the PAT[2]) and based on the established method for applying Article 92(3)(c) to regional aid schemes,[3] the Commission proposed that the French authorities exclude from the PAT scheme the areas currently eligible for the PAT in the departments of Charente, Cher, Indre, Landes, Mayenne, Orne, Bas-Rhin, Haut-Rhin, Ille-et-Vilaine, Vienne and Indre-et-Loire. Such exclusion should take effect on 1 July 1991, except in the case of Vienne, where it would take effect on 1 January 1992.

---

[1]   Nineteenth Competition Report, point 204.
[2]   OJ L 11, 12.1.1985.
[3]   OJ C 212, 12.8.1988.

In addition, the Commission informed the French authorities that it would once again analyze the economic and employment situation in several departments by 31 December 1991 or 31 December 1993 whose current situation appears to justify only temporary eligibility for the PAT.

The departments whose situation will be reviewed before the end of 1991 are Maine-et-Loire, Puy-de-Dôme and Saône-et-Loire, and those to be reviewed before the end of 1993 are Haute-Marne, Gers, Lot-et-Garonne, Haute-Garonne, Haute-Vienne and Hautes-Pyrénées.

The proposed appropriate measures on the areas took account of the Commission's decision in March agreeing to the reclassification of exceptional PAT areas as normal PAT areas. Exceptional PAT areas were areas eligible for the PAT subject to prior Commission control of large awards. The Commission took the view, on the basis of the standard method for assessing eligibility for aid under Article 92(3)(c), that the situation of the areas justified full classification as normal PAT areas.

Setting of aid ceilings for the remaining assisted areas

In view of the number of French regional aid schemes, the diversity of the forms they can take (grants, tax exemptions, subsidized loans, etc.) and the fact that the aids are granted by different ministries, the Commission thought that the situation should be simplified and it accordingly proposed the setting of regional aid ceilings. The ceilings, expressed in terms of net grant equivalent, represent the maximum acceptable for one and the same project under regional aid schemes. The main purpose of the ceilings is to improve the transparency of the French system given the abovementioned features. The ceilings should not result in any decrease in the level of aid that could previously be granted.

Clearer demarcation of the assisted areas covered by the
steel industry redevelopment corporations

The Commission asked the French authorities to delimit these areas precisely. It considered that, as with any regional aid, the activities of the redevelopment corporations set up in former steel areas must be confined to clearly defined areas.

In addition, the Commission would like the areas to be included in regions eligible for the PAT. Otherwise, the redevelopment corporations would have to confine their activities to firms employing fewer than 150 people and having a turnover of less than ECU 15 million and to limit the aid granted to 7.5% of the investment (or ECU 3 000 per job created or ECU 200 000 per recipient).

Restriction of the areas in which relief from local business tax and transfer duty are available

So as to ensure greater concentration, the Commission proposed that such aid should in future be granted only in PAT areas. However, since the intensity of such aid was low (4% net grant equivalent), the Commission indicated that, outside PAT areas, it would agree to firms with fewer than 150 persons and less than ECU 15 million turnover still begin able to receive such aid.

Size of firms eligible for assistance from coalfield redevelopment corporations in areas not eligible for regional aid

Hitherto, firms situated outside PAT areas could receive assistance from the coalfield redevelopment corporations only if they had fewer than 100 employees and sales of less than ECU 10 million. It was proposed to the French authorities that, if they so wished, they could raise the size limits to firms with 150 employees and ECU 15 million. This proposal, based on a similar change in the limits in the Commission decision on aids of minor importance,[1] is in line with the proposal relating to the redevelopment corporations for steel areas.

The Commission also began an investigation into the activities of certain public enterprises which also run schemes to attract alternative jobs to their areas. The Commission believes, on the basis of its present information, that such activities might involve aid (within the meaning of the Treaty) granted for regional purposes. However, the French authorities seem to take the view that such activities are not aid.

In view of this divergence of opinion and the fact that the Commission is under an obligation to determine the compatibility of all aid with the common market, Article 93(2) proceedings were initiated. This will enable the French authorities, the other Member States and other interested parties (including the public undertakings concerned) to express their views.

After having analysed such comments, the Commission will be in a position to determine:

(i) whether the activities in question constitute aid;

(ii) if so, whether such aid is compatible with the common market.

Redevelopment activities of this nature are carried on by EdF, Elf Aquitaine, Thomson, Péchiney, Rhône-Poulenc and EMC. Mostly through subsidiaries, these firms offer

---

[1] OJ C 40, 20.2.1990.

subsidized loans, equity stakes and other financial inducements to firms setting up or expanding their businesses in areas affected in which they themselves have made workers redundant or cut back their activities.

321. In February the Commission terminated the Article 93(2) proceedings initiated in November 1986 against France in respect of awards of regional aid in combination with aid of other types. The Commission had received an assurance from the French Government that the cumulation rules would be applied through the central government machinery at regional level; an administrative circular was being sent to the regional prefects for this purpose.

On 18 December 1984 the Commission had sent all the Member States, under Article 93(1), a notice providing that certain large awards of aid in which regional aid was combined with aid under other schemes for the same investment project had to be notified to it in advance so that it could assess whether they were compatible with the common market. All the Member States had eventually stated their agreement to the notice except France and Greece. In the case of France and Greece, the Commission opened Article 93(2) proceedings of which it served notice by letters dated 31 July 1987.

The proceedings against Greece were terminated in 1988. The proceedings against France were now also terminated as the administrative circular giving effect to the Community rules entered into force on 18 January 1990.

322. In February, the Commission cleared relief from corporation tax that had been granted to certain firms in Corsica in 1988 and 1989. The relief was granted for eight years to clearly defined firms that had set up in Corsica in those years.

In its decision the Commission took particular account of Corsica's economic and social situation, which is marked by high unemployment, handicapped by its island location and mountainous terrain which isolate communities and makes internal communications difficult, and the severe imbalance in trade between Corsica and the Continent. The Commission also obtained an assurance from the French Government that the regional aid ceiling applicable in Corsica had not been exceeded and that the rules on the cumulation of different types of aid had been complied with. It reminded the French Government that any extension of the scheme would have to be notified.

323. In October the Commission closed the file on the French authorities' failure to comply with one of the provisions of the Commission Decision of January 1987 on enterprise zones. Although the textile and clothing industry had been specifically excluded from the enterprise zone scheme, the Commission had noticed, on reading the quarterly reports on the implementation of the scheme forwarded by the French authorities, that several firms in the textile and clothing sector had set up in the Dunkirk enterprise zone with the benefit of the tax exemption.

The Commission approached the French authorities and received an assurance that the firms concerned would not be given the tax exemption.

324.   In November the Commission initiated Article 93(2) proceedings in respect of the possibility of combining the tax exemption provided for in enterprise zones with other types of aid. This followed the proposal of 'appropriate measures' under Article 93(1) in December 1989,[1] which the French authorities would not accept.

325.   In November the Commission approved a package of aid schemes on the island of Réunion. Some of the schemes were new (interest subsidies, guarantee funds, venture capital and measures to assist businesses), while some amended existing schemes (Fonds de redéveloppement industriel and Fonds régional d'aide au conseil).

In its decision, the Commission took account of the very difficult economic and social situation of the island, which is designated as an Article 92(3)(a) area and covered by the Poseidom (Programme d'options spécifiques à l'éloignement et à l'insularité des départements d'outre-mer) programme. The measures form part of the Community framework of support for Réunion approved by the Commission in 1989.

Ireland

326.   In January the Commission authorized the national programme for industrial development for the period 1989-93. Although most of the direct financial aid included in the programme, such as the capital grants provided by the Industrial Development Authority (IDA), Shannon Free Airport Development Company (Sfadco) and Údarás na Gaeltachta had already been approved by the Commission, the programme contained a number of new or existing types of aid that had not yet been formally examined by the Commission. The main new type of aid proposed was the marketing development subprogramme, with a planned budget of IRL 130 million. The subprogramme provides for a range of information, advice and support services intended to improve the marketing function of firms, which will be dispensed mainly by Coras Tráchtála and to a lesser extent the Irish Goods Council.

The national programme also contains various subprogrammes offering small and medium-sized businesses support for the cost of outside consultancy help and related services, or providing for recruitment and training aid, equity stakes by public authorities, research and development aid and special terms for the sale or rental of industrial land or buildings by the IDA and Sfadco.

In its decision, the Commission took account of the difficult economic and social situation in Ireland, which is characterized by below-average living standards and severe

---

[1]   Nineteenth Competition Report, point 204.

underemployment. At the Commission's request, the Irish authorities confirmed that in implementing the measures there would be no discrimination between Irish firms and those from other Member States. The Irish authorities will also have to provide annual reports on the programme so as to maintain transparency.

327. In July the Commission approved the extension of the special tax regime available to authorized firms in the Customs House Docks Area of Dublin. The Commission's approval relates to all the new firms authorized by the Irish authorities up to 1 January 1991. The Commission's previous approval[1] had been limited to a three-year period starting in July 1987. The firms concerned only pay a 10% rate of corporation tax until the year 2000.

Italy

328. In July the Commission took a final decision on aid measures under Law 120/87 for certain parts of the Mezzogiorno that had suffered natural disasters. Article 92(2) proceedings had been opened in the case in October 1989. The measures supplement industrial development action begun in 1981 under Article 32 of Law 219/81 following the Irpinia earthquake in 1980. The measures also provide for an increase, in certain areas of the Mezzogiorno affected by natural disasters from 1980 to 1986, in the investment aid provided for in Article 9 of Law 64/86 establishing the new aid scheme for the Mezzogiorno.

In the decision, the Commission allowed aid to be granted for investments costing up to LIT 32 billion under Article 32 of Law 219/81 in the 20 enterprise zones initially designated under the programme. However, aid was not allowed outside such zones or on sites added on to them or in respect of investment in excess of LIT 32 billion.

Furthermore, the Commission deemed the increase in aid provided for in Article 9 of Law 64/86 to be incompatible with the common market since it was not justified by a general worsening in the economic and social situation of the regions concerned.

The Italian Government was required to reclaim from the recipients aid that had been found unlawful and incompatible under Article 92.

329. In December the Commission also examined under Articles 92 and 93 of the EEC Treaty, Law 181/89 establishing special social provisions and redevelopment incentives accompanying the plan for restructuring the Italian public-sector steel industry.

In addition to the social measures introduced to assist directly workers in the sector (early retirement, aid for redeployment and training, etc.), the law provides for aid to assist

---

[1]   Seventeenth Competition Report, point 249.

investment by small and medium-sized firms in Resider areas (25% of the cost of eligible investment) which can be cofinanced by the structural Funds (Social Fund, ERDF, etc.).

Provision is also made for specific measures to assist the implementation of two programmes: a special reindustrialization programme covering investment projects by firms in the IRI group and an industrial promotion programme to aid business initiatives in mixed public and private ownership.

The measures applicable in the areas worst affected by the restructuring of the Italian public steel industry, i.e. mainly the provinces of Genoa, Terni, Naples and Taranto, were deemed compatible with the common market under Article 92(3)(a) and (c) of the EEC Treaty.

Netherlands

330. In May the Commission decided to terminate the Article 93(2) proceedings[1] which it had initiated in June 1989[2] with respect to regional aid programmes in the Netherlands.

During the proceedings, the Dutch authorities agreed to introduce restrictive criteria in implementing the programmes, which the Commission had previously accepted for other Dutch aid schemes. In view of these limitations on the areas eligible, the aid intensity and possibilities of cumulation, the Commission decided that the regional programmes qualified for an exemption under Article 92(3)(c) of the EEC Treaty.

In December the Commission also reached a decision on the overall plans of the Dutch Government in regional policy for the period 1991-94, which provide for a decrease in the rate of aid and in the coverage of assisted areas or regions eligible for investment aid.

The Commission agreed to investment aid up to 20% gross throughout the entire four-year period for the provinces of Groningen and Friesland, and for Lelystad. In the case of the south-east of Drenthe, however, the Commission's approval is restricted to two years; the situation in that region will be reviewed in 1992.

The Commission also agreed to the Dutch Government's plan to grant investment aid of up to 15% gross until 31 December 1992 in South Limburg, Helmond and Arnhem/Nijmegen.

As regards the region of Twente, where the Dutch Government had also proposed granting aid up to 31 December 1992, the Commission was unable to agree to such aid

---

[1]   OJ C 280, 8.11.1990.
[2]   Nineteenth Competition Report, point 207.

for more than a transitional period up to 1 July 1991, given the considerable improvement in unemployment and the level of GDP in the region.

Portugal

331.   In October, the Commission decided to approve an aid scheme to support
modernization of the distributive trades through technological innovation, restructuring
and projects to promote cooperation between firms. The maximum aid intensity varied
between 20 and 41% net grant equivalent (NGE). The scheme forms part of the
Community framework of support for Portugal approved by the Commission in 1989.
The budget allocated for financing the aid is ECU 33 million for the period 1990-93,
with ECU 23 million being provided by the Community.

United Kingdom

332.   In July the Commission decided not to raise any objections to the United Kingdom
authorities' proposed new aid scheme for the construction of industrial buildings, run
by the English Industrial Estates Corporation. The scheme is intended to encourage the
private sector to invest in industrial and commercial buildings in areas of England eligible
for regional aid. The grants will be paid to the investors and are intended to cover the
difference between the market price of the building and its construction cost. The grant
will be kept to the minimum necessary to ensure the scheme's success. In its decision,
the Commission took account of the regional development benefits of the scheme and
the transparency which it introduces in property transactions carried out by the public
authorities on behalf of firms.

333.   In December the Commission authorized the implementation of two new pilot
schemes by the Scottish Development Agency (SDA).

The Technology Development Fund is intended to strengthen Scottish industry through
the development of new or improved production processes, by promoting private sector
investment, particularly in biotechnology, electronics and oil and gas. The Fund has a
budget of UKL 78 million and will operate for four years. Only small and medium-sized
firms employing a maximum of 200 persons will be eligible for assistance. Aid from the
Fund will be taken into account in complying with regional aid ceilings. However, the
aid may also be granted outside of assisted areas at rates of up to 20% gross, with a
maximum amount per firm of ECU 200 000.

The Scottish Skills Foundation is intended to stimulate the provision of additional
training for employees to upgrade and broaden their skills. Grants up to 50% of training

costs, with a ceiling of UKL 250 000, may be provided. The Foundation has a budget of UKL 2 million and will operate for two years.

The Commission also approved a number of other schemes introduced by the SDA. The main ones are: local enterprise grants for urban projects (annual budget: UKL 7.5 million), training and employment grants and training programmes (UKL 5.3 million), a programme for rural and development initiatives (budget of UKL 5 million for 1988-92) and venture capital (UKL 7.5 million). The Commission approved this aid since it contributed to regional development and was intended for small and medium-sized firms.

§ 7 — Aid in the transport sector

Land transport

334.   The bulk of the aid provided for land transport continues to be that paid to national railways, either in compensation for public service obligations under Regulations (EEC) Nos 1191/69 and 1192/69, or as aid within the limits laid down by Regulation No 1107/70. The Commission informs the Council of such aid spending in the two-yearly reports provided for in Council Decision 75/327/EEC. The Commission has also reported to the Council on the aid granted for combined transport under Regulation No 1107/70.

The Commission scrutinized plans to introduce or alter specific aid schemes. These included an aid scheme for road transport in the Basque country in 1990-92. In view of the scheme's funding and the reduction in capacity, the Commission found the scheme compatible with the common market by virtue of the exception provided for in Article 92(3)(c).

Nor did the Commission raise objections to a scheme in Andalusia providing public aid for renovating and modernizing public transport road vehicles.

In the inland waterway sector, following the adoption of Council Regulation (EEC) No 1101/89 of 27 April 1989 on structural improvements in the industry,[1] a scrapping programme was launched on 1 January 1990 in order to reduce excess capacity. Under the scheme, owners were allowed to put in claims for a scrapping premium for up to 30 vessels with a deadweight of about 1 050 000 tonnes. These vessels had been permanently withdrawn from the inland waterway market by the end of 1990.

The Commission also defined its position on proposals for new or amended aid schemes in the industry notified to it by Member States.

The Commission ruled, for example, that a plan for restructuring the Belgian inland waterway fleet was not compatible with the common market under Article 92.[1] The plan's provisions for aid to certain categories of Belgian boatmen agreeing to leave the industry were, however, regarded as compatible with the common market and were therefore allowed to be implemented on their own.

After scrutinizing France's national rationalization plan for 1990-92 in inland waterway transport offering aid for vessels with a deadweight of under 450 tonnes and the public programme for 1990-94 for France's commercial fleet, the Commission had no objection to the plans.

---

[1]   OJ L 356, 6.12.1989.

Sea transport

335.   The Commission continued its scrutiny of State aids to Community shipowners. A number of studies were undertaken in that respect, dealing with, on the one hand, the structure of the Community fleet and the definition of competitive and representative model vessels and, on the other, the running costs of the various types of ships in absolute terms. Those studies proved indispensable in assessing, in the immediate context of the Community policy on sea transport, whether the aids in question were compatible with the common market. Moreover, the 'Guidelines for the examination of State aids to Community shipping companies', which the Commission adopted on 3 August 1989, had to be adjusted to take account of the latest economic data. That work is under way.

The Commission is still waiting for comments from a number of Member States on the 'General study of State aid in the port sector' which it prepared and distributed to the Member States. It is expected that once those comments have been received and analyzed the study will be presented to the Council.

Air transport

336.   Throughout 1990 the Commission continued to monitor developments in the area of State aids for Community air carriers with a view to ensuring that the liberalization process is not distorted by direct financial intervention at national level.

This work will become increasingly important in view of economic and financial strains imposed on many air carriers following the Gulf crisis.

In October 1990 the Commission approved, on the basis of Article 92(3)(c) of the EEC Treaty, a proposal from the German Federal Government to grant, in the context of a special Regional Development Programme covering the *Land* Bremen, investment aid aimed at increasing the capacity of a pilot school which Lufthansa operates at Bremen airport.

§ 8 — Aid in the agricultural sector

337. Agriculture within the Community continued to be subject to a wide range of pressures and influences that reflect the developing constraints and opportunities in which the sector now operates. The various market policy reforms, the most recent of which became effective from the 1988/89 marketing year, continued to be felt, particularly in terms of changes in prices for producers in the Community, which for certain key commodities were some 20 to 30% lower in real terms than in recent years. In addition to the impact of these price developments — for which the prospects for Community producers, irrespective of the outcome of the GATT Uruguay Round negotiations, were not good — exceptional weather conditions in 1990 had an adverse effect upon producers' returns in many regions of the Community.

The response of society in general to the wider recognition of environmental problems, and the part played by agriculture in this context, also played an increasing role in the development of the sector. Developments in consumer preferences, particularly for more sophisticated presentation of foods, for so-called biological produce and the highest possible standards of health and hygiene, likewise continued to exert their influences.

None of these pressures and influences were entirely new forces upon Community agriculture in 1990. Consequently they did not bring about any fundamental change in the Commission approach to State aid policy related to this sector. However, the Commission, in applying the aid policy to the agricultural sector, took full account of their significance both in terms of developing constraints upon the sector as well as potential opportunities. Accordingly, the Commission steadfastly continued to oppose any national aid measure which would run counter to the sound operation of the common agricultural policy or the free internal market. Such measures included those which, for example, attempt to switch the burden of change from domestic producers to those in other Member States. Consequently, the Commission, during the course of the year, opposed various forms of operating aid, and aided investments in sectors for which overcapacity was found at a Community level. The Commission was, however, hindered when faced with aid for agricultural products for which no market organization exists, such as potatoes. For these products the Treaty's provisions on State aid do not allow the Commission to prevent the grant of trade-distorting State aid, even when applied to intra-Community trade. The Commission is actively considering the options open to it to regularize the position in this area particularly in the run-up to 1992.

The Commission however authorized many State aids which enabled producers to benefit from processing and marketing opportunities where, through structural changes, greater value added may be realized or costs reduced. This aspect of Commission policy is particularly important under conditions where, as is now the case, the share of consumer expenditure on foodstuffs accruing to primary producers is for many products continuing to fall rapidly. Furthermore, the desires of consumers to obtain foods from artisan producers were often the subject of a positive response from the Commission in its aid policy. For example, the Commission had a positive approach to measures such as publicity measures which facilitated consumer recognition of foods from such producers. However, in this and all other areas the Commission insisted that no action be taken which could breach the provisions of Article 30 of the EEC Treaty.

When dealing with aid related to the environment, the Commission sought to strike a balance whereby the polluter-pays principle is applied while developments positive to the environment are stimulated, if necessary, by authorizing the grant of State aid.

338. The Commission also had to decide on aid funded by compulsory levies or contributions whose proceeds are used for certain specific areas of expenditure. The levies are generally made compulsory by legislation.

The funds concerned do not appear in the budget, but are channelled directly to cover expenditure in the sectors in which the levies are charged or in other sectors.

According to the case-law of the Court of Justice of the European Communities,[1] the way in which such a compulsory levy is raised is an essential component of the aid; the scrutiny of such schemes for the purpose of establishing whether they comply with the Community's rules should therefore cover both distribution of the aid itself and the manner in which it is financed.

Hence, even if an aid is compatible with the common market as regards both its form and its purpose, if it is funded by a levy that also applies to imported products produced in the Community it will have a protectionist effect which goes beyond the scope of the aids as such and makes it incompatible with the common market.

The Commission therefore decided to initiate the procedure provided for in Article 93(2) of the EEC Treaty in respect of the following aid measures:

(i)   aids and compulsory contributions for the promotion of pigmeat in Belgium;[2]

(ii) aids and levies for the benefit of the Comité national interprofessionnel de l'horti-culture florale, ornementale et des pépinières (CNIH) in France;[3]

(iii) aids and levies for the benefit of the Etablissement national technique pour l'amélioration de la viticulture (ENTAV) in France.[4]

---

[1]   In particular Case 47/69 *France* v *Commission* [1970] ECR 487.
[2]   OJ C 162, 3.7.1990.
[3]   OJ C 170, 12.7.1990.
[4]   OJ C 91, 9.4.1991.

339. Aid policy concerning agricultural incomes advanced significantly in 1990 which saw Commission approval for the first time of income aid schemes under Community rules introduced in 1989. This aspect of aid policy, although based on Article 43 of the Treaty rather than Articles 92 and 93, is now playing a role which has certain parallels with competition policy and is therefore worthy of mention in this Report. During 1990 schemes were approved for three Member States, the Netherlands, France and Italy. Although these schemes were each tailored to meet the particular circumstances encountered in the countries concerned they all exhibit several common features, in particular that of enabling incomes to be boosted without causing any market distortion. This result is achieved by decoupling the right to the aid, as well as its size, from any production decision which the beneficiaries may take. Several other Member States have already indicated their intention to apply the Community income aid policy.

Effective control by the Commission of national aid in the agricultural sector is of course essential if the distortions which may be associated with such aid, are to be avoided. In order to help to achieve this objective the Commission, in addition to reminding Member States from time to time of their obligations under the Treaty concerning such aids, applies a policy whereby infringements of these obligations which distort the costs normally borne under the common agricultural policy, may lead to a refusal by the Commission to charge to the Community budget expenditure which has been inflated by such aid. During the course of the year several cases where State aid was deemed to have had a distorting effect on the market were the subject of such refusal and consequently the costs had to be borne by the national resources of the Member State concerned. Although the total of this disallowed expenditure, at some ECU 13 million, was modest in relation to the EAGGF total, it does constitute a useful additional reminder to the Member States of their responsibilities in this policy area.

340. The following part of this subsection of the Report deals on a country-by-country basis with the most significant cases of State aid examined by the Commission in particular those that gave rise either to approvals or to final negative decisions.

Belgium

341. Having opened proceedings under Article 93(2) of the EEC Treaty in respect of investment aid for the Couplet sugar refinery at Brunehaut-Wez,[1] the Commission took a negative final decision and asked the Belgian authorities not to grant the aid.[2] The file was closed after the Belgian authorities had notified the Commission that the proposed aid had been cancelled.

---

[1]   Nineteenth Competition Report, point 218.
[2]   OJ L 186, 18.7.1990.

Denmark

342.   The Commission considered that existing aid granted to plant-multiplying stations with a view to covering their operating costs allowed producers to obtain propagating material at a price below that which reflected the cost of running the stations, and that the aid distorted competition between Danish suppliers to propagating material and those in other Member States.

In accordance with Article 93(1) of the EEC Treaty the Commission asked the Danish authorities to alter the existing aid scheme in such a way as to discontinue the aid by 1 January 1991 at the latest.

Federal Republic of Germany

343.   The Federal Republic of Germany notified the Commission of a number of aids granted on the territory of the former German Democratic Republic. They included aids which were similar to structural measures already in application in the Federal Republic (investment aid, land consolidation, improvement of the market structure, etc.), aids similar to existing Community schemes (set aside, extensification of agricultural production), as well as aids which related more closely to the specific situation of agriculture in the former German Democratic Republic. This last type of measure included in particular adjustment aid to compensate for losses resulting from the cut in agricultural prices due to the implementation of the provision of the common agricultural policy, aid for the restructuring of cooperatives as well as aid for the re-establishment and modernization of family farms. To the extent that these measures were not covered either by existing general Community legislation or by the special transitional measures for agriculture that had been adopted by the Council in the context of the German unification (see Council Regulation (EEC) No 3577/90, OJ L 353, 17.12.1990, in particular Article 4), they will have to be dealt with on the basis of Articles 92 and 93 of the Treaty.

Spain

344.   The Commission terminated the Article 93(2) proceedings in respect of aid in the form of equity investments (increase in capital) and subsidized loans to certain firms in the vegetable-oil sector (Mercosa, Olceca, Uteco-Jaen and Merco-Jaen). [1]

The Commission's decision took into account the information and supporting evidence provided by the Spanish authorities in the course of the proceedings showing that the

---

[1]   OJ C 315, 15.12.1989.

aid had been planned, granted and, with a few exceptions, paid prior to Spanish accession. Hence, the aid did not fall within the scope of Articles 92 to 94 of the Treaty.

The Commission decided not to object, under Articles 93 and 94 of the EEC Treaty, to aid schemes introduced under agrarian reform legislation in Andalusia and Extremadura, but indicated that it might take a decision on some of the measures at a later stage pursuant to Council Regulation (EEC) No 797/85 on improving the efficiency of agricultural structures.

The Commission regretted that most of the schemes had not been notified to it at the proposal stage in accordance with Article 93(3) of the EEC Treaty to enable the Commission to take a decision on them before they were put into effect.

France

345. The French Government notified the Commission of a proposed scheme to strengthen the strawberry industry. The measure involved aid for the marketing of strawberries, the amount of which depended on the quantities sold by the recognized producers' organizations. Strawberries fall within the scope of Regulation (EEC) No 1035/72 on the common organization of the market in fruit and vegetables.

The aid was to be considered as an operating aid to the said organizations. As such, it would have an indirect impact on the marketing costs of products subject to an EEC market organization and would therefore contravene the legal system laid down by the market organization and so constitute an infringement of Community provisions. The Commission consequently initiated the procedure provided for in Article 93(2) of the EEC Treaty in respect of this proposed aid.

On the same grounds the Commission regarded as an operating aid which — by contravening the rules of the common market organization — was incompatible with the common market, the aid granted to producers of cereal-based starch by way of a refund of the storage levy on cereals in the case of maize meal intended for the brewing industry. The Commission accordingly initiated Article 93(2) proceedings in respect of the aid.

Italy

346. The Commission also initiated proceedings provided for in Article 93(2) of the EEC Treaty in respect of aid which the Italian Government was planning to grant under an investment programme in the Mezzogiorno covering starch and glucose and products derived therefrom, vegetable protein and fermentation products. The aid which the

authorities planned to grant under the scheme totalled ECU 348.6 million (LIT 522.3 billion).

The Commission felt that, from the information in its possession the scheme appeared not to be compatible with the common market under Article 92(1) of the EEC Treaty or eligible for an exemption under paragraphs 2 and 3 of that Article.

It considered that aid that encouraged the installation of further production capacity in sectors where there was already structural overcapacity was likely to have an adverse effect on intra-Community trade and competition.

This was especially true in the case of the starch industry: boosting annual production capacity by 357 000 tonnes (equivalent to increasing Europe's production of wheat starch and starch generally by 25 and 7% respectively) could well place strain on the starch and starch products market and sharply reduce margins.

The Commission doubted whether a draft aid scheme operating under such constraints could provide a lasting solution to the development problems of regions such as the Mezzogiorno.

347.   The Commission also decided to initiate the Article 93(2) procedure in respect of six aid schemes planned by AIMA[1] in 1986 and 1987, namely:

(a) aid to pig farmers in parts of Emilia-Romagna hit by foot-and-mouth disease;

(b) aid for the buying-in and storage of Nocellara del Belice table olives;

(c) aid to extend local ham-curing times;

(d) public storage aid for hard and semi-hard cheese kept for average to long periods;

(e) aid for the buying-in of meat following the drought in Sardinia;

(f) aid for the buying-in and storage of Pecorino Romano cheese.

The Commission felt that the schemes constituted operating aid without any lasting effect on the development of the holdings receiving it and that the effects thereof would cease to be felt as soon as the aid was discontinued. Moreover the measures in question are not compatible with the Community provisions governing the market organizations concerned.

---

[1]   Azienda statale per gli Interventi sul Mercato Agricolo (Italian State intervention agency for agricultural produce).

Netherlands

348.   The Commission also opened proceedings under Article 93(2) against Part III of a tariff for natural gas that was to be applied to glasshouse growers in the Netherlands in 1989-94.[1] Part III of the tariff placed a partial ceiling on gas prices when the price of heavy fuel oil, which was used as a basis for calculating the price of natural gas, was HFL 415/tonne or more. The Commission concluded that the mechanism conferred a financial advantage on Dutch horticultural producers using natural gas which was equivalent to an operating aid. The aid was likely to distort competition and affect intra-Community trade; it should therefore be regarded as incompatible with the common market under Article 92 and not be put into effect.

United Kingdom

349.   The UK authorities notified the Commission of an aid for the advertising of agricultural products to be carried out by the British Egg Industry Council. The objective of the aid was to inform consumers of measures taken in the wake of the salmonella-in-eggs scare, in particular the policy of testing flocks of laying hens for this organism.

The Commission noted, in particular, the assurance given by the UK authorities that the advertising campaign would not infringe Article 30 of the EEC Treaty. Consequently, there would be no discriminatory surcharges for suppliers to the United Kingdom with flocks in other Member States, nor would the checking of the salmonella status of flocks in these States in order to benefit from the aid be subject to conditions more strict than those of equivalence. In view of fulfilment of these conditions the Commission raised no objections to the proposed aid.

---

[1]   OJ C 103, 25.4.1990.

§ 9 — State aid in the fisheries sector (Table 5)

350.   In 1990 the Commission examined 16 new cases of notified aids and seven cases of unnotified aids or aids notified late in the fisheries sector. It decided:

(i)   not to object to the implementation of the aid in 12 cases;

(ii)   to initiate the proceedings provided for in Article 93(2) of the EEC Treaty in two cases, which concerned Italy;

(iii)   to terminate the proceedings provided for in Article 93(2) of the EEC Treaty in two cases, which concerned Italy and Spain.

351.   The Commission adopted a negative final decision on certain aids granted by Spain, on the ground that they covered the regular revictualling of fishing vessels by means of logistical support vessels, in other words that they constituted operating aid which was incompatible with the common market.

352.   Table 5 summarizes developments in the number of aid cases dealt with in fisheries and the Commission's work on these aids. The figures are based on the date on which the decisions were taken and do not, therefore, necessarily tally with the number of cases registered or examined.

TABLE 5

Year	Total	No objection	Article 93(2) proceedings initiated	Article 93(2) proceedings terminated	Final decision under Article 93(2)
1985	12	8	4	2	2
1986	9	9	—	2	2
1987	43	24	3	2	1
1988	44	25	10	2	—
1989	45	11	18	9	1
1990	23	12	2	2	1

353.   In order not to jeopardize the attainment of common fisheries policy objectives, in particular as regards the problem of overcapacity of fleets, the Commission decided not to authorize national aids under the sixth Directive on shipbuilding for fishing vessels intended for the Community fleet.

354.   National aids for the construction of fishing vessels for the Community fleet may be authorized when they satisfy the conditions laid down by the guidelines for the assessment of national aids in the fisheries sector. These guidelines lay down that national aids must conform to the Community legislation governing the fishing industry structure (Regulation (EEC) No 4028/86).

Chapter II

Public undertakings

§ 1 — Telecommunications

355.   On 28 June, in line with the statement it made in 1989, the Commission adopted, pursuant to Article 90 of the EEC Treaty, Directive 90/388/EEC on competition in the markets for telecommunications services.[1] This coincided with the adoption, by the Council, of the Directive on open network provision (ONP).[1] The Commission had in fact already adopted the text of its Directive in June 1989, but decided not to notify it to the Member States until the Council adopted the ONP Directive, so that the two directives would take effect at the same time.[2] This was designed to maximize the benefits to users while ensuring that public undertakings in the telecommunications sector in the Member States are able to operate under optimum conditions.

The text of the Directive which the Commission adopted in 1990 differed in certain respects from the text adopted in 1989, since it took into account the results of the meeting held by the Council of Ministers on 7 December 1989.

The Directive provides for the abolition of the exclusive rights for the supply of telecommunications services other than voice telephony which Member States grant to their national administrations. With regard to switched data services the Directive provides for special transitional arrangements for the abolition of the prohibition on the simple resale of leased line capacity. The Directive does not apply to telex, mobile radiotelephony, paging and satellite services.

A complaint was referred to the Commission regarding the Dutch Government's refusal to approve a paging firm which was already operating in several other Member States. Paging services are not covered by Directive 90/388/EEC, but the competition rules are still applicable to them. The matter is still under consideration.

---

[1]   OJ L 192, 24.7.1990.
[2]   Nineteenth Competition Report, point 226.

The Commission continued its review of the measures adopted by Member States pursuant to Directive 88/301/EEC on telecommunications terminal equipment.[1] In 1990 a further three Member States (Federal Republic of Germany, Ireland and Denmark) complied with the Directive by terminating the exclusive rights which they had maintained in respect of the first telephone set and, in the case of Denmark, PABXs. Accordingly, only Belgium and Spain are still the subject of an infringement procedure.

---

[1]   OJ L 131, 27.5.1988; Eighteenth Competition Report, point 307 and Nineteenth Competition Report, point 226.

§ 2 — Individual cases

Denmark

356.   Following the action taken by the Commission in connection with a complaint brought by an international express courier service established in Denmark against some restrictive provisions of the 1983 law on postal services relating to express international courier and remailing services, the Danish Post Office undertook to amend that law with regard to international courier services.

Express international courier services will henceforth be allowed to provide such services in Denmark under conditions similar to those accepted by the other Member States following the action taken by the Commission. [1]

The Commission and the competent Danish authorities are proceeding with their discussions on the other aspect raised by the complainant, namely the provisions of the law which prohibit remailing services.

Federal Republic of Germany

357.   In line with the statement it made in 1989,[2] the Federal Republic of Germany repealed, with effect from 1 June 1990, a circular from the Ministry of the Interior dated 2 March 1980 which *inter alia* required certain civil servants to fly exclusively with Lufthansa or, failing that, with foreign companies which were associated with the German national airline.

The Commission had on several occasions pointed out to the Federal Government that those measures were not compatible with Community law. According to the Commission, the circular in question constituted a State measure in favour of a public undertaking which was clearly in breach of Article 90(1) of the EEC Treaty, in particular when taken in conjunction with Article 59 of the EEC Treaty, which requires that restrictions on freedom to provide services within the Community must be abolished.

The Commission has also set about examining whether Germany's *Arbeitsförderungsgesetz* of 25 July 1969, which grants to a public body, the Bundesanstalt für Arbeit, the exclusive right to provide a job-placement service, is compatible with Community law. Because of that monopoly, a private firm which specializes in finding employment for highly qualified executives was prevented from operating in this limited market, despite

---

[1]   Fifteenth Competition Report, point 259.
[2]   Nineteenth Competition Report, point 231.

the fact that the Bundesanstalt had not, until then, fully catered to the needs of that market. The Commission accordingly asked the German authorities for information on the extent of the monopoly. In other fields, in particular that of express courier services, the Commission has already pointed out that a Member State cannot, under Articles 86 and 90 of the EEC Treaty, grant exclusive rights to a public undertaking in respect of a service which it does not provide or provides in part only.

Greece

358.   Following the infringement proceedings which were brought against it pursuant to Article 169 of the EEC Treaty for failing to fulfil its obligations under Article 171 of the EEC Treaty,[1] Greece has brought its scheme of insurance for public property and loans granted by State-owned banks[2] into line with the Community provisions applicable.

It dit so in February by adopting provisions[3] whereby, in compliance with Commission Decision 85/276/EEC,[4] it discontinued the system of preference granted exclusively to Greek insurance companies in the public sector. All insurance firms operating on the Greek market will henceforth be treated in the same, non-discriminatory way.

Moreover, on 31 July, Greece adopted a law restricting the monopoly enjoyed by OTE, the Hellenic Telecommunications Institute, and opening up radiotelephony and certain other telecommunications services to competition. The law still prohibits, however, the retransmission of telex messages originating in Greece. The Commission notified the Greek authorities that, in its opinion, such a restriction was not compatible with the Treaty and that it might decide to oppose it. The matter is still under scrutiny.

Spain

359.   On 1 August, pursuant to Article 90(3) of the EEC Treaty, the Commission adopted a Decision[5] on the regulations covering postal services in Spain. These regulations stipulated that the Spanish Post Office alone was authorized to provide an international express courier service for items of mail weighing less than two kilograms.[6]

---

[1]   Nineteenth Competition Report, point 230.
[2]   Article 13 of Law No 1256/82 of 28 and 31 May 1982 (*Official Journal of the Hellenic Republic,* Part A, No 21).
[3]   Article 4 of Law No 1975/90 of 21 February 1990 (*Official Journal of the Hellenic Republic,* Part A, No 21).
[4]   Nineteenth Competition Report, point 308; OJ L 152, 11.6.1985.
[5]   OJ L 233, 28.8.1990.
[6]   Articles 10 to 12 of the Order of 19 May 1960 on postal services (*Boletín Oficial del Estado,* 15.6.1960) and Articles 19 to 22 of the Regulation of 14 May 1964 on postal services (*Boletín Oficial del Estado,* 9.6.1964).

The service provided by the Spanish Post Office in this respect does not cover every country in the world or indeed the whole of Spain: the door-to-door express courier service is limited to customers in provincial capitals and a few major cities and to countries and cities covered by the Postal Express International express courier service which belongs to the Express Mail Service — International Post Corporation network.

Together with the monopoly on postal services which is provided for under Spanish law, the fact that the Spanish Post Office was providing only a partial express courier service restricted the supply of express mail services to users and was thus in breach of Article 90(1) in conjunction with Article 86(b) of the EEC Treaty.

Accordingly, pursuant to Article 90(3) of the EEC Treaty, the Commission adopted a Decision under which Spain is obliged to open up that market.

Netherlands

360.   In February the Dutch Government appealed to the Court of Justice[1] against Commission Decision 90/16/EEC concerning the provision in the Netherlands of express delivery services.[2] Koninklijke PTT Nederland NV, a public undertaking, has also brought an action, although the Decision covers only a State measure which the Dutch Government does not regard as favouring the said public undertaking.[1]

The Dutch authorities have stated their intention to amend their legislation on postal services, although the changes in question have not yet been notified to the Commission.

---

[1]   OJ C 132, 11.5.1990.
[2]   OJ L 10, 12.1.1990.

Chapter III

Adjustment of State monopolies of a commercial character

Greece

361. With regard to the oil monopoly, the Greek authorities' reply of 18 January to the Commission's reasoned opinion of 18 October 1989 on the Greek rules on storage was not such that the Commission felt able to terminate the proceedings initiated on 16 August 1988 for infringement of Articles 30 and 37 of the EEC Treaty.[1]

As regards those aspects of the oil monopoly about which the Commission had decided on 8 June 1988 to make a reference to the Court of Justice,[2] the latter, by its judgment of 12 December, endorsed the Commission's view that the maintenance of exclusive rights in the importation and marketing of petroleum products is incompatible with Community law.[3]

Spain

362. The Commission continued to monitor compliance by the Spanish authorities with their commitments under the political agreement reached in January 1986 on the adjustment of the Spanish oil monopoly.[4]

The Commission expressed its agreement with the measures taken by the Spanish authorities to guarantee independent distributors access to large consumers of certain petroleum products and to abolish exclusive retailing rights.

However, the Commission drew the Spanish Government's attention to the fact that the parallel service-station network was not developing in the hoped-for manner, the proportion of the network accounted for by independent operators being barely significant. It reminded the Spanish Government that, at the end of the transitional period

---

[1] Nineteenth Competition Report, point 232.
[2] Eighteenth Competition Report, point 311.
[3] For a more detailed analysis of the judgment, see point 153 *et seq.* of this Report.
[4] Eighteenth Competition Report, point 312.

(31 December 1991), the application of the provisions of the EEC Treaty will mean that the system of restricting service stations in the monopoly network to monopoly products only will have to be reconsidered.

Lastly, the Commission exerted influence on the Spanish Government to ensure that the gradual adjustment of the tobacco products monopoly progressed in accordance with Article 48 of the Act of Accession.[1]

In this context Spain opened appropriate quotas for tobacco products from the Community and originating in Portugal for 1989[2] and 1990, the wholesale marketing of which cannot be covered by the exclusive monopoly right.

The Commission is seeing to it that, in practice, all interested traders may benefit from the opening of these quotas, which must, of course, be administered on the basis of objective, non-discriminatory criteria.

France

363.   The Commission took steps to ensure that the requirement to gradually adjust the French potassic fertilizer monopoly in relation to Spain and Portugal was complied with in accordance with Articles 48 and 208 of the Act of Accession.[3]

In response to the complaint lodged with it in 1989, the Commission requested the French Government to ensure that the quotas to be opened each year were fixed without discrimination having regard, in particular, to traditional patterns of trade.

France, for its part, opened the quotas for 1990 by publishing a notice to importers in the French Official Journal.[4] The administration of these new quotas has given rise to no further objections on the part of the complainant.

Portugal

364.   Following the Commission's reasoned opinion of 16 January concerning the oil monopoly, the Portuguese Government sent a reply which meets the Commission's demands.

The Portuguese Government has now undertaken to amend the rules governing the prices and taxation of petroleum products so that they no longer discriminate against

---

[1]   Nineteenth Competition Report, point 234.
[2]   Resolutions of 23 December 1988: *Boletín Oficial del Estado* No 311, 28.12.1988, p. 36383; 16 January 1990: *Boletín Oficial del Estado* No 17, 19.1.1990, p. 1793; and 26 April 1990: *Boletín Oficial del Estado* No 109, 7.5.1990, p. 12091.
[3]   Nineteenth Competition Report, point 237.
[4]   *Journal officiel de la République française*, 27.12.1989, p. 16193.

products imported from other Member States. The Commission has established that the various distributors operating on the Portuguese market have received quotas commensurate with their marketing capabilities.

Nevertheless, the Commission has decided not to terminate the infringement proceedings initiated on 21 February 1989[1] until the legislative measures announced by the Portuguese authorities have actually been adopted and their impact has been assessed. As in the case of the Spanish monopoly, the Commission is taking care to ensure that independent distributors are given access to the Petrogal network — the only major supply network in Portugal — under conditions which are compatible with Article 86 of the EEC Treaty.

With regard to the alcohol monopoly, despite the reasoned opinion announced in 1989[2] and sent to it on 16 January, the Portuguese Government has still not taken any specific adjustment measures as it is required to do by Article 208 of the Act of Accession. The bodies responsible for administering the monopoly therefore continue to exercise absolute control over imports both of ethyl alcohols of agricultural and non-agricultural origin and of wine spirits for use in the making of port wine.

This being so, the Commission felt obliged to refer the matter to the Court of Justice, which it proceeded to do on 11 December.

---

[1]   Eighteenth Competition Report, point 313.
[2]   Nineteenth Competition Report, point 236.

Chapter IV

Main decisions of the Court of Justice in the field of State aid

365. In 1990 the Court of Justice delivered seven judgments in State aid cases, including two concerned with agriculture.[1]

§ 1 — Recovery of aid unlawfully granted — Legitimate expectation

366. The judgment of the Court of Justice in Case C-5/89 *Commission* v *Germany* confirmed and developed the Court's previous rulings on the recovery of illegally granted aid.[2]

The facts of the case were similar to those of Case 94/87 *Commission* v *Germany*.[2] Neither the German Government nor the recipient firm had appealed the Commission Decision declaring the aid illegal and incompatible with the common market and ordering its recovery. However, when the German Government failed to comply with the Decision, the Commission brought an action for a declaration that it had breached its obligations under the EEC Treaty.

The German Government argued in its defence that it was absolutely impossible to implement the Decision for reasons concerning the principle of legitimate expectations as enshrined in Article 48 of the Administrative Procedure Act (Verwaltungs-verfahrensgesetz).

---

[1]   (a) Case C-301/87 *France* v *Commission*.
    (b) Case C-74/89 *Commission* v *Belgium*.
    (c) Case C-142/87 *Belgium* v *Commission*.
    (d) Case C-347/87 *Triveneta Zuccheri and Others* v *Commission* (agriculture).
    (e) Case C-169/84 *Cdf Chimie and Others* v *Commission*.
    (f) Case C-5/89 *Commission* v *Germany*.
    (g) Case C-86/89 *Italy* v *Commission* (agriculture).
[2]   Nineteenth Competition Report, point 239.

Finding for the Commission, the Court said that, while there was nothing in Community law to prevent national rules precluding the recovery of illegal aid from being based on such criteria as the protection of legitimate expectations, the Community interest must be taken fully into account.

In the Court's view, firms in receipt of State aid could not in principle have a legitimate expectation as to the lawfulness of the aid unless it had been granted in accordance with the procedure laid down in Article 93 of the EEC Treaty.

The Court introduced the concept of the diligent recipient who made sure that the procedure has been complied with, and made express reference to the Commission notice (*Official Journal of the European Communities* C 318, 24.11.1983, p. 3) informing potential recipients of State aid of the risks attaching to any aid granted to them illegally.

However, the Court did not exclude the possibility of a recipient of illegal aid being able to plead exceptional circumstances which might legitimately have given rise to his expectation as to the lawfulness of the aid received. In such a case the national court would either assess the circumstances independently or request a preliminary ruling under Article 177 of the EEC Treaty.

Lastly, the Court held that a Member State that granted aid in violation of the procedural rules laid down in Article 93 could not plead the legitimate expectations of recipients in order to evade the obligation to take the measures necessary to implement the Commission's Decision. Otherwise, it would, by its wrongful and unlawful conduct, deprive Articles 92 and 93 of the EEC Treaty of all practical effectiveness.

367.   The judgment in Case C-74/89 *Commission* v *Belgium* confirmed the established principle that a Member State may not plead provisions, practices or circumstances existing in its internal legal system in order to justify a failure to comply with obligations resulting from Community law. In the present case, Belgium did not deny having committed the breach of which it stood accused, but explained that, as a result of regionalization, responsibility for recovering the aid had passed from the State to the Flemish Region.

§ 2 — Action by a third party against a Commission Decision authorizing State aid

368.   In Case C-169/84 *Société Cdf Chimie et Fertilisants and Others* v *Commission* the Court had for the first time in the State aid field to give a ruling on the substance of a Commission Decision authorizing State aid. The Court had already had occasion to set aside a favourable Commission Decision clearing an aid scheme,[1] but the action had been brought by a Member State and not by a private firm and the ruling was based on a failure to comply with the procedural rules.

The case concerned the Dutch tariff system for the supply of natural gas. As regards the admissibility of the action, reference is made to the judgment of the Court in Case 169/84 *Cofaz* v *Commission*.[2]

On the substance of the case, the Court accepted, in the light of a report by independent technical experts, the applicants' submission that the Commission had committed manifest errors in the assessment of the facts.

---

[1]   Case 84/82 *Federal Republic of Germany* v *Commission*.
[2]   Sixteenth Competition Report, point 310.

§ 3 — Non-notified aid measures — Interim decisions

369.   In its judgments in Case C-301/87 *France* v *Commission* and Case C-142/87 *Belgium* v *Commission* the Court took a further step along the road towards ensuring full compliance with the system of monitoring State aids having regard, in particular, to the procedural rules contained in Article 93(3) of the EEC Treaty. For the conclusions that the Commission has drawn from these cases in respect of aids that have not been notified in advance in accordance with Article 93(3). [1]

On the various submissions of the applicant in Case C-301/87, namely infringement of procedural rules, breach of due process, the inadequate reasoning of the contested Decision and misapplication of Article 92 of the Treaty, the Court's judgment follows the well-established case-law on these subjects.

On the charge of inadequate reasoning, the Court found that the Decision was explicit, detailed and supported by precise reasons, and it dismissed the applicant State's submission that no consideration had been given to the substantive effect of the aid that had already been paid on competition and trade. The Court stated in this connection that, if the Commission were required to demonstrate in its Decision the substantive effect of aid already paid, that would give Member States that made payments of aid in contravention of the duty to notify, an advantage over those which had notified such aid at the proposal stage.

The submissions made by Belgium in Case C-142/87 are for the most part similar to those advanced by France in Case C-301/87 and were dismissed by the Court for the same reasons. With regard to the applicant State's submission that the aid granted was export aid and was therefore not covered by Articles 92 to 94 of the EEC Treaty and that, at all events, it could not affect trade between Member States, the Court held that Article 112 of the EEC Treaty did not preclude the application of Articles 92 to 94 and that, given the interdependence of the markets on which Community firms operate, it was not impossible for such aid to distort intra-Community competition even if the recipient firm exported almost all its production to non-member countries.

---

[1]   see point 172 of this Report.

Part Four

The development of concentration, competition and competitiveness

Chapter I

Mergers and acquisitions involving Community-scale firms in 1989/90

370. This chapter analyses the principal mergers, acquisitions and joint ventures that have taken place in the Community and gives some idea of changes in the pattern of competition during the reference period. The analysis is based on data published in the specialist press regarding operations involving the 1 000 leading industrial firms in the Community (ranked according to their turnover), the 500 largest firms world-wide and the largest firms in the service sector, as represented by distribution, banking and insurance.

The Commission's aim is thus to produce realistic data, chiefly on mergers and acquisitions, of value to the single market programme. The reasons behind the operations and their impact on competition are also analysed.

The following operations are examined:

(i)   acquisitions of majority holdings, including mergers;

(ii) acquisitions of minority holdings;

(iii) industrial and commercial joint ventures.

The reference period is June 1989 to May 1990.

§ 1 — Overview (Tables 6 and 7)

371.   The total number of operations reached 1 384, an increase of 23% ; the number of acquisitions of majority holdings (including mergers) rose by as much as 25% to 833. Once more, three-quarters of these operations occurred in industry, with a distinct tendency towards cross-border deals. There was a surge in merger activity during the second half of the period, when some three-quarters of all operations took place. It would appear that the adoption of the merger control Regulation in December 1989 prompted many firms to make acquisitions before the Regulation entered into force in September 1990.

In industry, especially, there was an above-average increase in the number of 'big' cases, i.e. those in which the combined turnover of the firms concerned exceeded ECU 5 000 million. In the service sector, on the other hand, this phenomenon was confined to banking.

Most operations again took place in the four largest Member States: the Federal Republic of Germany, the United Kingdom, Italy and France. In Spain, the number of mergers, especially large-scale ones, increased considerably.

Once more, the sector most affected by this activity was the chemical industry, followed by the food and drink industry and the paper and printing industry.

Purely national operations accounted for no more than 40% of cases, whereas the previous year the corresponding figure was over 50%. On the other hand, there was a considerable increase in operations between firms from different Member States (+45%) and operations involving firms from non-EEC countries (+74%).

The form most frequently used remained, by and large, the majority acquisition (60% of cases), but banks and insurance companies were quite often interested in minority acquisitions or joint ventures.

TABLE 6

National, Community and international mergers (a), acquisitions of minority holdings (b) and joint ventures (c) in the Community in 1989/90

Sector	National[1]			Community[2]			International[3]			Total			Grand total
	(a)	(b)	(c)	(a)	(b)	(c)	(a)	(b)	(c)	(a)	(b)	(c)	
Industry	241	73	41	257	62	55	124	45	60	622	180	156	958
Distribution	31	15	4	17	2	6	4	4	3	52	21	13	86
Banking	65	40	10	23	33	12	25	23	8	113	96	30	239
Insurance	16	13	6	18	24	2	12	7	3	46	44	11	101
Total	353	141	61	315	121	75	165	79	74	833	341	210	1 384

Source: Data gathered by the Commission from the specialist press.
[1] Operations of firms from the same Member State.
[2] Operations of firms from different Member States.
[3] Operations of firms from Member States and third countries with effects on the Community market.

TABLE 7

Breakdown of national, Community and international majority acquisitions (including mergers) in industry, distribution, banking and insurance (combined turnover >1 000 >2 000 >5 000 >10 000 million ecus)

Sector	Year	National[1]				Community[2]				International[3]				Total			
		>1	>2	>5	>10	>1	>2	>5	>10	>1	>2	>5	>10	>1	>2	>5	>10
Industry	1986/87	111	73	42	18	52	42	24	13	8	3	2	—	171	118	67	31
	1987/88	135	84	48	24	86	61	34	22	47	40	28	15	268	185	110	61
	1988/89	163	118	60	29	148	110	72	53	62	60	38	24	373	288	170	106
	1989/90	183	117	66	44	212	158	102	70	118	109	56	26	513	384	224	140
Distribution	1986/87	19	12	6	1	2	2	2	—	—	—	—	21	14	8	1	1
	1987/88	15	11	6	2	5	3	1	—	2	2	2	—	22	16	9	2
	1988/89	21	17	8	—	1	1	1	—	1	1	1	—	23	19	10	—
	1989/90	13	11	3	2	6	3	3	1	2	2	2	1	21	16	8	4
Banking	1986/87	9	6	5	3	2	2	1	1	9	7	5	3	20	15	11	7
	1987/88	19	14	7	4	10	10	8	4	7	5	4	2	36	29	19	10
	1988/89	22	15	3	1	11	9	4	2	8	8	5	4	41	32	12	7
	1989/90	22	19	14	10	10	9	7	2	5	4	1	0	37	32	22	12
Insurance	1986/87	5	3	2	2	1	—	—	—	2	1	—	—	8	4	2	2
	1987/88	1	1	—	—	7	6	1	—	8	3	1	—	16	10	2	—
	1988/89	5	5	3	—	3	3	2	—	4	3	2	—	12	11	7	—
	1989/90	1	—	—	—	9	6	3	1	2	1	—	—	12	7	3	1
Total	1986/87	144	94	55	24	57	46	27	14	19	11	7	3	220	151	88	41
	1987/88	170	110	61	30	108	80	44	26	64	50	35	17	342	240	140	73
	1988/89	211	155	74	30	163	123	79	55	75	72	46	28	449	350	199	113
	1989/90	219	147	83	56	237	176	115	74	127	116	59	27	583	439	257	157

Source: See Table 6.
[1] Operations of firms from the same Member State.
[2] Operations of firms from different Member States.
[3] Operations of firms from Member States and third countries with effects on the Community market.

§ 2 — Mergers, acquisitions and joint ventures in industry

Mergers (Tables 8 and 9)

372.   Total mergers increased by 26% to 622. The marked trend towards cross-border mergers continued. For the first time, there were more Community than national operations, and there were twice as many acquisitions of Community firms by third-country firms as a year earlier.

The chemical industry again topped the league, followed by food and drink, the increase being well above average in both sectors. Paper and printing still ranked third. The metals and motor-vehicle industries saw appreciable increases in the number of operations, whereas electrical and mechanical engineering experienced a reduction.

In the four largest Member States, mergers involving combined turnovers in excess of ECU 5 000 million occurred mainly in the chemicals, food and drink, electrical engineering and metals sectors. In the Federal Republic of Germany, as in the previous year, many mergers took place in mechanical engineering. In the other Member States, it was in chemicals and food and drink that most operations occurred. In Spain, there was also a considerable amount of merger activity in the motor industry.

The breakdown by combined turnover of the firms concerned confirms the trend towards an increase in large-scale operations. One operation in five had a combined turnover exceeding ECU 10 000 million, and one in three ECU 5 000 million. Large-scale mergers took place above all in the chemicals, food and drink, metals and electrical engineering sectors.

Large-scale operations have for many years occurred mainly in the Federal Republic of Germany, the United Kingdom, Italy and France, but Spain is coming increasingly to the fore. During the reference period, it was in those Member States that almost 90% of all mergers involving a combined turnover in excess of ECU 5 000 million or 10 000 million took place. Against the trend, the number of large-scale mergers fell sharply in France, but there was a wave of such activity in the United Kingdom.

In all the large Member States, foreign investors outnumbered domestic investors when it came to participating in mergers involving a combined turnover of more than ECU 5 000 million. This was especially apparent in the United Kingdom, where only 20% of all large-scale mergers were between national firms. The Netherlands continued to be an exception in this respect, with national mergers predominating. In the smaller Member States, all large-scale mergers were carried out by foreign investors; even in Spain, only two mergers out of a total of 23 were national operations.

The sharpest increase recorded during the reference period was in acquisitions by third-country firms within the Community. Such firms invested not only in chemicals and food and drink, but also, relatively often compared with Community firms, in paper and printing and mechanical engineering.

In one-third of cases, the purchasers were American; next came the Swedes, the Swiss and the Japanese. Nearly 90% of all operations were initiated by firms from this group of countries, with the result that acquisitions by other non-Community firms were isolated cases.

Detailed analysis of two industrial sectors

373.   The following sectors were chosen because of their significance in relation to mergers.

Chemicals

374.   It was in this sector that by far the largest number of acquisitions took place (148, up 38% on the previous year, or 24% of all operations in industry). The 20 largest chemical companies in the Community account for some two-thirds of total turnover in this sector. In 1989/90 almost all these companies took part in at least one operation, the largest of them taking part as a rule in several. However, with one or two exceptions, the companies acquired were relatively small.

Nevertheless, the competitive situation may have worsened more in certain important market segments such as plastics, paints and varnishes or detergents and household-cleaning materials, where small and medium-sized firms abound, than in sectors which already had an oligopolistic structure.

Although three-quarters of all acquisitions (compared with two-thirds the previous year) were made at international level, a number of national mergers, some of them sizeable, also took place, notably in the large Member States (apart from Italy and Spain). Account must also be taken of those cases where the acquiring company has its head office in the same Member State as the target company, but where the parent company is foreign. Such operations could in fact also be regarded as national mergers, although they appear in the statistics as transnational operations. During the reference period there were 13 such operations, including six in the United Kingdom alone.

Mergers where the company acquired had a turnover of more than ECU 250 million, the threshold laid down in the merger control Regulation which has since entered into force, were confined more or less to the Federal Republic of Germany and the United Kingdom. In the Federal Republic of Germany, the operations were essentially national in character.

The acquiring companies were almost exclusively French, German, Dutch and British, but American, Swiss and Swedish companies also played a part.

Among the companies acquired, there were, besides UK, German and French companies, many Spanish and Italian companies, the latter numbering rarely among the acquirers. On the other hand, there was only one instance of a Dutch company being bought. Overall, therefore, there was a very clear-cut north-south divide as regards merger operations in the chemicals sector. It can be said, however, at least as far as Spain is concerned, that this phenomenon will enhance the competitiveness of the national industry.

Food and drink

375. The number of mergers in this sector increased considerably in 1989/90. During this period there were 102 such operations (+34%), or one sixth of all operations in industry. Compared with chemicals, national operations have a greater weight, but an intensification of Community operations is undeniably taking place.

The degree of concentration is much lower than in the chemical industry, but it is generally higher nationally than at Community level because of the barriers to trade which continue to exist. Owing to the still highly compartmentalized nature of the Community market, firms with a comparatively small turnover are able to occupy a leading position in their home market.

Some of the largest firms made selective acquisitions, apparently so as to be able to face up to competition from multinational companies, and US multinationals in particular. In the case of cross-border operations, the acquiring companies came predominantly (85%) from the Netherlands, France, the United Kingdom and the USA. Only two German companies made acquisitions abroad, and Italian companies made none. On the other hand, firms from these Member States were often the subject of successful bids, as were French, Spanish and UK firms.

The top spot occupied by the Netherlands is due almost entirely to the numerous majority acquisitions by Unilever. This multinational company acquired holdings in top-rank companies in all the large Member States. In France and the United Kingdom, it was above all the industry leaders BSN and Hillsdown that made acquisitions abroad.

Generally speaking, given that the intense acquisition activity on the part of large firms was coupled with only modest growth in demand in the food and drink sector, the trend towards a higher degree of concentration perceptible the previous year should continue.

TABLE 8

National, Community and international margers (including acquisitions of majority holdings) in the Community

Sector[1]	National				Community				International				Total			
	1986/ 1987	1987/ 1988	1988/ 1989	1989/ 1990	1986/ 1987	1987/ 1988	1988/ 1989	1989/ 1990	1986/ 1987	1987/ 1988	1988/ 1989	1989/ 1990	1986/ 1987	1987/ 1988	1988/ 1989	1989/ 1990
1. Food	39	25	35	41	11	18	27	44	2	8	14	17	52	51	76	102
2. Chem.	38	32	37	38	27	38	56	75	6	15	14	35	71	85	107	148
3. Elec.	33	25	23	20	6	4	18	16	2	7	8	10	41	36	49	46
4. Mech.	21	24	31	25	8	5	17	13	2	9	7	14	31	38	55	52
5. Comp.	2	2	3	1	—	1	—	1	—	—	1	0	2	3	4	2
6. Meta.	15	28	16	29	4	9	13	28	—	3	6	7	19	40	35	64
7. Trans.	15	3	7	11	6	9	6	13	—	3	1	8	21	15	14	32
8. Pap.	17	24	32	28	7	6	26	30	1	4	7	21	25	34	61	79
9. Extra.	8	9	11	10	1	2	5	8	—	1	3	1	9	12	19	19
10. Text.	4	11	11	4	2	2	7	8	—	1	2	1	6	14	20	13
11. Cons.	13	21	20	19	3	12	19	17	3	—	—	3	19	33	39	39
12. Other	6	10	7	15	—	5	3	4	1	7	3	7	7	22	13	26
Total	211	214	233	241	75	111	197	257	17	58	62	124	303	383	492	622

Source: See Table 6.

[1] Key:

Food :   Food and drink.
Chem. : Chemicals, fibres, glass, ceramic wares, rubber.
Elec. : Electrical and electronic engineering, office machinery.
Mech. : Mechanical and instrument engineering, machine tools.
Comp. : Computers and data-processing equipment.
Meta. : Production and preliminary processing of metals, metal goods.
Trans. : Vehicles and transport equipment.
Pap. :   Wood, furniture and paper (including printing and publishing).
Extra. : Extractive industries.
Text. : Textiles, clothing, leather and footware.
Cons. : Construction.
Other : Other manufacturing industry.

TABLE 9

**Breakdown of national, Community and international acquisitions of majority holdings
by sector in 1989/90 and by combined turnover of firms
involved >1 000, >2 000, >5 000, >10 000 million ecus**

Sector[1]	National[2]				Community[3]				International[4]				Total			
	>1	>2	>5	>10	>1	>2	>5	>10	>1	>2	>5	>10	>1	>2	>5	>10
1. Food	32	16	8	5	37	32	24	14	17	13	9	3	86	61	41	22
2. Chem.	27	20	12	10	68	55	35	22	34	33	16	7	129	108	63	39
3. Elec.	17	14	7	6	12	11	9	7	10	10	7	4	39	35	23	17
4. Mech.	18	11	8	3	12	7	0	0	12	11	6	3	42	29	14	6
5. Comp.	1	1	1	1	1	1	1	1	—	—	—	—	2	2	2	2
6. Meta.	21	16	9	6	25	19	15	14	7	7	2	1	53	42	26	21
7. Trans.	10	7	6	4	10	10	7	5	8	5	4	2	30	22	17	11
8. Pap.	19	9	3	2	16	6	3	3	20	20	6	3	55	34	12	8
9. Extra.	10	7	5	1	8	8	4	3	1	1	1	0	19	16	10	4
10. Text.	2	0	0	0	7	3	2	1	1	1	1	1	10	4	3	2
11. Cons.	15	12	4	3	10	4	1	0	2	2	2	0	27	18	8	3
12. Other	11	5	3	3	4	2	1	0	6	6	2	2	21	13	6	5
Total	183	117	66	44	212	158	102	70	118	109	56	26	513	384	224	140

Source: See Table 6.
[1] Key: See Table 8, note 1.
[2] Mergers of firms from the same Member State.
[3] Mergers of firms from different Member States.
[4] Mergers of firms from Member States and third countries with effects on the Community market.

Acquisitions of minority holdings (Table 10)

376.   The number of acquisitions of minority holdings was only slightly up on the previous year. While purely national operations actually decreased by nearly 30 %, firms from other Member States and third countries were particularly active in the Community.

Among foreign buyers, it was above all the Americans who thus gained a foothold in the common market, but Swedish, Japanese and Swiss firms were also very active.

Surprisingly, besides the food and drink, chemicals and electrical engineering sectors, interest centred mainly on the construction industry, which accounted for one-sixth of all new acquisitions. Only two-thirds of these transactions were between Community firms. They may herald future mergers.

TABLE 10

National, Community and international acquisitions of minority holdings in the Community

Sector[1]	National				Community				International				Total			
	1986/ 1987	1987/ 1988	1988/ 1989	1989/ 1990	1986/ 1987	1987/ 1988	1988/ 1989	1989/ 1990	1986/ 1987	1987/ 1988	1988/ 1989	1989/ 1990	1986/ 1987	1987/ 1988	1988/ 1989	1989/ 1990
1. Food	13	17	15	13	7	9	4	9	1	9	2	4	21	31	21	26
2. Chem.	16	9	10	7	6	6	5	5	1	2	2	11	23	17	18	23
3. Elec.	9	8	18	7	2	4	5	8	—	3	2	9	11	15	25	24
4. Mech.	10	10	7	4	2	—	1	3	1	3	—	3	13	13	8	10
5. Comp.	1	1	—	1	—	—	1	0	—	—	1	2	1	1	2	3
6. Meta.	9	11	6	9	2	2	7	3	1	2	3	1	12	15	16	13
7. Trans.	4	8	4	3	1	1	1	3	—	—	3	6	5	9	8	12
8. Pap.	7	19	15	8	—	7	9	5	4	3	1	5	11	29	25	18
9. Extra.	5	5	11	8	—	2	2	4	2	5	1	1	7	12	14	13
10. Text.	2	5	5	4	1	1	—	2	1	—	1	1	4	6	6	7
11. Cons.	8	15	6	8	—	5	2	20	1	1	2	2	9	21	10	30
12. Other	—	7	5	1	—	—	—	0	—	1	1	0	—	8	6	1
Total	84	115	102	73	21	37	37	62	12	29	20	45	117	181	159	180

Source: See Table 6.
[1] Key: See Table 8, note 1.

Joint ventures (Table 11)

377. The number of joint ventures was 20% up on the previous year. A regional breakdown shows, as in the case of minority acquisitions, a fall in the number of national operations and a sharp rise in that of cross-border operations, which accounted for nearly three-quarters of the total. This form of operation seems to be viewed by non-Community firms as an effective means of gaining access to the Community market.

Joint ventures are a common form of link-up in the chemicals and electrical engineering sectors, where research plays a particularly important role. The surprisingly big increase recorded in the motor industry is entirely due to cross-border operations; the same applies to the paper and printing industry.

TABLE 11

Joint ventures in the Community

Sector [1]	National				Community				International				Total			
	1986/1987	1987/1988	1988/1989	1989/1990	1986/1987	1987/1988	1988/1989	1989/1990	1986/1987	1987/1988	1988/1989	1989/1990	1986/1987	1987/1988	1988/1989	1989/1990
1. Food	—	6	4	5	1	3	2	2	4	1	3	4	5	10	9	11
2. Chem.	3	7	8	12	1	5	9	9	10	12	11	16	14	24	28	37
3. Elec.	4	8	8	2	3	5	7	8	14	7	14	13	21	20	29	23
4. Mech.	9	4	6	5	—	—	2	3	8	3	2	4	17	7	10	12
5. Comp.	1	2	—	0	1	1	2	0	3	2	3	0	5	5	5	0
6. Meta.	1	2	9	6	1	6	3	6	1	2	3	4	3	10	15	16
7. Trans.	1	1	4	5	3	4	2	12	—	1	1	5	4	6	7	22
8. Pap.	3	7	4	3	1	1	5	6	2	1	—	5	6	9	9	14
9. Extra.	—	3	2	1	1	1	—	0	—	1	—	0	1	5	2	1
10. Text.	—	—	3	0	—	2	—	2	—	1	—	2	—	3	3	4
11. Cons.	3	1	4	2	2	2	3	2	—	3	—	1	5	6	7	5
12. Other	4	4	4	0	2	1	1	5	3	1	—	6	9	6	5	11
Total	29	45	56	41	16	31	36	55	45	35	37	60	90	111	129	156

Source: See Table 6.
[1] Key: See Table 8, note 1.

Main motives for mergers and joint ventures (Table 12)

Mergers

378. It is not easy as a rule to identify the different motives for mergers and joint ventures. Owing to the large number of motives given and to the fact that they are sometimes interlinked, it is impossible to avoid overlapping; in some cases, moreover, no one motive was decisive. The motives mentioned in the specialist press for the various operations must therefore be interpreted with care.

Strengthening of market position and development of commercial activities continued to head the list, being mentioned in some three-quarters of cases. It is therefore undeniable that firms are continuing to prepare intensively for more competition and larger markets. This is true in general of all the sectors studied, but these motives are given relatively often in the construction, metals, food and drink and mechanical engineering sectors.

TABLE 12

**Main motives for mergers
and joint ventures in 1989/90**

Motive	Mergers (including acquisitions of majority holdings)	Joint ventures
Strengthening of market position	212	38
Expansion	126	15
Complementarity	26	3
Diversification	14	3
Restructuring (including rationalization and synergy)	57	22
R&D and production and marketing	3	18
Cooperation	6	18
Other	24	12
Not specified	154	27
Total	622	156

Joint ventures

379.   Joint ventures doubtless also serve to strengthen market position or develop commercial activities, but the main motives given here are cooperation, synergy and R&D.

§ 3 — Mergers, acquisitions and joint ventures in services

380.   In services sectors there was an increase in mergers, acquisitions and joint ventures in banking and insurance, but a decline in distribution. Although the operations recorded in the latter sector were still essentially national in character, there were, as in the financial sector, signs of a more outward-looking attitude than the previous year.

The breakdown by size of firm is based on turnover in the case of distribution (as in that of industry), on one-tenth of assets in the case of banks and gross premium income in the case of insurance companies. These are the same criteria as those adopted for the merger control Regulation.

Acquisitions of majority holdings (including mergers) (Table 13)

381.   While there was a sharp increase in acquisitions of majority holdings in the financial sector, the corresponding number in the distribution sector was down on the previous year. Generally speaking, a stronger trend towards internationalization was noted, with in particular more transactions between firms from different Member States.

In the case of large-scale operations, i.e. those exceeding ECU 5 000 million, a sharp increase occurred in banking; however, contrary to the general trend, these operations were almost all national in character. In the other two sectors, 'big' mergers were few in number.

TABLE 13

National, Community and international mergers (including acquisitions of majority holdings) in the Community

Services

Sector	National				Community				International				Total			
	1986/ 1987	1987/ 1988	1988/ 1989	1989/ 1990	1986/ 1987	1987/ 1988	1988/ 1989	1989/ 1990	1986/ 1987	1987/ 1988	1988/ 1989	1989/ 1990	1986/ 1987	1987/ 1988	1988/ 1989	1989/ 1990
Distribution	40	40	53	31	5	8	4	17	4	9	1	4	49	57	58	52
Banking	22	53	51	65	3	12	16	23	10	13	16	25	35	78	83	113
Insurance	17	14	15	16	7	14	8	18	4	12	10	12	28	40	33	46
Total	79	107	119	112	15	34	28	58	18	34	27	41	112	175	174	211

Source: See Table 6.

Acquisitions of minority holdings (Table 14)

382. As with majority acquisitions, minority acquisitions were much more numerous in banking and insurance than the previous year. The companies buying into Community banks and insurance companies came mainly from other Member States and from third countries. On the other hand, firms in the distribution sector were less active in this respect and most investments were essentially at national level.

TABLE 14

National, Community and international acquisitions of minority holdings in the Community

Services

Sector	National				Community				International				Total			
	1986/ 1987	1987/ 1988	1988/ 1989	1989/ 1990	1986/ 1987	1987/ 1988	1988/ 1989	1989/ 1990	1986/ 1987	1987/ 1988	1988/ 1989	1989/ 1990	1986/ 1987	1987/ 1988	1988/ 1989	1989/ 1990
Distribution	7	13	8	15	3	4	6	2	1	5	8	4	11	22	22	21
Banking	11	38	32	40	9	15	19	33	13	28	11	23	33	81	62	96
Insurance	5	8	9	13	1	4	13	24	5	7	7[1]	7	11	19	29[1]	44
Total	23	59	49	68	13	23	38	59	19	40[1]	26	34	55	122[1]	113	161

Source: See Table 6.
[1] Figures in the Eighteenth Competition Report amended.

Joint ventures (Table 15)

383. Overall the number of new joint ventures was the same as the previous year. The trend was downward in insurance, whereas a sharp increase was recorded in banking. In all areas, however, the trend towards an increase in Community and international activities continued.

TABLE 15

Joint ventures in the Community

Services

Sector	National				Community				International				Total			
	1986/ 1987	1987/ 1988	1988/ 1989	1989/ 1990	1986/ 1987	1987/ 1988	1988/ 1989	1989/ 1990	1986/ 1987	1987/ 1988	1988/ 1989	1989/ 1990	1986/ 1987	1987/ 1988	1988/ 1989	1989/ 1990
Distribution	3	4	7	4	1	3	4	6	1	—	3	3	5	7	14	13
Banking	18	16	11	10	5	7	6	12	1	7	7	8	24	30	24	30
Insurance	1	10	8	6	1	3	5	2	—	3	3	3	2	16	16	11
Total	22	30	26	20	7	13	15	20	2	10	13	14	31	53	54	54

Source: See Table 6.

§ 4 — Conclusions

384.   The analysis of mergers, acquisitions and joint ventures reported in the specialist press prompts the following conclusions for the period 1989/90:

(i)   The total number of operations increased by 23 %; once more, nearly 70 % concerned industry, two thirds of which were majority acquisitions. There was a renewed strengthening of the trend towards cross-border mergers. These accounted for 60 % of all cases, whereas in the previous year the proportion was below 50 %. In industry, this trend was even more marked.

(ii)   More than half of all mergers occurred in three sectors: chemicals, food and drink, and paper. It was in these sectors, and in metals and electrical engineering, that most majority acquisitions involving a combined turnover in excess of ECU 2 000 million took place. Large-scale operations, with a combined turnover of between ECU 5 000 million and 10 000 million, increased especially in the food and drink sector.

(iii)   In industry, the number of mergers involving a combined turnover of more than ECU 5 000 million was up 30 % on the previous year. This increase is almost entirely due to cross-border operations. In services, the number of large-scale operations increased only in banking, and they were carried out mainly at national level.

(iv)   Given that the number of company mergers was again substantial, the degree of concentration must have increased, especially in those sectors which experienced a considerable growth in the number of large-scale operations, namely food and drink, metals, motor vehicles and paper (including printing and publishing). However, a more detailed study of the various markets is needed in order to evaluate the impact of this increase on concentration and competition.

(v)   Although mergers can improve the competitiveness of Community firms both within the Community and *vis-à-vis* non-EEC firms, they must not lead to restrictions of competition within the common market.

The regulation on the control of mergers came into force in September 1990 and constitutes for the Commission an important legal instrument to guard against these risks of restrictions to competition. If the scale of mergers, which were observed in the first half of 1990 and were for the most part acquisitions in anticipation, continues one can expect as a result a significant slow-down in the number of cases. It is not yet possible to know in what way this tendency will be compensated by an intensification of acquisition activity in the unified Germany as well as other merger cases having a tangible effect in the Community.

Chapter II

The programme of studies and its results

§ 1 — Objectives of the 1990 programme of studies

385.　The aim of the studies published or completed in 1990 was to provide support for the three main areas of competition policy: State aids, deregulation and mergers. They will either assist the Commission's staff in their daily work or serve as a basis for more detailed thinking on general policy. A brief summary of the studies is given below.

The studies were commissioned from independent consultants who are responsible for the data and views set out therein. Some of them have been published by the Office for Official Publications of the European Communities.

Several studies are not intended for publication. They include analyses of certain sectors from the point of view of competition policy where the confidential nature of the content rules out publication, and studies covering specific aspects of competition policy which are of limited interest to the general public.

§ 2 — Studies published or intended for publication

The use made by Member States' public authorities of R&D contracts and the importance of such contracts compared with more conventional types of aid

386.   The Commission undertook in the Community framework for State aids for research and development to carry out an examination of the extent to which Article 93(3) of the EEC Treaty should apply to large research and development contracts awarded by government departments to companies in the competitive market sector.

This study places R&D contracts in the general context of public funding of research in the Community and examines the various beneficiaries and aims of such funding. On the basis of direct contacts with the public authorities in France, the Federal Republic of Germany, Italy and the United Kingdom, the study furnishes the main budgetary, legal and conceptual information needed to analyse the problem from the State aid point of view.

In those four Member States, the value of civilian R&D contracts is put at ECU 930 million in 1987, or approximately 20% of the public funds made available to businesses that year for civilian R&D. Approximately one half of these contracts may contain an aid element owing to a variety of factors, notably the grant of industrial property rights, the contract award procedure, the purpose of the contract and the extent to which the contractor is free to determine its content. These factors differ, however, not only from one country to another and from one government department to another, but also from one contract to another, and knowledge of each individual contract awarded and of the true nature of the contract award process is necessary in order to detect any aid element. Moreover, the lack of suitable quantitative criteria makes it impossible to work out a methodology similar to that used to determine the intensity of 'conventional' aid.

The study therefore proposes that guidelines be published defining an appropriate method of awarding R&D contracts consisting essentially in subjecting them to an award procedure along the lines of that governing works and supply contracts and proposed for services contracts.

Predation in air transport

387.   This report is concerned with policy towards predatory behaviour in European aviation, with particular reference to policy within a more liberalized regulatory regime. The report provides a definition of predatory behaviour and a brief introduction to some of the main concepts of relevance in identifying predatory practices in the airline industry and a discussion of these concepts and issues in detail.

Industry and firm-specific conditions in the airline industry are such that predation can be both rational and feasible in this industry. Predation in the airline industry might take the form of action both to increase capacity by scheduling more services and to reschedule flights to reduce the demand for entrants' services, as well as action in cutting prices. Increase of capacity by the incumbent after entry is a strong signal that predation may be taking place. So too would be a price increase once (and if) exit takes place. It is important to be aware that predation can take place in markets other than the one in which entry takes place (or is planned), since predation might occur in other markets where the incumbent and entrant already compete. Price-matching by a high-cost incumbent could be a non-predatory competitive response to the entry of low-cost firms when there are high exit costs and/or sunk re-entry costs.

§ 3 — Summaries of studies not intended for publication

Strategic mergers and cooperation agreements in air transport

388.   The study describes first of all the development of the regulatory framework surrounding scheduled air-transport services in Europe. It then examines the economic factors which determine the competitive strategy of airlines, notably configuration and the striving after dominant positions at airports. It also analyses the components of competition in air transport. Certain factors which influence competition are examined in greater detail.

The study stresses the need for a Community policy to safeguard competition. It draws upon the American experience and gives guidance on how to analyse link-ups, including mergers, between airlines on the basis of, among other things, the configuration of their networks. The study distinguishes between cooperation agreements concerning fares and those concerning capacity (the anti-competitive effect of which predominates) or technical matters. It concludes that flanking policies are needed to promote workable competition.

Non-conference shipping lines operating in Community maritime trade

389.   The study examines the position of independent shipping lines in the Community, the quality of the service they provide, the opportunities for access to the liner shipping market, the pricing policy of the independents, competition from tramp services, competition from transhipment and other competitive pressures on the liner shipping market in general, and on liner conferences in particular.

The study detects fairly stiff competition in the open trades, and difficulties over market access in trade with certain countries where government intervention at the other end seeks to prevent free access to cargoes by independent operators. The study also indicates that there is a tendency towards over-capacity in liner shipping in the 1990s. It ends by proposing that the various Community trades should remain subject to control in future.

Studies relating to a Directive on telecommunications services

390.   Two studies were carried out as part of the Commission's drive to apply the competition rules to telecommunications. One of the basic aims was to determine what restrictions, if any, of competition are justified by the performance by telecommunications administrations of public tasks, in particular the setting up of a universal network and the supplying thereof under non-discriminatory conditions. Such was the purpose of the first of the two studies. First of all it analyses the US experience. It concludes therefrom that a legislative distinction between basic (data-transmission) services and value-added services will, owing to technological development, always be inadequate. It gives rise to legal uncertainty which handicaps new services and small businesses, which are more numerous in Europe than in the USA. A different approach must therefore be worked out for the Community. The study suggests a distinction based on the economic risk involved in establishing each of the two types of network. The first type is set up in advance of the development of terminals and the services they can render. The second is developed with a view to satisfying the need for interconnection of existing equipment and is intended for a smaller number of users. The study concludes, therefore, that only the protection of networks of the first type by legislative measures can be justified.

The second study concerns the legal basis adopted by the Commission for opening up telecommunications services markets to competition, namely Article 90(3) of the EEC Treaty. It examines in detail the legal arguments against using that provision. It concludes first of all that, apart from exclusive rights granted in respect of services for non-economic reasons, the grant of any other exclusive right to public enterprises or enterprises already enjoying special or exclusive rights must be considered a measure within the meaning of paragraph 1 of the Article. The Commission must therefore examine its compatibility with the Treaty. As to paragraph 2 of the Article, the study views this as a transitional measure which the Member States can rely upon only until such time as the Commission adopts directives or decisions specifying the Community interest in this field. Article 90(3) requires a systematic examination of all sectors in which services monopolies have been granted to public enterprises for economic reasons, and an assessment of the compatibility of those measures with the EEC Treaty.

When it comes to choosing between directives or individual decisions, the study considers that the Treaty offers no guidance. The Commission must therefore base its choice on sound administrative practice. Any directives adopted would be of a legislative nature and would harmonize the provisions in force in the Member States.

Studies relating to the electricity industry

391. The Commission had two in-depth analyses carried out on the production and distribution of electricity. The possibility of introducing a certain amount of competition into this field was considered as was that of adopting a more harmonized Community policy on increasing rationalization of structural investments, optimizing the use of

distribution networks and introducing more transparency into rating formulas. This could have a positive impact on supplies, while allowing greater flexibility in relations between certain consumer groups and producers.

In the first of the two studies, a cost-benefit analysis is made of open access in electricity by reference to the concept of natural monopoly. The supposed existence of a natural monopoly in the electricity industry may justify economically the industry's present structure. However, such a natural monopoly does not necessarily exist at all levels of the industry. Structural changes are at all events conceivable as long as they do not call into question the benefits that may be obtained from the existence of a natural monopoly in certain segments of the industry. Such changes may also be justified where there is a natural monopoly. They must, however, involve competitive benefits which outweigh the cost involved in introducing several firms into a market characterized by the existence of a natural monopoly.

The study concludes that economic benefits may be expected to be obtained by extending the transit Directive to autoproducers and independent producers and by extending the Directive on public contracts to electricity purchases. An essential precondition for introducing more competition is that various charging problems, in particular charges for transport, should be resolved on a sound economic basis.

The second study starts from the premise of the Commission's possible use of Article 90(3) of the EEC Treaty to adopt a Directive to put an end to the practice whereby network operators combine two services: that of producing or obtaining supplies of electricity, and that of transporting it. The report concentrates on ways of giving third parties access to the electricity network. A striking conclusion is the importance of the distinction between guaranteed supply contracts and those which are interruptible. In the opinion of the study's authors, the latter pose fewer problems for network operators inasmuch as they can, in the event of their having difficulty supplying their traditional captive customers, temporarily cut off supplies to third parties with access to their networks but having interruptible contracts.

Study of the shipbuilding market in 1989

392.   This study, finished in 1990, is based on Article 4(3) of the sixth Council Directive on aid to shipbuilding which requires a regular review of the maximum level of aid that Member States can grant. The purpose of the ceiling is to enable the gap between the costs of the most efficient Community shipyards and the (below-cost) prices of Far Eastern competitors to be bridged. A study of this nature was first carried out in 1986 and has been updated in each of the years 1987 and 1988.

The study, as in the previous one made in 1989, concentrates on ship types which are most commonly constructed within the Community and for which the EC yards are in most direct competition with third-country producers. The study then establishes the cost estimates of the most effective yard for each vessel type. The conclusion of the study is that as regards three of the ship types examined there is at present no longer a gap between the costs of the most effective Community yards and the Far Eastern prices, while for the other vessel types a gap continues to exist.

Quantification of State aids in Greece (1981-88)

393. The first and second surveys on State aids (Article 92) published by the Commission did not contain any reliable estimates for Greece. The purpose of the study was to estimate the Greek Government's budgetary expenditure on State aids.

With a view to quantifying these aids, the consultants examined systematically, placing the stress on grants, every sector of manufacturing industry. They then proceeded in the same way for the other categories, i.e. risk capital, loans, accelerated depreciation and guarantees, albeit in a more condensed fashion owing to the incompleteness and lack of transparency of the sources available. When the study was being prepared, the targets imposed by the Commission were adhered to despite the difficulties encountered as regards the availability and reliability of sources.

In conclusion, the present document might serve as a basis for close collaboration in future between the Greek authorities and the Commission in the field of the quantification of State aids, notably with a view to updating the second survey on State aids.

Merger control — collection and analysis of data on the insurance markets

394. This study is a complementary instrument for the application of the EC merger control Regulation in the field of insurance.

Whereas the information that must be provided by the parties when notifying a merger is restricted to information on the companies involved in a merger, the study provides general background information on the insurance markets. Both types of information are necessary to make a well-reasoned decision on whether or not a merger is compatible with the common market. This study describes — in summary fashion — the 12 national insurance markets of the European Community and the three major 'foreign' markets, i.e. Switzerland, USA and Japan. The study is preceded by an introduction which analyses the EC insurance market. It describes its position in the world insurance economy and indicates major trends and influences.

Background information on the Community beer market[1]

395.   In addition to studies made by external consultants, the Commission undertook internally a study of the EEC beer market. The European Community is the world's largest beer-producing area. The following generalized characterization of the market may be made.

The EEC beer market appears to be made up of a number of distinct relevant geographic markets for the purposes of the application of anti-trust law. Only three brewers, BSN (France), Heineken (the Netherlands) and Carlsberg (Denmark), are present on most markets and even these three are relatively minor players outside their home countries. Only approximately 4% of all beer consumed in the EEC has crossed a national border: this is a reflection not only of significantly different demand patterns in Member States, but also of the high unit costs involved in transporting beer.

Although a certain number of major breweries are and show an increasing tendency to be internationalized, they remain relatively small on a world scale. Indigenous breweries remain active and profitable in most Member States. Although a considerable degree of merger/takeover activity has persisted in the sector in recent years, the European Community has a far greater number of breweries than any other comparable land mass.

This has advantages and disadvantages: the majority of EC breweries are unable to enjoy the economies of scale exploited by the 'mega-breweries' in the USA and Japan; on the other hand the consumer enjoys unrivalled choice of types and brands.

The reasons for this diversity of supply are difficult to identify. It is however notable that in countries where a 'tied-house' system operates (e.g. Federal Republic of Germany, United Kingdom, Belgium) a proliferation of small and medium-sized breweries compete. On the other hand, in countries where a completely 'open' system operates, few brands compete on a market dominated by one or two large brewers which benefit from significant economies of scale (Carlsberg in Denmark, Guinness in Ireland, Budweiser/Miller in the USA, Bond/Elders in Australia).

The Community is the world's largest exporter of beer; in the 1980s exports accounted for an almost constant 95% of total trade in beer (exports plus imports). In 1988, beer generated a trade surplus of ECU 606 million.

A marked difference exists between the conditions prevalent on the markets in Northern and Southern Europe. Northern markets are static of declining, characterized by overcapacity and in many cases strong brand loyalty, and are difficult to penetrate. Southern markets, with no history of beer drinking, are expanding from a low per capita consumption level. Expansion is largely fuelled by Northern European groups (notably

---

[1]   The figures contained herein are deduced by the Commission on the basis of interventions from a variety of sources, including estimates of professional bodies and experts.

Heineken, BSN and Carlsberg), which are making considerable direct investment in these areas.

Although it could be stated that the concentration level of breweries on each national market is high compared to most other industrial sectors, it is low compared to that for the beer sector in the other major industrialized nations. In particular, concentration levels are high (in descending order) in Ireland, Denmark, Greece, Portugal, Belgium, France, the Netherlands, Luxembourg and Italy. Moderate concentration levels prevail in Spain and Great Britain, low levels at the Community level as a whole and in West Germany.

Only in the developed and static North European markets does the tied-house system exist. It is most prevalent in the United Kingdom where, according to Commission figures, approximately 62% of total beer sales pass through tied channels. This figure is much lower in other Member States; the approximate equivalent statistic for other Member States is the following:

Belgium	35%
Germany	25%
France	10%
Luxembourg	40%
Netherlands	10%

The countries in which the system does operate (Belgium, West Germany, France, the Netherlands, Luxembourg, United Kingdom) account for 78% of total EC sales, and are host to approximately 93% of all EC breweries. The countries in which over 20% of total national beer sales pass through tied outlets (Belgium, West Germany, Luxembourg, United Kingdom) account for 65% of total EC sales and are host to over 90% of all EC breweries.

In the Community as a whole, less than 30% of all beer sales pass through tied outlets.

The proportion of total beer sold through on- and off-licensed premises differs significantly according to the Member State in question, as do sales by draught or packaged. In particular a high proportion of total beer sales passes through the on-licensed sector in Ireland (>90%), United Kingdom (>80%), Spain (>75%), Greece and Portugal (>60%) and Belgium (55%). In the other Member States approximately 40% of total beer sales pass through on-licensed outlets (West Germany and France approximately 35%). Only in Ireland (>85%) and in the United Kingdom (>70%) do draught beer sales exceed packaged.

Annex

European Parliament:

Resolution on the Nineteenth Report on Competition Policy of the Commission of the European Communities

Response of the Commission of the European Communities to the Resolution on the Nineteenth Report on Competition Policy

Economic and Social Committee:

Opinion on the Nineteenth Report on Competition Policy of the Commission of the European Communities

Commission Regulation (EEC) No 2367/90 of 25 July 1990 on the notifications, time-limits and hearings provided for in Council Regulation (EEC) No 4064/89 on the control of concentrations between undertakings

Commission notice regarding restrictions ancillary to concentrations (90/C 203/05)

Commission notice regarding the concentrative and cooperative operations under Council Regulation (EEC) No 4064/89 of 21 December 1989 on the control of concentrations between undertakings (90/C 203/06)

Commission Decision of 23 November 1990 on the implementation of hearings in connection with procedures for the application of Articles 85 and 86 of the EEC Treaty and Articles 65 and 66 of the ECSC Treaty

I — Competition policy towards enterprises — List of Decisions, Notices and Judgments
1. Decisions pursuant to Articles 85 and 86 of the EEC Treaty
2. Notices pursuant to Articles 85 and 86 of the EEC Treaty
   (a) Pursuant to Article 19(3) of Council Regulation No 17
   (b) Pursuant to Article 5(2) of Council Regulation (EEC) No 3975/87
   (c) Pursuant to Article 12(2) of Council Regulation (EEC) No 4056/86
3. Decisions pursuant to Articles 65 and 66 of the ECSC Treaty
4. Decisions pursuant to Article 6 of Council Regulation (EEC) No 4064/89
5. Judgments of the Court of Justice

II — Competition policy and government assistance to enterprises
1. Aid cases in which the Commission raised no objection
2. Aid cases in which the Commission decided to open the Article 93(2) EEC procedure
3. Aid cases in which the Commission decided to open the procedure provided for in Article 6(4) of Decision No 322/89/ECSC
4. Aid cases in which the Commission decided to close the Article 93(2) EEC procedure
5. Aid cases in which the Commission decided to close the procedure provided for in Article 6(4) of Decision No 3484/85/ECSC
6. Aid cases in which the Commission took a negative final decision under Article 93(2) of the EEC Treaty

European Parliament

Resolution on the Nineteenth Report on Competition Policy of the Commission of the European Communities

The European Parliament,

— having regard to the Nineteenth Report on Competition Policy of the Commission of the European Communities,

— having regard to its earlier resolutions on competition policy,

— having regard to the report of the Committee on Economic and Monetary Affairs and Industrial Policy and the opinion of the Committee on Legal Affairs and Citizens' Rights and the Committee on Agriculture, Fisheries and Rural Development (Doc. A3-0374/90);

1. Emphasizes that the process of completing the single market, and the approach of the 1992 deadline for this task, gives an ever greater significance to Community competition policy; affirms that this requires:

(i)   regular and clear reporting on competition policy developments to ensure democratic accountability to the European Parliament and a clear understanding of these issues by the general public,

(ii) vigorous, rapid and efficient administration of competition policy,

(iii) a proper balance between competition policy and the other policy objectives of the European Community;

Timing and structure of the Commission's competition policy reports

2. Considers that the Commission's annual competition policy reports have a vital role to play in ensuring democratic accountability of the Commission to the European Parliament in a policy area where the Commission has very considerable power, and the final say on many sensitive issues; believes that the annual reports help to publicize competition policy developments at European Community level, and to increase awareness of their implications;

3. Regrets, therefore, that yet again the Commission does not appear to give a sufficiently high priority to its annual report, with the result that its presentation to Parliament is delayed year after year in spite of repeated protests by Parliament; considers it wholly unacceptable that its request (in paragraph 40 of its resolution on the Eighteenth Report) for the Nineteenth Report to be submitted by 30 April 1990 was disregarded; insists that the report be given a higher priority in the future, and that sufficient staff and other resources are provided by the Commission to DG IV to ensure that it can be presented in subsequent years by 30 April at the latest;

4. Further notes that the structure of the report has remained largely unchanged for the last 15 years while the complexity of the issues involved, the number of areas covered by competition policy, and experience in the application of the Treaty regulations have also expanded greatly;

5. Suggests, in order to ensure the full appreciation of major developments in competition policy as well as giving the vital technical details on particular sectors, firms, countries and business practices that the annual competition policy report should be reorganized as follows:

(i) the general introduction to include a 1 500 word summary of the whole report (which could also be published separately on a stand-alone basis);

(ii) a detailed index to be provided to the report (as suggested in point 42 of its resolution on the Eighteenth Report) so as to enable, for example, easier location of the six separate sections in the Nineteenth Report, where air transport is discussed;

6. Further believes, in view of the great expansion in the work of the Commission on State aids, and its forthcoming new activities in the field of merger controls, that the Commission should consider publication of its annual report in three separate parts: (i) general competition policy, (ii) State aids, and (iii) mergers, with a summary and complete index for each part;

7. Emphasizes finally the need for wider awareness of the obligations of Community competition law among the public in general, and among undertakings, and national, regional and local governments in particular; welcomes, in this context, the recent publication by the Commission of the consolidated Community rules applicable to undertakings, and trusts that this will be regularly updated; underlines, moreover, the importance of providing clear and concise summaries of these rules for the attention of small and medium-sized enterprises in particular;

Administration of competition policy

8. Notes that Community competition policy has had to confront two major new challenges in 1990:

(i) the unification of Germany;

(ii) the implementation of the recently adopted Regulation on merger controls;

9. Further notes that, in addition to these new tasks, the Commission will have to pursue a number of other key policy objectives, and in particular:

(i) effective follow-up to its second survey on State aids, and the major problems that it has revealed,

(ii) consistent and effective application of Community competition policy in sectors such as automobiles, financial services, air transport and telecommunications,

(iii) extension of Community competition policy in fields where the Commission has been inadequately involved, or not at all, such as the liberal professions;

10. Emphasizes that these new or reinforced tasks involve a great increase in an already heavy workload for the competition policy services of the Commission (DG IV); notes with concern, in this context, that there were already 3 239 cases pending at the end of 1989, and that only a small proportion of these cases were submitted during 1989, with many cases pending for several years;

11. Considers, therefore, that there must be an urgent and immediate increase in the staff available for implementing Community competition law;

12. Further considers that any reinforcement of DG IV staff should take into sufficient account the need for a wide mix of skills, in view especially of the increased complexity of the economic analysis that is required; suggests, in this context, that the Commission should look at the countries with the longest history of anti-trust legislation, both inside the Community and outside (such as Canada and the United States) for their experience in handling staff requirements when faced with expansions in case load, case-law and additional fields of activity, noting their widespread use of applied economists, those with joint economics and law degrees and those with business experience, especially in marketing;

13. Considers that the Commission's programme of research as outlined in Part IV of the report should be conceived as a valuable instrument in the implementation of Community competition policy, and that it needs, therefore, to be better integrated into the day-to-day work programme of DG IV; requests information on the criteria used by the Commission in defining its research priorities;

Welcomes the valuable data that is provided in Chapter 1, Part IV of the report on mergers, acquisitions and recent structural changes in EC industry, but regrets the lack of detail in Chapter 2 on the programme of studies and their results; asks the Commission to state briefly the countries and sectors covered by each research project, as was the custom in earlier reports, as well as giving full details in the Annex;

14. Considers that the right balance must be struck in the administration of Community competition policy between the need for speed, efficiency and fairness, and recalls its previously expressed concern (as in paragraph 44 of its resolution on the Eighteenth Report) that there should be an effective separation of the Commission's functions of investigation, promotion of fairness and delivery of final judgment in its administrative procedures, to achieve which it calls for an updated assessment of the role of the Hearing Officer. Welcomes the fact that legal safeguards on competition policy matters have been strengthened as a result of the creation of the Court of First Instance;

15. Calls for a report on the advisability of establishing a separate European Cartel Office responsible to the European Parliament; considers that this could have some advantages in terms of guaranteeing greater administrative independence, but points out that it could also lead to greater bureaucracy and duplication of functions between the proposed cartel office and the Commission; believes that the effective staffing of DG IV is the priority at the present time;

16. Welcomes the recent decisions by the Court of Justice in the Hoechst, Dow Chemical and Dow Benelux cases which strengthen the Commissions's investigation powers, including surprise investigations, in order to provide better factual evidence about particular enterprises; further requests the Commission, however, to give better particulars in its decisions ordering investigations of undertakings and thereby to respond to the critical remarks made by the Court of Justice in its judgment in Joined Cases 46/87 and 227/88 *Hoechst* v *Commission*;

17. Considers, in the interest of furthering democratic accountability, that the European Parliament should be informed of proposed Community competition policy initiatives earlier than at present; calls, in particular for

– all draft block exemptions or other implementing Commission decisions to be sent to the Parliament at the same time as they are sent to the Advisory Committee on Restrictive Practices and Dominant Positions, the Advisory Committee on Mergers and to other interested parties;

German unification

18. Considers that German unification, and the process of incorporating the former GDR within the European Community and within a social market rather than a centrally planned economy, has major consequences for Community competition policy:

(i) in terms of evaluating the State aids that are provided to reshape the former GDR's infrastructure and economy,

(ii) in terms of evaluating the impact on competition of the privatization process being carried out by the State Holding Company (Treuhandanstalt);

19. Recognizes the need for State aids from the German Government to help in the former GDR, but insists that they be fully transparent, and that they do not create new distortions of competition at the expense, in particular, of other disadvantaged and peripheral regions of the Community;

20. Supports the Commission view that the aid to Berlin and the intra-German border areas contributed under the German budget must be reduced as quickly as possible, since the legal basis for such aid (Article 92(2)(c)) of the EEC Treaty) is no longer available following German unification and Berlin and the old intra-German border areas should, in the interests of equal competition with other regions, be incorporated into the standard aid arrangements;

21. Notes that the unprecedentedly rapid and far-reaching process of selling off the assets of the former 'Kombinate' by the Treuhandanstalt should greatly increase economic efficiency but also poses considerable risks as far as fair and equal competition are concerned;

22. Warns against the possible creation of new monopolies and dominant positions as a result of takeovers of former GDR enterprises by German firms. Insists that there be fully transparent public sales procedures by the Treuhandanstalt, and that there should be no discrimination of any kind between German and other Community firms in this process; calls on the Commission to draw up and submit to Parliament a report on such takeovers and public-sales procedures;

The Regulation on merger control

23. Welcomes the fact that the Council finally took the decision to adopt a Regulation on merger control in December 1989 after so many years of stalemate;

24. Congratulates the Commission, and in particular its mergers task force, on its rapid adoption of the implementing Regulation and its creation of the necessary infrastructure so that the Regulation on merger control was able to come into force on 21 September 1990;

25. Regrets, however, that the first draft of the implementing Regulation was prepared in April 1990 and circulated to interested parties, but that Parliament was only informed in June, giving it inadequate time to comment before the Regulation's adoption in July;

26. Considers the aggregate world turnover threshold of ECU 5 billion to be unrealistically high; this high threshold, allied to the express provision that Articles 85 and 86, shall not apply to concentrations irrespective of the turnover of the undertakings involved, prevents the Commission from scrutinizing, on the basis of Regulation No 17, many concentrations which restrict competition within the EEC and have an effect on inter-State trade, the Commission thus being obliged to operate on the inadequate basis of Article 89; therefore supports any proposal to reduce the thresholds provided for in Article 1 of the Regulation on merger control;

27. Considers that the unsatisfactory relationship between the competences of the Commission and the Member States on merger controls must also be improved;

Considers, in this context, that there are too many exceptions to the basic rules in Council Regulation No 4064/89 and that too much legal uncertainty is created as a result; believes that unnecessary overlap and uncertainty are created, for example, by those provisions of the Regulation which allow national scrutiny of certain mergers on the basis of criteria such as considerations of public security, plurality of the media, prudential control of financial institutions and even vaguer 'other public interest' considerations pursuant to Article 21 of the Regulation;

Calls on the Commission, moreover, to have recourse only in the most exceptional circumstances to Article 9 of the Regulation on merger control, whereby it may refer a notified concentration to the competent authorities of a Member State in the event of a threat to competition in a distinct market in that Member State and to consider the repeal of this provision when it comes up for review before 21 December 1993;

Recognizes that the Regulation has now just come into operation, but believes that the problems outlined above should be immediately examined, with a view to eliminating them as soon as possible, taking account of the need first to gain adequate experience of the Regulation and to ensure DG IV has sufficient resources to cope with any extension of competence;

28. Calls on the Commission further to reduce the amount of information required in form CO from the companies concerned, when notifying the Commission of a proposed concentration, thereby saving them unnecessary time and financial costs;

29. Calls on the Commission to report back on other aspects of the functioning of the Regulation on merger control as soon as sufficient practical experience has been gained;

30. Welcomes the Commission's Notice regarding the concentrative and cooperative operation under the Regulation on merger control, (1990, OJ C 203, p. 10) as being a very necessary clarification of its thinking as to when minority share acquisitions, partial mergers or concentrative joint ventures may fall within the scope of the regulation;

31. Requests the Commission to submit its promised complementary guidelines on joint ventures;

Need for a proper balance between competition policy and the other policy objectives of the European Community

32. Affirms that competition is a complex interaction of economic forces and not a simple solution to all economic problems, and that therefore the major objective of competition policy must be to create and maintain workable and effective competition in all sectors, rather than to strive for the unrealistic theoretical model of perfect competition;

33. Welcomes, for example, the Commission's widespread use of block exemptions (as in its latest proposals on insurance), in order to give firms the appropriate balance between legal security and freedom to compete; calls, however, for continued careful monitoring of how the adopted block exemptions are working in practice to see if they are really achieving their objectives;

34. Insists, moreover, that competition policy should not be carried out in isolation from other vital policy objectives of the Community, such as increasing Community industrial competitiveness, and strengthening economic and social cohesion and the achievement of sustainable development; considers that these objectives must be closely coordinated, and believes that one of the key ways of judging the effectiveness of Community competition policy is by reference to whether those wider objectives are being met;

35. Considers that this would be facilitated by systematic review of the impact of Commission decisions in the field of competition; calls, therefore, upon the Commission to include in each such decision 'an economic, social and environmental audit', looking at the impact on economic competitiveness, levels of employment, social security costs, regional development and the environment;

36. Considers, finally, that in some cases Community competition policy has had too great a burden placed upon it, as in certain industrial sectors where the Community's competition rules have had to be interpreted by DG IV in the absence of a Community industrial strategy for the sector concerned, which would include aid criteria within a wider policy context;

37. Considers, therefore, that for this reason, and in the interests of maximum transparency in the Community's competition policy, the Commission should give further consideration to defining more clearly how industrial, regional and other policy considerations should be taken into account in decisions on competition policy, including State aids, and should report thereon;

38. Believes that the above principles are of particular importance in assessing the Commission's policy on State aids;

State aids

39. Welcomes the publication of the Commission's second survey on State aids as an invaluable instrument for analysing the different types and volume of State aid within the Community and the distortions that they can cause; regrets that certain countries (notably Belgium and Greece) have not fully cooperated with the Commission in preparing the survey; requests clarification from the Commission as to how and when its proposed standardized system of annual reporting on State aids will be fully introduced, and what sanctions there will be for non-compliance;

40. Reaffirms that State aids should not be judged as a good or bad phenomenon in their own right, nor in terms of their absolute levels, but according to the purpose for which they are used and the effects they may have on economic and social cohesion;

41. Believes, however, that differentials in levels of State aid for the same objective from one Community country to another may cause severe distortions of competition, and could be one of the key factors in impeding the creation of a true internal market by 1992;

42. Calls, therefore, for:

(i)   the fullest possible transparency of aids granted by national and regional authorities,

(ii) a clearer and more effective Community framework for national and regional aids, which would require any such aids to be justified in terms of consistent and strictly defined social, environmental, regional or industrial policy considerations,

(iii) a sustained effort at Community level to reduce aid differentials from one country to another where this is needed in order to ensure fairer conditions of competition;

43. Calls in particular on the Commission to submit proposals for determining the conditions in which the undertakings which are most affected by environmental protection measures or are located in ecologically fragile areas may be granted assistance;

44. Believes, however, that significant and real differentials should be permitted in favour of disadvantaged areas within the Community, in order to take due account of differences in levels of employment and economic development between different regions and countries;

45. Believes that the considerable experience acquired to date and the breadth of understanding and analysis of the situation in the sector are now sufficient to enable consistent arrangements to be laid down in all parts of Community territory; calls, therefore, on the Commission to draw up a code of rules providing for uniform enforcement of provisions in the individual sectors, based on the principles set out in paragraphs 40 to 44 above;

46. Calls on the Commission to vigorously apply Articles 92 and 93 to both public and privately owned companies; regrets the tendency of certain Member States to unduly favour certain of their own private or public companies by means of illegal and disguised aids;

47. Draws the attention of the Member States to the need to comply with the provisions of Article 93(3) concerning the obligation to inform the Commission in sufficient time of all plans to grant or alter aid; urges the Commission to use all means at its disposal to enforce the law in this respect; further urges the Commission to use all means at its disposal to enforce the law in this respect; further urges the Commission to continue to impose the paying back of any sums illegally paid by Member States by way

of State aid, and to make a formal proposal to Council and Parliament so that in future the amounts paid back become Community budget revenue;

48. Insists that all Community countries fully respect the Commission's framework of State aids for the motor vehicle sector, and that the Commission takes tough action to combat abuses throughout the Community; calls, moreover, for a Commission investigation as to whether unreasonable differences in prices and delivery times for similar vehicles have again opened up within the Community;

49. Requests clarification as to why the recent Commission guidelines for the examination of State aids to Community shipping companies were forwarded to the Council but not apparently to the European Parliament;

50. Welcomes the Commission's acceptance of certain State aids to help the long-term unemployed, which could be of particular value as Europe faces the prospect of an economic downturn in the light of the Gulf crisis, the fall in agricultural prices and other factors;

Other specific issues

51. Welcomes the Commission's increased emphasis on opening up competition in the audio-visual media, but calls on the Commission to take whatever additional legal measures are necessary to safeguard pluralism and freedom of expression and to reduce the concentration of ownership in the hands of transnational multimedia groups, such as those led by Murdoch, Maxwell and Berlusconi;

52. Calls on the Commission to specify what new measures it will take:

(i)   to apply competition rules in the energy sector more strictly than in the past, in particular by ensuring greater transparency in the prices charged and in production costs (especially in the nuclear sector),

(ii) to open up competition in the often closed 'liberal' professions,

(iii) to carry out a more detailed assessment of the actual importance and impact — in competition terms — of factors such as conglomerate company forms, joint ventures and management behaviour; and to determine, in particular, whether it will draw up blueprints for action in relation to those factors which have been brought to light by research in the field;

53. Demands that the Commission, in the run-up to further liberalization of competition in the air transport sector after 1 January 1993, remains extremely vigilant in ensuring that currently proposed cooperation agreements and practices between the flag-carrying airlines (for example the proposed joint venture or merger between British Airways, Sabena and KLM, the 'cooperation agreement' between Air France and Lufthansa or the proposed absorption of UTA by Air France) do not serve as a means for these airlines further to secure their already dominant market positions before greater liberalization measures are introduced;

54. Notes with concern the increased concentration in the food sector caused by many acquisitions and mergers; commends the Commission's decision to keep a close watch on restructuring in this sector, and asks for this vigilance to include the distribution of food products by the grocery trade, and concentration in retailing more generally;

55. Welcomes the Belasco judgment of the Court of Justice which made it clear that a Belgian cartel concerned with the marketing of products purely within Belgium could have a significant influence on intra-Community trade through its restrictions on foreign competition in Belgium, and believes this has important implications for Community competition law;

56. Considers that increased cooperation leading to convergence on competition policy should be an important objective of the current negotiations for a European economic space with the EFTA countries;

believes that this should also apply to the countries of Central and Eastern Europe which are developing a social market economy, although their special problems in the short and medium-term should also be recognized;

57. Supports the concept of closer cooperation between the Community and US competition authorities on the issue of extra-territorial application of Community and US law;

58. Calls on the Commission to provide, within eight weeks of receipt of this report, a point-by-point initial written response indicating the Commission's views and intended actions and, where the initial response indicates a need for further consideration and/or further action, the timescale for such consideration and/or action;

59. Instructs its President to forward this resolution to the Commission, the Council, the competition authorities in the Member States and the governments and parliaments of the Member States.

Response of the Commission of the European Communities to the Resolution on the Nineteenth Report on Competition Policy

Parliament's Resolution
(Desmond Report)

Commission's response

The annual Competition Report

Point 3. Request that the report be given a higher priority and that sufficient staff and other resources be provided to DG IV to ensure that the report can be presented by 30 April.

The Commission continues to give the report the highest priority, but administrative constraints, in particular the need to publish the report in the Community's nine official languages, limit the scope for shortening the deadline. It will do everything it can, however, to ensure that the report is presented in future by 30 April.

Points 5 and 6. Suggestion that the report be restructured along certain lines.

The report's present layout is based on that of Articles 85 to 93 of the EEC Treaty. Thus it deals first of all with competition policy towards enterprises and then with that towards government assistance to enterprises. The Commission does not deny that the report's structure can be improved. However, this cannot be done before the Twenty-first Report, the Twentieth having already been finalized.

Administration of competition policy

Point 11. Considers that there must be an increase in the staff available for implementing Community competition law.

The Commission agrees.

Point 12. Suggestion that more use should be made of applied economists, those with joint economics and law degrees and those with business experience.

The staff of the Commission's DG IV consists of Community officials with degrees mainly in law and/or economics and a number of national officials with experience in competition matters.

Point 13. Asks to be informed of the criteria governing the choice of studies. Requests an indication as to which countries and which sectors are covered by the studies.

DG IV's research budget is very limited. Consequently, the studies have to be selected carefully. The selection is made on the basis of the priorities established for competition policy. During the period covered by the Nineteenth Report, the studies concentrated on two aspects: the modification of market structures and the impact of State aids from the point of view of competition policy. The first was aimed at developing guidelines for a realistic application of merger control. In the second case, the aim was to gain a better understanding of certain types of State aid in order to strengthen and buttress Community policy in this area. The studies do not have any academic purpose, but are intended to help the Commission in its daily work. The more practical the studies are and the more they are oriented towards certain political objectives, the less they are of general interest.

In so far as the studies concern the conduct of certain companies or groups of companies, their publication also provides pointers to the individual decisions which the Commission might take, something which often has to be avoided for a certain length of time.

Point 14. Calls for an effective separation of the Commission's functions of investigator, prosecutor and judge in its administrative procedures. Requests an updated assessment of the role of the Hearing Officer.

In its Nineteenth Competition Report, the Commission stated (pp. 21 and 22) that it had taken note of the statements and comments made by Parliament on this question and that it would take account thereof. In the past, it was the Commission's practice to separate inspection (on-the-spot investigation) from the processing of individual cases by rapporteurs. This system was subsequently abandoned because the separation of the two tasks essential to the preparation of the decision, that is to say the establishment of the facts, on the one hand, and the legal assessment, on the other, had given rise to a considerable number of problems as regards planning and coordinating the respective work and was therefore not conducive to the effective handling of cases.

Individual cases are now dealt with by the operational directorates within DG IV. These directorates must submit the draft decision both to the directorate responsible for coordination within DG IV and to the Legal Service, which is administratively separate from DG IV. This procedure already provides several guarantees of checks and balances. Moreover, the Hearing Officer is responsible for ensuring that the parties are heard in an objective manner and that their right to a fair hearing is respected. Draft decisions are also submitted to the Advisory Committee for its opinion. The Committee consists of national experts on competition matters and is chaired by an official from Directorate A other than the official who initiated the case. The case is presented in detail before the committee by one of the national experts. The Commission is of the opinion that this affords a sufficient guarantee of the effective separation of the various functions in the administrative procedure. A further safeguard is provided by the existence of a two-stage judicial review procedure, namely by the Court of First Instance and by the Court of Justice.

Point 15. Calls for a report on the advisability of establishing a separate European Cartel Office.

The departments of the Directorate-General for Competition have recently undergone major structural changes, as a result of, among other things, the adoption of the Merger Control Regulation. The Commission does not think it necessary to set up a European Cartel Office.

Point 17. Wishes to be informed earlier of proposed Commission competition policy initiatives, and in particular to be informed of all draft block exemptions or other implementing Commission decisions at the same time as the Advisory Committee.

The Commission's departments, adopting a pragmatic attitude, have worked out, together with the Committee on Economic and Monetary Affairs and Industrial Policy, an informal procedure which enables that Committee to take note of such proposals at an appropriate stage. The Commission's departments intend to continue this procedure.

German unification

Point 22. Asks for a report on take-overs of companies in the former GDR and on the public sales procedures of the Treuhandanstalt.

In view of the fact that German unification took place after the period covered by the Nineteenth Report, the Commission's policy towards its impact on the competitive situation in the common market is discussed in detail in the Twentieth Report.

However, the Commission can already indicate here that it is seeing to it that the unification process takes place with due regard for competition policy considerations, both from the traditional anti-trust point of view and from that of State aids. The Commission has played an active part in this process, with the result that it has not been pursued as a national matter, but instead in an entirely Community-minded way.

Merger Control Regulation

Point 26. Is in favour of reducing the thresholds laid down in Article 1 of the Regulation.

The Commission whole-heartedly agrees. It intends to propose such a reduction at the time of the review provided for in Article 1(3) of the Regulation.

Point 27. Considers it necessary to study without delay the problems connected with the division of powers between the Community and the Member States.

The Commission will carry out such a study as part of the preparations for the review mentioned in the reply to point 26.

Point 28. Calls on the Commission to reduce the amount of information required in Form CO.

The Merger Control Regulation lays down a procedure with relatively strict time-limits. If it is to adhere to those time-limits, the Commission must have all the necessary information at its disposal. Form CO was therefore designed along relatively perfectionist lines. The Commission would point out, however, that Article 4(3) of the Regulation provides for the possibility for the Commission to reduce, in certain cases, the amount of information that has to be given. Initial practical experience with the application of the Regulation has shown that, in most cases, formal notifications are preceded by informal contacts. It is in the course of such contacts that the Commission has often been able to waive the obligation to supply certain information.

Point 29. Calls on the Commission to report back on other aspects of the functioning of the Merger

The Commission intends to give an account of all important aspects of the functioning of the

Control Regulation as soon as sufficient practical experience has been gained.

Point 31. Requests the Commission to submit its promised complementary guidelines on joint ventures.

Need for a proper balance between competition policy and the other policy objectives of the European Community

Point 35. Calls upon the Commission to include in each decision in the field of competition an economic, social and environmental audit.

Regulation in its annual account on competition policy. The first such account can be found in the Twentieth Report.

The guidelines will be presented in the course of 1991.

It has never been the intention that competition policy, as pursued by the Community, should create a model of perfect competition. According to Article 3(f) of the Treaty, the Community must ensure that competition in the common market is not distorted. Competition policy is thus directed towards attaining the objectives set by the Treaty, primarily the establishment of a genuine single market which is both open and competitive.
An active competition policy contributes substantially to the attainment of the objective of increasing industrial competitiveness and strengthening economic and social cohesion. By stimulating economic growth, it promotes employment and regional development. The benefits to the consumer are also evident.
Consequently, it will not be necessary to carry out systematically an 'economic, social and environmental audit' in every case.

Point 37. Considers that the Commission should define how industrial, regional and other policy considerations should be taken into account in decisions on competition policy, and should report thereon.

As far as the Community's industrial strategy is concerned, it has long been acknowledged that an effective industrial policy rests on an active competition policy, both in the anti-trust field and in that of State aids. It should be stressed, moreover, that competition policy necessarily applies to all economic activities and cannot be used in a 'discriminatory' manner with a view to taking action 'à la carte' in specific sectors.

State aids

Point 42. Calls for the fullest possible transparency of aids granted by national and regional authorities. Calls for a Community framework which would require any such aids to be justified in terms of social, environmental, regional or industrial policy considerations. Calls for an effort to reduce aid differentials from one country to another.

The Commission has decided to publish a summary, of varying length depending on the importance of the cases dealt with, of all the decisions it takes on aid schemes to which it does not raise any objections. The summary is published in the *Official Journal of the European Communities.* Decisions regarding aid schemes in respect of which the Commission initiates the Article 93(2) procedure or in respect of which it takes a negative decision under that Article are already published in full in the Official Journal. The Commission is currently carrying out a review of all existing aid schemes. One of its reasons for so

Point 43. Calls for proposals for determining the conditions in which the undertakings which are most affected by environmental protection measures or are located in ecologically fragile areas may be granted assistance.

Point 46. Calls on the Commission to vigorously apply Articles 92 and 93 to both public and privately owned companies.

Point 48. Calls for an investigation into whether unreasonable differences in prices and delivery times for similar vehicles have again opened up within the Community.

Other specific issues

Point 52. Calls on the Commission to specify what new measures it will take:
(i)   to apply competition rules more strictly in the energy sector;

(ii) to open up competition in the 'liberal' professions;

(iii) to carry out a more detailed assessment of the importance and impact — in competition terms — of conglomerate company forms, joint ventures and management behaviour.

doing is to reduce aid differentials from one country to another.

The existing framework on State aids in environmental matters is being revised and a new framework will be proposed to Member States in late 1991 or early 1992. The questions raised in Parliament's Resolution will be taken into account in the new framework.

In 1991 the Commission will adopt a proposal aimed at strengthening the application of Articles 92 and 93 to public companies.

The findings of the car-price survey (January 1988, January 1989, January 1990 and April 1990) mentioned in the Twentieth Competition Report are being evaluated to ascertain whether the differences in prices from one Member State to another are, in fact, justified. There is a need for further studies on such specific aspects as differences in trim or equipment levels between the models in the survey, in order to arrive at prices between which a valid comparison may be made. The results of this exercise will be published in the Twenty-first Competition Report.

The Commission is currently pursuing a more active policy as regards the application of the existing competition rules, notably those of the EEC Treaty, in the energy sector.
It already has the means (such as Article 37/EEC) of ensuring a more open energy market. It is considering whether new measures will be useful, not to say necessary, and hopes to be in a position to announce this summer what new steps it intends to take or propose.

In this sector, also, the Commission considers that the existing rules provide it with the means it needs to pursue an active competition policy. It has recently received informal requests and a number of complaints and notifications relating to alleged distortions of competition in certain 'liberal' professions and other professional services, including the medical professions, consultancy services, customs agents, estate agents, and in sports; it is investigating these matters under the existing rules.

The Commission would point out that Article 1 of the proposal for a Council Regulation enabling the Commission to grant exemption for certain categories of agreements in the insurance sector provides that such categories may include involving the 'common coverage of certain types of risks'. The enabling Regulation was adopted on

Point 53. Asks the Commission to ensure that further liberalization in the air transport sector after 1 January 1993 is not frustrated by the strengthening of the dominant positions of certain national airlines before that date.

31 May 1991. The Commission is about to start drafting the exemption Regulation. It does not for the time being intend to prepare other provisions in the areas mentioned.

The Commission is pursuing a very active competition policy in this sector in order to ensure, among other things, that airlines in a dominant position do not abuse that position. The Twentieth Competition Report already mentions several Commission measures — both formal and informal — in this field.

Other steps are being taken to ensure that the competitive situation in the sector does not worsen before the liberalization measures enter into force at the beginning of 1993.

Point 56. Considers that increased cooperation leading to convergence on competition policy, such as is being negotiated with the EFTA countries, should also apply to the countries of central and eastern Europe which are developing a social market economy.

The Community intends to include in the draft European agreements with certain central and eastern European countries clauses on competition policy similar to those already contained in the association agreements with the EFTA countries; moreover, the Commission is actively cooperating with certain countries of Central and Eastern Europe, in particular to help them establish a body of competition law and a competition policy.

Economic and Social Committee

Opinion on the Nineteenth Report on Competition Policy of the Commission of the European Communities

On 23 July 1990 the Commission decided to consult the Economic and Social Committee, under Article 198 of the Treaty establishing the European Economic Community, on the abovementioned report.

The Section for Industry, Commerce, Crafts and Services, which was responsible for preparing the Committee's work on the subject, adopted its Opinion on 5 December 1990. The Rapporteur was Mr Bagliano.

At its 282nd Plenary Session (meeting of 19 December 1990), the Economic and Social Committee adopted the following Opinion with no dissenting votes and three abstentions.

1. General introduction

1.1. A goal achieved at last

The Nineteenth Report on Competition Policy opens by highlighting the successful conclusion — at the very end of the year — of work on merger controls.

The *ad hoc* Regulation was approved on 21 December 1989 and entered into force on 21 September.

The Committee shares the Commission's satisfaction at this, although it remains concerned about possible problems of interpretation and implementation.

1.2. The Commission and the ESC

It is right and proper to be pleased with the results achieved over the year under review. It is, however, equally helpful to examine the quality of these results, and to consider how complete they are, how easy to implement, and what reactions they have aroused or are likely to arouse.

Regular criticism (and self-criticism) can only be healthy, particularly if it is offered in a spirit of cooperation and of participation in the pursuit of the Commission's annual goals for completion of the internal market.

It is in this spirit that the Committee approaches its tasks. The present Opinion will thus offer assessments, reiterate a few criticisms, put forward new recommendations, and provide the Commission with support and a stimulus, as regards guidelines for competition policy.

The Committee notes the Commission's assurance that when formulating policy, it will take account of the suggestions made in the ESC Opinion on the Eighteenth Report on Competition Policy. The Committee trusts that the Commission will respect this commitment.

1.3. The overall competition balance

EC competition rules have now been extended to further sectors of the economy, including transport, telecommunications, broadcasting and energy.

It is worth highlighting the concept of 'overall competition balance' which the Commission sees as an essential yardstick for assessing concrete cases.

The Committee has always stressed the need to adopt a wide outlook, embracing not only the Community and international markets but also the links between the various Community policies, in order to build up a coherent and realistic, overall geographic and political picture.

1.4. What is the position of national competition laws?

Although the competition rules of the Treaty are directly applicable in national legislation, the dividing line between EC competition policy and national policies is becoming increasingly blurred. While national legislation is becoming more aligned with Community legislation (a number of modifications have been made to national laws, and the new Italian law in large measure reflects the spirit and letter of the Treaty), there is still a grey area of legal uncertainty which needs clarification.

The Committee asks the Commission to consider and clarify this area, for example by means of *ad hoc* communications which provide guidance not just for companies, but also — more important — for the national courts.

The Community and national levels are not separated by rigid, uncrossable boundaries; they are flexible elements of a competition policy which, by means of the principle of subsidiarity, can and must retain its original spirit, pursue the objectives of the Treaty, and be applied consistently throughout the Community.

2. Specific problems

2.1. Distributive trades

These are a delicate, complex part of the economic production chain, and the Commission has always paid them considerable attention.

The many block exemption regulations bear witness to this attention, which is also made necessary by the wealth of agreements in this area. There is now a consolidated body of Community legislation and case-law on the subject.

These block exemptions — like all exemptions covered by Article 85(3) of the Treaty — are made for a specified period, and it is legitimate that the sectors concerned should be able to rely, during this specific period, on the legal framework laid down in the exemption Regulation itself.

However, the Commission seems unhappy with the situation and appears to be reviewing it, although the reasons for the Commission's unhappiness, and the possible alternatives, are not yet clear.

2.2. Controls for mergers and other forms of amalgamation

The revised 'basic' Regulation was published in the Official Journal of 21 September 1990,[1] with corrections of inaccuracies in the various language versions (some of these corrections do make the Regulation much easier to understand and interpret).

---

[1]   OJ L 257, 21.9.1990, p. 14.

The Committee issued its Opinion on the subject on 2 June 1988.[1] Here it would confirm its generally favourable assessment, subject to a few reservations which can only be cleared up by practical experience of implementation. Such experience may also suggest that certain points of the Regulation should be amended.

More particularly, precisely because the threshold at which a merger takes on a 'Community dimension' is high (at least during the first few years of implementation), the criteria and parameters must now fit into a broad geographical and temporal perspective. Any definition of 'relevant market' will have to take account of not only current but, more importantly, future potential competition, and not just in the Community but more especially at international level.

The completion of the internal market means that the geographical market is now at least the common market, and for many sectors is worldwide.

2.3. Services

Competition rules are being extended to cover a number of service industries (the two best-known examples being telecommunications and air transport). *Ad hoc* regulations take account of the special features of the service sector.

However, as in the case of mergers, the application of Community rules is not enough. Action must be taken to deal with national regulations which impede effective competition in certain sectors such as postal services, commercial monopolies and services carried out under State licence.

2.4. Public aids

The Committee has on several occasions insisted that public aid — where authorized — must always be transparent and degressive.

Although this must be the guiding principle and the final goal, some aid may, under precise conditions, still be compatible with the continuing process of Community integration. Exceptional circumstances and difficulties in particular sectors, regions or Member States have always been carefully considered by the Commission.

Aid which is incompatible with the Treaty is in any case clearly defined, not least by sectoral framework rules and by the large body of case-law.

Now more than ever, completion of the internal market brings a need for a dynamic competition policy, in parallel with a more robust industrial policy which makes allowances for the Herculean efforts which Community industry must make to adjust. The impact which third country competition is already exerting in the Community (and in certain Member States in particular) is an important consideration in the restructuring of supply in the internal market.

Small and medium-sized firms in particular face serious risks and need to make significant investment if they are to find a new competitive niche in the run-up to 1993.

There have now been two White Papers on State aids. This fact in itself shows how difficult it is to gain an accurate picture of the situation in the Member States. An accurate picture in a *sine qua non* for a proper intervention policy — one which does not simply inhibit, but also authorizes. We should therefore support the flexible and, in a certain sense, self-critical attitude adopted by the Commission in updating and amending these White Papers, which also refer to competition policy initiatives.

However, the exceptional circumstances faced by some sectors mean that a forward-looking, realistic evaluation is needed; while rigorously respecting the rules of the Treaty, this evaluation must take account of the fact that in many sectors, third-country competitors enjoy State support in various guises.

---

[1]   OJ C 208, 8.8.1988, p. 11.

The Committee shares the Commission's concern to apply the same rules to nationalized industries as to private industry, although the rules must be carefully designed to avoid any risk of discrimination between these two categories.

2.5. Prices — Comparisons between Member States — National price control legislation

2.5.1. The Committee has already drawn the Commission's attention to the fact that many comparable products still vary in price — sometimes considerably — within the Community.

The continuing nature of this phenomenon suggests that the problem is a complex one and that there is still a long and difficult path to negotiate before we achieve a real single market. The fact of the matter is that a large number of factors play a direct or indirect role in price formation.

The Committee and the European Parliament have often stressed the importance and tricky nature of studies of pricing in the various markets. They have urged the Commission not to overlook the structural, sectoral and general differences which persist in the Member States.

Comparison of the prices charged in each Member State for an identical product is a useful analytical instrument but perhaps not an adequate way to assess competition between Member States. Price variation is certainly indicative of a situation which is bound *inter alia* to distort competition. But although this is the most obvious aspect for the consumer, many other factors also come in to play, such as the diversity of tax systems, of technical standards, of administrative systems and of the rules governing distribution systems.

Comparison of Member States' prices in any given sector is a vital way of gleaning information and carrying out checks, but it must be accompanied by careful study of the continuing, structural and socio-economic differences between national markets.

Further harmonization and approximation is therefore needed in order to achieve the greater uniformity which is a minimum prerequisite for accurate comparisons and conclusions.

2.5.2. As a rule, prices must be determined by the market, i.e. by the free play of economic forces. Competition policy must ensure that this is achieved with respect for the roles of all the socio-economic partners, for consumer interests and for legislation protecting the environment (to cite the most topical and significant examples).

Accordingly, neither companies nor national authorities must play an undue part in price formation or price levels. Their task is to administer the few remaining exceptions, which, in any case, are governed by national control/monitoring systems.

As full market integration has not yet been achieved, national laws still have a role to play in controls designed to avoid abuses and, in certain cases, to ensure a degree of price stability.

The levers of short-term economic policy are still to a large extent in national hands, despite the growing interest in inter-bank cooperation and coordination, particularly between central banks.

While the Commission has direct instruments of investigation it has no direct powers of intervention in the implementation of competition rules. Although Articles 85 and 86 refer to businesses rather than Member States, use could be made of Article 3(f) and the second paragraph of Article 5.[1] Furthermore, the Commission can find broader (but equally clear and precise) legitimation in the first indent of Article 155, which states that the Commission shall 'ensure that the provisions of this Treaty and the measures taken by the institutions pursuant thereto are applied'.

A list of each Member State's laws and regulations with the potential to affect competition could however be drawn up, as the first step towards more effective monitoring.

---

[1]   Article 3(f) states that the activities of the Community include: 'the institution of a system ensuring that competition in the common market is not distorted'. Article 5 (second paragraph) states that the Member States 'shall abstain from any measure which could jeopardize the attainment of the objectives of this Treaty'.

2.6. Dumping

The Committee feels that a responsible and attentive policy on trade and competition must pay special attention to the problem of dumping.

The Commission has sufficient experience, particularly in those sectors where improper export pricing is a regular occurrence.

Trade barriers are disappearing almost everywhere and duties and quotas are being reduced, although admittedly at differing speeds. The only form of defence is thus to ascertain whether dumping is taking place, and to take defensive action.

The Commission has shown its readiness to act, and to complete the necessary procedures calmly and dispassionately

This strategy of responsible vigilance is the Commission's correct interpretation of the concept of a competition policy designed to boost and protect the internal market whilst respecting the rules of the General Agreement on Tariffs and Trade (GATT) (despite the absence within GATT of the 'social clause' which has been called for by many parties).

2.7. Procedure

The Regulation on merger control contains some important innovations concerning time-limits, arrangements for the participation of the parties concerned, and cooperation from national administrations.

2.7.1. The time-limits are very short, particularly when compared with those normally required to reach a Commission decision.

The Regulation very realistically acknowledges that in the case of prior notification, a faster procedure is needed. The Committee trusts that this laudable intention will be respected fairly, and that 'incomplete information' will not be used as an expedient for extending the deadlines.

2.7.2. The preliminary informal meetings proposed in the Regulation are an interesting innovation. They should help the Commission to respect the one-month deadline, or at all events to make the procedure as rapid as possible.

This approach is to be supported, not least because it will help to offset the complete nature of the form CO, the compilation of which will in practice be simplified by experience and the goodwill of all parties.

2.7.3. The heightened role of national authorities, and the requirement that they should cooperate effectively with the Commission, is also noteworthy.

The Court of Justice has, on several occasions, confirmed the Commission's power to carry out its duties within Member States and with the Member States' cooperation, in cases where a matter apparently of exclusively national interest in fact has possible implications for intra-EC trade.

The primacy of Community law over national provision is no longer in question, but it is worth stressing that this also affects relations between national authorities and the Commission.

2.7.4. For the implementation of Articles 85 and 86 of the Treaty, the Commission has quasi-legal powers under Regulation No 17 (first Regulation implementing Articles 85 and 86 of the Treaty, OJ 13, 21.2.1962). Article 19 of this Regulation gives the parties the opportunity of being heard on the matters to which the Commission has taken objection, under conditions designed to guarantee the rights of the defendant and ensure that the Commission is able to take an independent, impartial decision.

However, before taking a decision, the Commission has in some cases issued press communiqués stating its objections *vis-à-vis* particular undertakings.

The Committee would ask the Commission to reconsider this practice. It might be felt that in publishing these objections, the Commission could prejudice the final decision. Moreover, the Commission could find itself in a delicate position if the final decision fails to uphold objections which have already been released to the press.

2.8. Community legislation and national legislation

The recent Regulation on merger control will provide a valuable tool for assessing the link between EC law and national laws.

The existence of a Regulation specifically dealing with merger controls must not lead the Commission to limit its vigilance to Community-dimension mergers.

A high level of concentration is already apparent in a number of sectors. Nor is vigilance — outside Regulation (EEC) No 4064/89 — exercised solely by repressing abuses of dominant positions (Article 86).

The Commission must thus identify and keep tabs on the actual competition conditions in particular sectors. Mergers in some of these sectors will never have the 'Community dimension' specified by Article 1 of Regulation (EEC) No 4064/89 simply because of the way these sectors are structured.

In any case, all mergers which do not have a Community dimension should come under national legislation (although this may not in practice always be the case). Some instances may even be covered by the national legislation of several Member States simultaneously.

Differences and conflicts — and therefore problems — cannot be ruled out in such cases, and the Commission would not be justified in acting as a 'super partes' judge on its own initiative. The powers and instruments conferred on it by Regulation (EEC) No 4064/89 are subject to a number of conditions and limitations.

However, the Committee would reiterate (see point 2.5) that Treaty Articles 3(f) and 155 contain powers and instruments which enable the Commission to take firmer and more effective action when and where necessary.

Hence the clear need for staunch cooperation between Member States, and for closer cooperation between the Commission and the national governments.

2.9. Studies and research

Earlier ESC Opinions have dwelt on the studies and research which the Commission has entrusted to outside experts. A summary of their findings appears in the last chapter of the annual report.

On each occasion, the Commission specifies that responsibility for 'the data and views set out therein' rests with the universities and independent consultants who carried out the study. As the studies are published separately, the Committee would prefer to see the Commission set out its own thoughts and conclusions in the report, and bear the same degree of responsibility for them as for the report as a whole.

Publications dealing with competition rules should be more widely circulated at all levels, particularly to the small and medium-sized firms of the newer Member States. In addition to the work already done or under way, a study or guide to technology transfer contracts would be particularly helpful not just to the newer Member States but also to firms in the developing countries.

2.10. The resources of DG IV

As the Regulation on merger control is an *ad hoc* instrument, the Commission has chosen to set up a 'merger task force', bringing together manpower resources already available and Member State nationals with special experience.

It is difficult to judge the accuracy of the forecast for the workload which the Regulation will generate for the task force. Fifty notifications could be an under- or an over-estimate. Reinforcement of Directorates B, C and D might also have allowed greater internal flexibility and, more important, made use of the sectoral experience of each department.

The Committee has no doubts about the need to bolster the aggregate resources of DG IV. It has always stressed this point, being aware of the workload and responsibilities faced by this DG.

3. International relations

3.1. The Commission's international activities

More vigorous cooperation with the United Nations and the Organization for Economic Cooperation and Development (OECD) must be underpinned by increasing Community solidarity.

In GATT too — as ESC Opinions on the GATT negotiations have made clear — the Commission must hold firm, in order to ensure fair competition between the international economic powers.

3.2. The EC and the European Free Trade Association (EFTA)

The Committee has already given a full account of its views on EC-EFTA relations and their future development.[1] The problems stem partly from the differing institutional structures of the two areas, and it is thus pointless to pursue forms of integration which are impossible in the short term at least.

However, competition policy is an exception to this rule : the trading situation calls for respect of common rules, and the safeguarding of a few minimum standards of fairness.

3.3. EC-USA and EC-Japan cooperation

Contact with third countries' anti-trust authorities is always useful and indeed necessary.

The recent Regulation on merger control should not alter communication channels with the USA and Japan, the two main non-EC areas.

The matter is best dealt with by informal bilateral contacts and information swapping. Formal agreements are unnecessary and their drafting would pose legal problems.

Formal commitments have manifold and complex implications (we need only cite the question of extra-territoriality, or the principle of reciprocity which is often invoked improperly or solely as a bargaining chip).

Although the final goal may seem distant, work should continue on the internationalization of anti-trust rules, and harmonization (even partial and gradual) of the rules of international trade.

Done at Brussels, 19 December 1990.

The Chairman
of the Economic and Social Committee

François STAEDELIN

---

[1]   OJ C 182, 23.7.1990, p. 33.

Commission Regulation (EEC) No 2367/90 of 25 July 1990 on the notifications, time-limits and hearings provided for in Council Regulation (EEC) No 4064/89 on the control of concentrations between undertakings

THE COMMISSION OF THE EUROPEAN COMMUNITIES

Having regard to the Treaty establishing the European Economic Community,

Having regard to Council Regulation (EEC) No 4064/89 of 21 December 1989 on the control of concentrations between undertakings,[1] and in particular Article 23 thereof,

Having regard to Council Regulation No 17 of 6 February 1962, First Regulation implementing Articles 85 and 86 of the Treaty,[2] as last amended by the Act of Accession of Spain and Portugal, and in particular Article 24 thereof,

Having regard to Council Regulation (EEC) No 1017/68 of 19 July 1968 applying rules of competition to transport by rail, road and inland waterway,[3] as last amended by the Act of Accession of Spain and Portugal, and in particular Article 29 thereof,

Having regard to Council Regulation (EEC) No 4056/86 of 22 December 1986 laying down detailed rules for the application of Articles 85 and 86 of the Treaty to maritime transport,[4] and in particular Article 26 thereof,

Having regard to Council Regulation (EEC) No 3975/87 of 14 December 1987 laying down detailed rules for the application of the competition rules to undertakings in air transport,[5] and in particular Article 19 thereof,

Having consulted the Advisory Committee on Concentrations, as well as the Advisory Committee on Restrictive Practices and Monopolies in the Transport Industry, in Maritime Transport and in Air Transport,

1. Whereas Article 23 of Regulation (EEC) No 4064/89 empowers the Commission to adopt implementing provisions concerning the form, content and other details of notifications pursuant to Article 4, time-limits pursuant to Article 10, and hearings pursuant to Article 18;

2. Whereas Regulation (EEC) No 4064/89 is based on the principle of compulsory notification of concentrations before they are put into effect; whereas, on the one hand, a notification has important legal consequences which are favourable to the parties, while, on the other hand, failure to comply with the obligation to notify renders the parties liable to a fine and may also entail civil law disadvantages for them; whereas it is therefore necessary in the interests of legal certainty to define precisely the subject matter and content of the information to be provided in the notification;

---

[1]   OJ L 395, 30.12.1989, p. 1.
[2]   OJ 13, 21.2.1962, pp. 204-62.
[3]   OJ L 175, 23.7.1968, p. 1.
[4]   OJ L 378, 31.12.1986, p. 4.
[5]   OJ L 374, 31.12.1987, p. 1.

3. Whereas it is for the parties concerned to make full and honest disclosure to the Commission of the facts and circumstances which are relevant for taking a decision on the notified concentration;

4. Whereas in order to simplify and expedite examination of the notification it is desirable to prescribe that a form be used;

5. Whereas since notification sets in motion legal time-limits for initiating proceedings and for decisions, the conditions governing such time-limits and the time when they become effective must also be determined;

6. Whereas rules must be laid down in the interests of legal certainty for calculating the time-limits provided for in Regulation (EEC) No 4064/89; whereas in particular the beginning and end of the period and the circumstances suspending the running of the period must be determined; whereas the provisions should be based on the principles of Regulation (EEC, Euratom) No 1182/71 of 3 June 1971 determining the rules applicable to periods, dates and time-limits,[1] subject to certain adaptations made necessary by the exceptionally short legal time-limits referred to above;

7. Whereas the provisions relating to the Commission's procedure must be framed in such way as to safeguard fully the right to be heard and the rights of defence;

8. Whereas the Commission will give the parties concerned, if they so request, an opportunity before notification to discuss the intended concentration informally and in strict confidence; whereas in addition it will, after notification, maintain close contact with the parties concerned to the extent necessary to discuss with them any practical or legal problems which it discovers on a first examination of the case and if possible to remove such problems by mutual agreement;

9. Whereas in accordance with the principle of the right to be heard, the parties concerned must be given the opportunity to submit their comments on all the objections which the Commission proposes to take into account in its decisions;

10. Whereas third parties having sufficient interest must also be given the opportunity of expressing their views where they make a written application;

11. Whereas the various persons entitled to submit comments should do so in writing, both in their own interest and in the interest of good administration, without prejudice to their right to request an oral hearing where appropriate to supplement the written procedure; whereas in urgent cases, however, the Commission must be able to proceed immediately to oral hearings of the parties concerned or third parties; whereas in such cases the persons to be heard must have the right to confirm their oral statements in writing;

12. Whereas it is necessary to define the rights of persons who are to be heard, to what extent they should be granted access to the Commission's file and on what conditions they may be represented or assisted;

13. Whereas it is also necessary to define the rules for fixing and calculating the time-limits for reply fixed by the Commission;

14. Whereas the Advisory Committee on Concentrations shall deliver its opinion on the basis of a preliminary draft decision; whereas it must therefore be consulted on a case after the inquiry into that case has been completed; whereas such consultation does not, however, prevent the Commission from re-opening an inquiry if need be,

---

[1]   OJ L 124, 8.6.1971, p. 1.

HAS ADOPTED THIS REGULATION:

SECTION I

NOTIFICATIONS

Article 1

Persons entitled to submit notifications

1. Notifications shall be submitted by the persons or undertakings referred to in Article 4(2) of Regulation (EEC) No 4064/89.

2. Where notifications are signed by representatives of persons or of undertakings, such representatives shall produce written proof that they are authorized to act.

3. Joint notifications should be submitted by a joint representative who is authorized to transmit and to receive documents on behalf of all notifying parties.

Article 2

Submission of notifications

1. Notifications shall be submitted in the manner prescribed by form CO as shown in Annex I. Joint notifications shall be submitted on a single form.

2. Twenty copies of each notification and 15 copies of the supporting documents shall be submitted to the Commission at the address indicated in form CO.

3. The supporting documents shall be either originals or copies of the originals; in the latter case the notifying parties shall confirm that they are true and complete.

4. Notifications shall be in one of the official languages of the Community. This language shall also be the language of the proceedings for the notifying parties. Supporting documents shall be submitted in their original language. Where the original language is not one of the official languages, a translation into the language of the proceedings shall be attached.

Article 3

Information to be provided

1. Notifications shall contain the information requested by form CO. The information must be correct and complete.

2. Material changes in the facts specified in the notification which the notifying parties know or ought to have known must be communicated to the Commission voluntarily and without delay.

3. Incorrect of misleading information shall be deemed to be incomplete information.

Article 4

Effective date of notifications

1. Subject to paragraph 2 notifications shall become effective on the date on which they are received by the Commission.

2. Subject to paragraph 3, where the information contained in the notification is incomplete in a material respect, the Commission shall without delay inform the notifying parties or the joint representative in writing and shall fix an appropriate time-limit for the completion of the information; in such cases, the notification shall become effective on the date on which the complete information is received by the Commission.

3. The Commission may dispense with the obligation to provide any particular information requested by form CO where the Commission considers that such information is not necessary for the examination of the case.

4. The Commission shall without delay acknowledge in writing to the notifying parties or the joint representative receipt of the notification and of any reply to a letter sent by the Commission pursuant to paragraph 2 above.

Article 5

Conversion of notifications

1. Where the Commission finds that the operation notified does not constitute a concentration within the meaning of Article 3 of Regulation (EEC) No 4064/89 it shall inform the notifying parties or the joint representative in writing. In such a case, the Commission may, if requested by the notifying parties, as appropriate and subject to paragraph 2 below, treat the notification as an application within the meaning of Article 2 or a notification within the meaning of Article 4 of Regulation No 17, as an application within the meaning of Article 12 or a notification within the meaning of Article 14 of Regulation (EEC) No 1017/68, as an application within the meaning of Article 12 of Regulation (EEC) No 4056/86 or as an application within the meaning of Article 3(2) or of Article 5 of Regulation (EEC) No 3975/87.

2. In cases referred to in paragraph 1, second sentence, the Commission may require that the information given in the notification be supplemented within an appropriate time-limit fixed by it in so far as this is necessary for assessing the operation on the basis of the abovementioned Regulations. The application or notification shall be deemed to fulfil the requirements of such Regulations from the date of the original notification where the additional information is received by the Commission within the time-limit fixed.

SECTION II

TIME-LIMITS FOR INITIATING PROCEEDINGS AND FOR DECISIONS

Article 6

Beginning of the time-limit

1. The periods referred to in Article 10(1) of Regulation (EEC) No 4064/89 shall start at the beginning of the day following the effective date of the notification, within the meaning of Article 4(1) and (2) of this Regulation.

2. The period referred to in Article 10(3) of Regulation (EEC) No 4064/89 shall start at the beginning of the day following the day on which proceedings were initiated.

3. Where the first day of a period is not a working day within the meaning of Article 19, the period shall start at the beginning of the following working day.

Article 7

End of the time-limit

1. The period referred to in the first subparagraph of Article 10(1) of Regulation (EEC) No 4064/89 shall end with the expiry of the day which in the month following that in which the period began falls on the same date as the day from which the period runs. Where such a day does not occur in that month, the period shall end with the expiry of the last day of that month.

2. The period referred to in the second subparagraph of Article 10(1) of Regulation (EEC) No 4064/89 shall end with the expiry of the day which in the sixth week following that in which the period began is the same day of the week as the day from which the period runs.

3. The period referred to in Article 10(3) of Regulation (EEC) No 4064/89 shall end with the expiry of the day which in the fourth month following that in which the period began falls on the same date as the day from which the period runs. Where such a day does not occur in that month, the period shall end with the expiry of the last day of that month.

4. Where the last day of the period is not a working day within the meaning of Article 19, the period shall end with the expiry of the following working day.

5. Paragraphs 2 to 4 above shall be subject to the provisions of Article 8.

Article 8

Addition of holidays

Where public holidays or other holidays of the Commission as defined in Article 19 fall within the periods referred to in Article 10(1) and in Article 10(3) of Regulation (EEC) No 4064/89, these periods shall be extended by a corresponding number of days.

Article 9

Suspension of the time-limit

1. The period referred to in Article 10(3) of Regulation (EEC) No 4064/89 shall be suspended where the Commission, pursuant to Articles 11(5) or 13(3) of the same Regulation, has to take a decision because:

(a) information which the Commission has requested pursuant to Article 11(2) of Regulation (EEC) No 4064/89 from an undertaking involved in a concentration is not provided or not provided in full within the time-limit fixed by the Commission;

(b) an undertaking involved in the concentration has refused to submit to an investigation deemed necessary by the Commission on the basis of Article 13(1) of Regulation (EEC) No 4064/89 or to cooperate in the carrying out of such an investigation in accordance with the abovementioned provision;

(c) the notifying parties have failed to inform the Commission of material changes in the facts specified in the notification.

2. The period referred to in Article 10(3) of Regulation (EEC) No 4064/89 shall be suspended:

(a) in the cases referred to in subparagraph 1(a) above, for the period between the end of the time-limit fixed in the request for information and the receipt of the complete and correct information required by decision;

(b) in the cases referred to in subparagraph 1(b) above, for the period between the unsuccessful attempt to carry out the investigation and the completion of the investigation ordered by decision;

(c) in the cases referred to in subparagraph 1(c) above, for the period between the occurrence of the change in the facts referred to therein and the receipt of the complete and correct information requested by decision or the completion of the investigation ordered by decision.

3. The suspension of the time-limit shall begin on the day following that on which the event causing the suspension occurred. It shall end with the expiry of the day on which the reason for suspension is removed. Where such day is not a working day within the meaning of Article 19, the suspension of the time-limit shall end with the expiry of the following working day.

Article 10

Compliance with the time-limit

The time-limits referred to in Article 10(1) and (3) of Regulation (EEC) No 4064/89 shall be met where the Commission has taken the relevant decision before the end of the period. Notification of the decision to the undertakings concerned must follow without delay.

SECTION III

HEARING OF THE PARTIES AND OF THIRD PARTIES

Article 11

Decisions on the suspension of concentrations

1. Where the Commission intends to take a decision under Article 7(2) of Regulation (EEC) No 4064/89 or a decision under Article 7(4) of that Regulation which adversely affects the parties, it shall, pursuant to Article 18(1) of that Regulation, inform the parties concerned in writing of its objections and shall fix a time-limit within which they may make known their views.

2. Where the Commission pursuant to Article 18(2) of Regulation (EEC) No 4064/89 has taken a decision referred to in paragraph 1 provisionally without having given the parties concerned the opportunity to make known their views, it shall without delay and in any event before the expiry of the suspension send them the text of the provisional decision and shall fix a time-limit within which they may make known their views.

Once the parties concerned have made known their views, the Commission shall take a final decision annulling, amending or confirming the provisional decision. Where the parties concerned have not made known their view within the time-limit fixed, the Commission's provisional decision shall become final with the expiry of that period.

3. The parties concerned shall make known their views in writing or orally within the time-limit fixed. They may confirm their oral statements in writing.

Article 12

Decisions on the substance of the case

1. Where the Commission intends to take a decision pursuant to Article 8(2), second subparagraph, Article 8(3)(4) and (5), Article 14 or Article 15 of Regulation (EEC) No 4064/89, it shall, before consulting the Advisory Committee on Concentrations, hold a hearing of the parties concerned pursuant to Article 18 of that Regulation.

2. The Commission shall inform the parties concerned in writing of its objections. The communication shall be addressed to the notifying parties or to the joint representative. The Commission shall, when giving notice of objections, fix a time-limit within which the parties concerned may inform the Commission of their views.

3. Having informed the parties of its objections, the Commission shall upon request give the parties concerned access to the file for the purposes of preparing their observations. Documents shall not be accessible in so far as they contain business secrets of other parties concerned or of third parties, or other confidential information including sensitive commercial information the disclosure of which would have a significant adverse effect on the supplier of such information or where they are internal documents of the authorities.

4. The parties concerned shall, within the time-limit fixed, make known in writing their views on the Commission's objections. They may in their written comments set out all matters relevant to the case and may attach any relevant documents in proof of the facts set out. They may also propose that the Commission hear persons who may corroborate those facts.

Article 13

Oral hearings

1. The Commission shall afford parties concerned who have so requested in their written comments the opportunity to put forward their arguments orally, if those persons show a sufficient interest or if the Commission proposes to impose a fine or periodic penalty payment on them. It may also in other cases afford the parties concerned the opportunity of expressing their views orally.

2. The Commission shall summon the persons to be heard to attend on such date as it shall appoint.

3. It shall forthwith transmit a copy of the summons to the competent authorities of the Member States, who may appoint an official to take part in the hearing.

Article 14

Hearings

1. Hearings shall be conducted by persons appointed by the Commission for that purpose.

2. Persons summoned to attend shall either appear in person or be represented by legal representatives or representatives authorized by their constitution. Undertakings and associations of undertakings may be represented by a duly authorized agent appointed from among their permanent staff.

3. Persons heard by the Commission may be assisted by lawyers or university teachers who are entitled to plead before the Court of Justice of the European Communities in accordance with Article 17 of the Protocol on the Statute (EEC) of the Court of Justice, or by other qualified persons.

4. Hearings shall not be public. Persons shall be heard separately or in the presence of other persons summoned to attend. In the latter case, regard shall be had to the legitimate interest of the undertakings in the protection of their business secrets.

5. The statements made by each person heard shall be recorded.

Article 15

Hearing of third parties

1. If natural or legal persons showing a sufficient interest, and especially members of the administrative or management organs of the undertakings concerned or recognized workers' representatives of those undertakings, apply in writing to be heard pursuant to the second sentence of Article 18(4) of Regulation (EEC) No 4064/89, the Commission shall inform them in writing of the nature and subject matter of the procedure and shall fix a time-limit within which they may make known their views.

2. The third parties referred to in paragraph 1 above shall make known their views in writing or orally within the time-limit fixed. They may confirm their oral statements in writing.

3. The Commission may likewise afford to any other third parties the opportunity of expressing their views.

SECTION IV

MISCELLANEOUS PROVISIONS

Article 16

Transmission of documents

1. Transmission of documents and summonses from the Commission to the addressees may be effected in any of the following ways:

(a) delivery by hand against receipt;

(b) registered letter with acknowledgement of receipt;

(c) fax with a request for acknowledgement of receipt;

(d) telex.

2. Subject to Article 18(1), paragraph 1 above also applies to the transmission of documents from the parties concerned or from third parties to the Commission.

3. Where a document is sent by telex or by fax, it shall be presumed that it has been received by the addressee on the day on which it was sent.

Article 17

Setting of time-limits

1. In fixing the time-limits provided for in Articles 4(2), 5(2), 11(1) and (2), 12(2) and 15(1), the Commission shall have regard to the time required for preparation of statements and to the urgency of the case. It shall also take account of public holidays in the country of receipt of the Commission's communication.

2. The day on which the addressee received a communication shall not be taken into account for the purpose of fixing time-limits.

Article 18

Receipt of documents by the Commission

1. Subject to Article 4(1), notifications must be delivered to the Commission at the address indicated in form CO or have been dispatched by registered letter before expiry of the period referred to in Article 4(1) of Regulation (EEC) No 4064/89. Additional information requested to complete notifications pursuant to Article 4(2) or to supplement notifications pursuant to Article 5(2) of this Regulation must reach the Commission at the aforesaid address or have been dispatched by registered letter before the expiry of the time-limit fixed in each case. Written comments on Commission communications pursuant to Articles 11(1) and (2), 12(2) and 15(1) must be delivered to the Commission at the aforesaid address before the time-limit fixed in each case.

2. Where the last day of a period referred to in paragraph 1 is a day by which documents must be received and that day is not a working day within the meaning of Article 19, the period shall end with the expiry of the following working day.

3. Where the last day of a period referred to in paragraph 1 is a day by which documents must be dispatched and that day is a Saturday, Sunday or public holiday in the country of dispatch, the period shall end with the expiry of the following working day in that country.

Article 19

Definition of Commission working days

The term 'working days' in Articles 6(3), 7(4), 9(3) and 18(2) means all days other than Saturdays, Sundays, public holidays set out in Annex II and other holidays as determined by the Commission and published in the *Official Journal of the European Communities* before the beginning of each year.

Article 20

Entry into force

This Regulation shall enter into force on 21 September 1990.

This Regulation shall be binding in its entirety and directly applicable in all Member States.

Done at Brussels, 25 July 1990.

For the Commission

Leon BRITTAN

Vice-President

Annex I

Form CO relating to the notification of a concentration pursuant to Council Regulation (EEC) No 4064/89

A — Introduction

This form specifies the information to be provided by an undertaking or undertakings when notifying the Commission of a concentration with a Community dimension. A 'concentration' is defined in Article 3 and 'Community dimension' by Article 1 of Regulation (EEC) No 4064/89.

Your attention is particularly drawn to Regulation (EEC) No 4064/89 and to Commission Regulation (EEC) No 2367/90. In particular you should note that:

(a) all information requested by this form must be provided. However if, in good faith, you are unable to provide a response to a question or can only respond to a limited extent on the basis of available information, indicate this and give reasons. If you consider that any particular information requested by this form may not be necessary for the Commission's examination of the case, you may ask the Commission to dispense with the obligation to provide that information, under Article 4(3) of Regulation (EEC) No 2367/90;

(b) unless all sections are completed in full or good reasons are given explaining why it has not been possible to complete unanswered questions (for example, because of the unavailability of information on a target company during a contested bid) the notification will be incomplete and will only become effective on the date on which all the information is received. The notification will be deemed to be incomplete if information is incorrect or misleading;

(c) incorrect or misleading information where supplied intentionally or negligently could make you liable to a fine.

B — Who must notify

In the case of a merger (within the meaning of Article 3(1)(a) of Regulation (EEC) No 4064/89 or the acquisition of joint control in an undertaking within the meaning of Article 3(1)(b) of Regulation (EEC) No 4064/89, the notification shall be completed jointly by the parties to the merger or by those acquiring joint control as the case may be.

In the case of the acquisition of a controlling interest in an undertaking by another, the acquirer must complete the notification.

In the case of a public bid to acquire an undertaking, the bidder must complete the notification.

Each party completing the notification is responsible for the accuracy of the information which it provides.

For the purposes of this form 'the parties to the concentration' ('the parties') includes the undertaking in which a controlling interest is being acquired or which is the subject of a public bid.

C — Supporting documentation

The completed notification must be accompanied by the following:

(a) copies of the final or most recent versions of all documents bringing about the concentration, whether by agreement between the parties concerned, acquisition of a controlling interest or a public bid:

(b) in a public bid, a copy of the offer document. If unavailable on notification it should be submitted as soon as possible and not later than when it is posted to shareholders;

(c) copies of the most recent annual reports and accounts of all the parties to the concentration;

(d) copies of reports or analyses which have been prepared for the purposes of the concentration and from which information has been taken in order to provide the information requested in Sections 5 and 6;

(e) a list and short description of the contents of all other analyses, reports, studies and surveys prepared by or for any of the notifying parties for the purpose of assessing or analysing the proposed concentration with respect to competitive conditions, competitors (actual and potential), and market conditions. Each item in the list must include the name and position held of the author.

D — How to notify

The notification must be completed in one of the official languages of the European Community. This language shall thereafter be the language of the proceedings for all notifying parties.

The information requested by this form is to be set out using the sections and paragraph numbers of the form.

Supporting documents shall be submitted in their original language; where this is not an official language of the Community they shall be translated into the language of the proceedings (Article 2(4) of Regulation (EEC) No 2367/90).

The supporting documents may be originals or copies of the originals. In the latter case the notifying party shall confirm that they are true and complete.

The financial data requested in Section 2.4 below must be provided in ecus at the average conversion rates prevailing for the years or other period in question.

Twenty copies of each notification and 15 copies of all supporting documents must be provided.

The notification should be sent to:

Commission of the European Communities,
Directorate-General for Competition (DG IV),
Merger Task Force (Cort. 150),
200 rue de la Loi,
B-1049 Brussels;

or be delivered by hand during normal Commission working hours at the following address:

Commission of the European Communities,
Directorate-General for Competition (DG IV),
Merger Task Force,
150 avenue de Cortenberg,
B-1040 Brussels.

E — Secrecy

Article 214 of the Treaty and Article 17(2) of Regulation (EEC) No 4064/89 require the Commission and the Member States, their officials and other servants not to disclose information they have acquired through the application of the Regulation of the kind covered by the obligation of professional secrecy. The same principle must also apply to protect confidentiality as between notifying parties.

If you believe that your interests would be harmed if any of the information you are asked to supply was to be published or otherwise divulged to other parties, submit this information separately with each page clearly marked 'Business secrets'. You should also give reasons why this information should not be divulged or published.

In the case of mergers or joint acquisitions, or in other cases where the notification is completed by more than one of the parties, business secrets may be submitted under separate cover, and referred to in the notification as an annex. In such cases the notification will be considered complete on receipt of all the annexes.

F — References

All references contained in this form are to the relevant articles and paragraphs of Council Regulation (EEC) No 4064/89.

SECTION I

1.1. *Information on notifying party (or parties)*

Give details of:

1.1.1. name and address of undertaking,

1.1.2. nature of the undertaking's business,

1.1.3. name, address, telephone, fax and/or telex of, and position held by, the person to be contacted.

1.2. *Information on other parties to the concentration*[1,2]

For each party to the concentration (except the notifying party) give details of:

1.2.1. name and address of undertaking,

1.2.2. nature of the undertaking's business,

1.2.3. name, address, telephone, fax and/or telex of, and position held by, the person to be contacted.

---

[1]   A concentration is defined in Article 3.
[2]   This includes the target company in the case of an contested bid, in which case the details should be completed as far as is possible.

1.3. *Address for service*

Give an address in Brussels if available to which all communications may be made and documents delivered in accordance with Article 1(4) of Commission Regulation (EEC) No 2367/90.

1.4. *Appointment of representatives*

Article 1(2) of Commission Regulation (EEC) 2367/90 states that where notifications are signed by representatives of undertakings, such representatives shall produce written proof that they are authorized to act. Such written authorization must accompany the notification and the following details of the representatives of the notifying party or parties and other parties to the concentration are to be given below:

1.4.1. is this a joint notification?

1.4.2. if 'yes', has a joint representative been appointed?

if 'yes', please give the details requested in 1.4.3. to 1.4.6. below;

if 'no', please give details of the representatives who have been authorized to act for each of the parties to the concentration indicating who they represent;

1.4.3. name of representative;

1.4.4. address of representative;

1.4.5. name of person to be contacted (and address if different from 1.4.4);

1.4.6. telephone, fax and/or telex.

SECTION 2

Details of the concentration

2.1. Briefly describe the nature of the concentration being notified. In doing so state:

(i)   whether the proposed concentration is a full legal merger, an acquisition, a concentrative joint venture or a contract or other means conferring direct or indirect control within the meaning of Article 3(3);

(ii) whether the whole or parts of parties are subject to the concentration;

(iii) whether any public offer for the securities of one party by another has the support of the former's supervisory boards of management or other bodies legally representing the party concerned.

2.2. List the economic sectors involved in the concentration.

2.3. Give a brief explanation of the economic and financial details of the concentration. In doing so provide, where relevant, information about the following:

(i)   any financial or other support received from whatever source (including public authorities) by any of the parties and the nature and amount of this support,

(ii) the proposed or expected date of any major events designed to bring about the completion of the concentration,

(iii) the proposed structure of ownership   control after the completion of the concentration.

2.4. For each of the parties, the notifying party shall provide the following data for the last three financial years;

2.4.1. worldwide turnover, [1]

2.4.2. Community-wide turnover, [1][2]

2.4.3. turnover in each Member State, [1,2]

2.4.4. the Member State, if any, in which more than two-thirds of Community-wide turnover is achieved, [1,2]

2.4.5. profits before tax worldwide, [3]

2.4.6. number of employees worldwide. [4]

SECTION 3

Ownership and control [5]

For each of the parties provide a list of all undertakings belonging to the same group. This list must include:

3.1. all undertakings controlled by the parties, directly or indirectly, within the meaning of Article 3(3);

3.2. all undertakings or persons controlling the parties directly or indirectly within the meaning of Article 3(3);

3.3. for each undertaking or person identified in 3.2 above, a complete list of all undertakings controlled by them directly or indirectly, within the meaning of Article 3(3).

For each entry to the list the nature and means of control shall be specified;

3.4. provide details of acquisitions made during the last three years by the groups identified above, of undertakings active in affected markets as defined in Section 5 below.

The information sought in this section may be illustrated by the use of charts or diagrams where this helps to give a better understanding of the pre-concentration structure of ownership and control of the undertakings.

SECTION 4

Personal and financial links

With respect to each undertaking or person disclosed in response to Section 3 provide:

---

[1]   See Article 5 for the definition of turnover and note the special provisions for credit, insurance, other financial institutions and joint undertakings.
  For insurance undertakings, credit and other financial institutions, Community residents and residents of a Member State are defined as natural or legal persons having their residence in a Member State, thereby following the respective national legislation. The corporate customer is to be treated as resident in the country in which it is legally incorporated. For the calculation of turnover, the notifying party should also refer to the examples: Guidance Note I for credit and other financial institutions: Guidance Note II for insurance undertakings: Guidance Note III for joint undertakings.
[2]   See Guidance Note IV for the calculation of turnover in one Member State with respect to Community-wide turnover.
[3]   'Profits before tax' shall comprise profit it on ordinary activities before tax on profit.,
[4]   Employees shall comprise all persons employed in the enterprise who have a contract of employment and receive remuneration.
[5]   See Article 3(3) to (5).

4.1. a list of all other undertakings which are active on affected markets (affected markets are defined in Section 5) in which the undertakings of the group hold individually or collectively 10% or more of the voting rights or issued share capital. In each case state the percentage held;

4.2. a list of all other undertakings which are active on affected markets in which the persons disclosed in response to Section 3 hold 10% or more of the voting rights or issued share capital. In each case state the percentage held;

4.3. a list for each undertaking of the members of their boards of management who are also members of the boards of management or of the supervisory boards of any other undertaking which is active on affected markets; and (where applicable) for each undertaking a list of the members of their supervisory boards who are also members of the boards of management of any other undertaking which is active on affected markets;

in each case stating the name of the other undertaking and the position held.

Information provided here may be illustrated by the use of charts or diagrams where this helps to give a better understanding.

SECTION 5

Information on affected markets

The notifying party shall provide the data requested having regard to the following definitions:

Product markets

A relevant product market comprises all those products and/or services which are regarded as interchangeable or substitutable by the consumer, by reason of the product's characteristics, their prices and their intended use.

A relevant product market may in some cases be composed of a number of individual product groups. An individual product group is a product or small group of products which present largely identical physical or technical characteristics and are fully interchangeable. The difference between products within the group will be small and usually only a matter of brand and/or image. The product market will usually be the classification used by the undertaking in its marketing operations.

Relevant geographic market

The relevant geographic market comprises the area in which the undertakings concerned are involved in the supply of products or services, in which the conditions of competition are sufficiently homogeneous and which can be distinguished from neighbouring areas because, in particular, conditions of competition are appreciably different in those areas.

Factors relevant to the assessment of the relevant geographic market include the nature and characteristics of the products or services concerned, the existence of entry barriers or consumer preferences, appreciable differences of the undertakings' market shares between neighbouring areas or substantial price differences.

Affected markets

Affected markets consist of relevant product markets or individual product groups, in the Common Market or a Member State or, where different, in any relevant geographic market where:

(a) two or more of the parties (including undertakings belonging to the same group as defined in Section 3) are engaged in business activities in the same product market or individual product group and where the concentration will lead to a combined market share of 10% or more. These are horizontal relationships; or

(b) any of the parties (including undertakings belonging to the same group as defined in Section 3) is engaged in business activities in a product market which is upstream or downstream of a product market or individual product group in which any other party is engaged and any of their market shares is 10% or more, regardless of whether or not there is any existing supplier/customer relationship between the parties concerned. These are vertical relationships.

1 — Explanation of the affected relevant product markets

5.1. Describe each affected relevant product market and explain why the products and/or services in these markets are included (and why others are excluded) by reason of their characteristics, their prices and their intended use.

5.2. List the individual product groups defined internally by your undertaking for marketing purposes which are covered by each relevant product market described under 5.1 above.

II — Market data on affected markets

For each affected relevant product market and, where different, individual product group, for each of the last three financial years:

(a) for the Community as a whole;

(b) individually for each Member State where the parties (including undertakings belonging to the same group as defined in Section 3) do business;

(c) and where different, for any relevant geographic market,

provide the following:

5.3. an estimate of the value of the market and, where appropriate, of the volume (for example in units shipped or delivered) of the market. [1] If available, include statistics prepared by other sources to illustrate your answers. Also provide a forecast of the evolution of demand on the affected markets;

5.4. the turnover of each of the groups to which the parties belong (as defined in Section 3);

5.5. an estimate of the market share of each of the groups to which the parties belong;

5.6. an estimate of the market share (in value and where appropriate volume) of all competitors having at least 10% of the geographic market under consideration. Provide the name, address and telephone number of these undertakings;

5.7. a comparison of prices charged by the groups to which the parties belong in each of the Member States and a similar comparison of such price levels between the Community and its major trading partners (e.g. the United States of America, Japan and EFTA);

5.8. an estimate of the value (and where appropriate volume) and source of imports to the relevant geographic market;

5.9. the proportion of such imports that are derived from the groups to which the parties belong;

5.10. an estimate of the extent to which any of these imports are affected by any tariff or non-tariff barriers to trade.

III — Market data on conglomerate aspects

In the absence of horizontal or vertical relationships, where any of the parties (including undertakings belonging to the same group as defined in Section 3) holds a market share of 25% or more for any product market or individual product group, provide the following information:

---

[1]   The value and volume of a market should reflect output less exports plus imports for the geographic market under consideration.

5.11. a description of each relevant product market and explain why the products and/or services in these markets are included (and why others are excluded) by reason of their characteristics, their prices and their intended use;

5.12. a list of the individual product groups, defined internally by your undertaking for marketing purposes which are covered by each relevant product market described;

5.13. an estimate of the value of the market and the market shares of each of the groups to which the parties belong for each affected relevant product market and, where different, individual product group, for the last financial year:

(a) for the Community as a whole;

(b) individually for each Member State where the groups to which the parties belong do business;

(c) and where different, for any relevant geographic market.

In each response in Section 5 the notifying party shall explain the basis of the estimates used or assumptions made.

SECTION 6

General conditions in affected markets

The following information shall be provided in relation to the affected relevant product markets and, where different, affected individual product groups:

Record of market entry

6.1. Over the last five years (or a longer period if this is more appropriate) has there been any significant entry to these markets in the Community? If the answer is 'yes', provide information on these entrants, estimating their current market shares.

6.2. In the opinion of the notifying party are there undertakings (including those at present operating only in extra-Community markets) that could enter the Community's markets? If the answer is 'yes', provide information on these potential entrants.

6.3. In the opinion of the notifying party what is the likelihood of significant market entry over the next five years?

Factors influencing market entry

6.4. Describe the various factors influencing entry into affected markets that exist in the present case, examining entry from both a geographical and product viewpoint. In so doing take account of the following where appropriate:

(i) the total costs of entry (capital, promotion, advertising, necessary distribution systems, servicing, etc.) on a scale equivalent to a significant viable competitor, indicating the market share of such a competitor;

(ii) to what extent is entry to the markets influenced by the requirement of government authorization or standard setting in any form? Are there any legal or regulatory controls on entry to these markets?

(iii) to what extent is entry to the markets influenced by the availability of raw materials?

(iv) to what extent is entry to the markets influenced by the length of contracts between an undertaking and its suppliers and/or customers?

(v) describe the importance of licensing patents, know-how and other rights in these markets.

Vertical integration

6.5. Describe the nature and extent of vertical integration of each of the parties.

Research and development

6.6. Give an account of the importance of research and development in the ability of a firm operating on the relevant market to compete in the long term. Explain the nature of the research and development in affected markets carried out by the undertakings to the concentration.

In so doing take account of the following where appropriate:

(i) the research and development intensities[1] for these markets and the relevant research and development intensities for the parties concerned;

(ii) the course of technological development for these markets over an appropriate time period (including developments in products and/or services, production processes, distribution systems, etc.);

(iii) the major innovations that have been made in these markets over this time period and the undertakings responsible for these innovations;

(iv) the cycle of innovation in these markets and where the parties are in this cycle of innovation;

(v) describe the extent to which the parties concerned are licensees or licensors of patents, know-how and other rights in affected markets.

Distribution and service systems

6.7. Explain the distribution channels and service networks that exist on the affected markets. In so doing take account of the following where appropriate:

(i) the distribution systems prevailing on the market and their importance. To what extent is distribution performed by third parties and/or undertakings belonging to the same group as the parties as disclosed in Section 3?

(ii) the service networks (for example maintenance and repair) prevailing and their importance in these markets. To what extent are such services performed by third parties and/or undertakings belonging to the same group as the parties as disclosed in Section 3?

Competitive environment

6.8. Give details (names, addresses and contacts) of the five largest suppliers to the notifying parties and their individual share of the purchases of the notifying parties.

6.9. Give details (names, addresses and contacts) of the five largest customers of the notifying parties and their individual share of the sales of the notifying parties.

6.10. Explain the structure of supply and demand in affected markets. This explanation should allow the Commission to appreciate further the competitive environment in which the parties carry out their business. In so doing take account of the following where appropriate:

(i) the phases of the markets in terms of, for example, take-off, expansion, maturity and decline. In the opinion of the notifying party, where are the affected products in these phases?

(ii) the structure of supply. Give details of the various identifiable categories that comprise the supply side and describe the 'typical supplier' of each category;

(iii) the structure of demand. Give details of the various identifiable groups that comprise the demand side and describe the 'typical customer' of each group;

---

[1] Research and development intensity is defined as research and development expenditure as a proportion of turnover.

(iv) whether public authorities, government agencies or State enterprises or similar bodies are important participants as sources of supply or demand. In any instance where this is so give details of this participation;

(v) the total Community-wide capacity for the last three years. Over the period what proportion of this capacity is accounted for by the parties and what have been their rates of capacity utilization?

Cooperative agreements

6.11. To what extent do cooperative agreements (horizontal and/or vertical) exist in the affected markets?

6.12. Give details of the most important cooperative agreements engaged in by the parties in the affected markets, such as licensing agreements, research and development, specialization, distribution, long-term supply and exchange of information agreements.

Trade associations

6.13. List the names and addresses of the principal trade associations in the affected markets.

World-wide context

6.14. Describe the worldwide context of the proposed concentration indicating the position of the parties in this market.

SECTION 7

General matters

7.1. Describe how the proposed concentration is likely to affect the interests of intermediate and ultimate consumers, and the development of technical progress.

7.2. In the event that the Commission finds that the operation notified does not constitute a concentration within the meaning of Article 3 of Regulation (EEC) No 4064/89, do you request that it be treated as an application within the meaning of Article 2 or a notification within the meaning of Article 4 of Regulation No 17, as an application within the meaning of Article 12 or a notification within the meaning of Article 14 of Regulation (EEC) No 1017/68, as an application within the meaning of Article 12 of Regulation (EEC) No 4056/86 or as an application within the meaning of Article 3(2) or Article 5 of Regulation (EEC) No 3975/87?

SECTION 8

Declaration

The notification must conclude with the following declaration which is to be signed by or on behalf of all the notifying parties.

The undersigned declare that the information given in this notification is correct to the best of their knowledge and belief, that all estimates are identified as such and are their best estimates of the underlying facts and that all the opinions expressed are sincere.

They are aware of the provisions of Article 14(1)(b) of Regulation (EEC) No 4064/89.

Place and date:

Signatures:

GUIDANCE NOTE I[1]

Calculation of turnover for credit and other financial institutions

(Article 5(3)(a))

For the calculation of turnover for credit institutions and other financial institutions, we give the following example (proposed merger between bank A and bank B)

I — Consolidated balance sheets

(in million ECU)

Assets	Bank A	Bank B
Loans and advances to credit institutions	20 000	1 000
to credit institutions within the Community	(10 000)	(500)
to credit institutions within one (and the same) Member State X	(5 000)	(500)
Loans and advances to customers	60 000	4 000
to Community residents	(30 000)	(2 000)
to residents of one (and the same) Member State X	(15 000)	(500)
Other assets	20 000	1 000
Total assets	100 000	6 000

II — Calculation of turnover

In place of turnover, the following figures shall be used:

	Bank A	*Bank B*
1. *Aggregate worldwide turnover* is replaced by one-tenth of total assets the total sum of which is more than ECU 5 000 million.	10 000	600

2. *Community-wide turnover*

is replaced by, for each bank, one-tenth of total assets multiplied by the ratio between loans and advances to credit institutions and customers within the Community and the total sum of loans and advances to credit institutions and customers.

---

[1]   In the following guidance notes, the terms 'institution' or 'undertaking' are used subject to the exact delimitation in each case.

	Bank A	Bank B
This is calculated as follows:		
one-tenth of total assets	10 000	600
which is multiplied for each bank by the ratio between:		
loans and advances to credit institutions and customers	10 000	500
within the Community	30 000	2 000
	40 000	2 500
and		
the total sum of loans and advances to credit institutions	20 000	1 000
and customers	60 000	4 000
	80 000	5 000

For
Bank A: 10 000 multiplied by (40 000 : 80 000) = 5 000
Bank B: 600 multiplied by (2 500 : 5 000) =   300
which exceeds ECU 250 million for each of the banks.

3. *Total turnover within one (and the same) Member State X*

	Bank A	Bank B
is replaced by one-tenth of total assets:	10 000	600

which is multiplied for each bank by the ratio between loans and advances to credit institutions and customers within one and the same Member State X and to the total sum of loans and advances to credit institutions and customers.

	Bank A	Bank B
This is calculated as follows:		
loans and advances to credit institutions and customers	5 000	500
within one (and the same) Member State X	15 000	500
	20 000	1 000
and		
the total sum of loans and advances to credit institutions		
and customers	80 000	5 000

For
Bank A: 10 000 multiplied by (20 000 : 80 000) = 2 500
Bank B: 600 multiplied by (1 000 : 5 000) =   120

Result:
50% of bank A's and 40% of bank B's Community-wide turnover are achieved in one (and the same) Member State X.

III — Conclusion

Since

(a) the aggregate worldwide turnover of bank A plus bank B is more than ECU 5 000 million;

(b) the Community-wide turnover of each of the banks is more than ECU 250 million; and

(c) each of the banks achieves less than two-thirds of its Community-wide turnover in one (and the same) Member State,

the proposed merger would fall under the scope of the Regulation.

GUIDANCE NOTE II

Calculation of turnover for insurance undertakings

(Article 5(3)(a))

For the calculation of turnover for insurance undertakings, we give the following example (proposed concentration between insurances A and B):

I — Consolidated profit and loss account

(in million ECU)

Income	Insurance A		Insurance B	
Gross premiums written	5 000		300	
gross premiums received from Community residents		(4 500)		(300)
gross premiums received from residents of one (and the same) Member State X		(3 600)		(270)
Other income	500		50	
Total income	5 500		350	

II — Calculation of turnover

1. *Aggregate worldwide turnover*

is replaced by the value of gross premiums written worldwide, the sum of which is ECU 5 300 million.

2. *Community-wide turnover*

is replaced, for each insurance undertaking, by the value of gross premiums written with Community residents. For each of the insurance undertakings, this amount is more than ECU 250 million.

3. *Turnover within one (and the same) Member State X*

is replaced, for insurance undertakings, by the value of gross premiums written with residents of one (and the same) Member State X.

For insurance A, it achieves 80% of its gross premiums written with Community residents within Member State X, whereas for insurance B, it achieves 90% of its gross premiums written with Community residents in that Member State X.

III — Conclusion

Since

(a) the aggregate worldwide turnover of insurances A and B, as replaced by the value of gross premiums written worldwide, is more than ECU 5 000 million;

(b) for each of the insurance undertakings, the value of gross premiums written with Community residents is more than ECU 250 million; but

(c) each of the insurance undertakings achieves more than two-thirds of its gross premiums written with Community residents in one (and the same) Member State X,

the proposed concentration would not fall under the scope of the Regulation.

GUIDANCE NOTE III

Calculation of turnover for joint undertakings

A — Creation of a joint undertaking (Article 3(2))

In a case where two (or more) undertakings create a joint undertaking that constitutes a concentration, turnover is calculated for the undertakings concerned.

B — Existence of a joint undertaking (Article 5(5))

For the calculation of turnover in case of the existence of a joint undertaking C between two undertakings A and B concerned in a concentration, we give the following example:

I — Profit and loss accounts

(in million ECU)

Turnover	Undertaking A	Undertaking B
Sales revenues worldwide	10 000	2 000
Community	(8 000)	(1 500)
Member State Y	(4 600)	(900)

(in million ECU)

Turnover	Joint undertaking C	
Sales revenues worldwide	100	
with undertaking A		(20)
with undertaking B		(10)
Turnover with third undertakings	70	
Community-wide		(60)
in Member State Y		(50)

II — Consideration of the joint undertaking

(a) The undertaking C is jointly controlled (in the meaning of Article 3(3) and (4)) by the undertakings A and B concerned by the concentration, irrespective of any third undertaking participating in that undertaking C.

(b) The undertaking C is not consolidated by A and B in their profit and loss accounts.

(c) The turnover of C resulting from operations with A and B shall not be taken into account.

(d) The turnover of C resulting from operations with any third undertaking shall be apportioned equally amongst the undertakings A and B, irrespective of their individual shareholdings in C.

(e) Any joint undertaking existing between one of the undertakings concerned and any third undertaking shall (unless already consolidated) not be taken into account.

III — Calculation of turnover

(a) Undertaking A's aggregate worldwide turnover shall be calculated as follows: ECU 10 000 million and 50% of C's worldwide turnover with third undertakings (i.e. ECU 35 million), the sum of which is ECU 10 035 million.

Undertaking B's aggregate worldwide turnover shall be calculated as follows: ECU 2 000 million and 50% of C's worldwide turnover with third undertakings (i.e. ECU 35 million), the sum of which is ECU 2 035 million.

(b) The aggregate worldwide turnover of the undertakings concerned is ECU 12 070 million.

(c) Undertaking A achieves ECU 4 025 million within Member State Y (50% of C's turnover in this Member State taken into account), and a Community-wide turnover of ECU 8 030 million (including 50% of C's Community-wide turnover);

and undertaking B achieves ECU 925 million within Member State Y (50% of C's turnover in this Member State taken into account), and a Community-wide turnover of ECU 1 530 million (including 50% of C's Community-wide turnover.

IV — Conclusion

Since

(a) the aggregate worldwide turnover of undertakings A and B is more than ECU 5 000 million,

(b) each of the undertakings concerned by the concentration achieves more than ECU 250 million within the Community,

(c) each of the undertakings concerned (undertaking A 50.1% and undertaking B 60.5%) achieves less than two-thirds of its Community-wide turnover in one (and the same) Member State Y,

the proposed concentration would fall under the scope of the Regulation.

GUIDANCE NOTE IV

Application of the two-thirds rule

(Article 1)

For the application of the two-thirds rule for undertakings, we give the following examples (proposed concentration between undertakings A and B):

I — Consolidated profit and loss accounts

Example 1

(in million ECU)

Turnover	Undertaking A	Undertaking B
Sales revenues worldwide	10 000	500
within the Community	(8 000)	(400)
in Member State X	(6 000)	(200)

Example 2(a)

(in million ECU)

Turnover	Undertaking A	Undertaking B
Sales revenues worldwide	4 800	500
within the Community	(2 400)	(400)
in Member State X	(2 100)	(300)

Example 2(b)

same figures as in example 2(a), *but* undertaking B achieves ECU 300 million in Member State Y.

II — Application of the two-thirds rule

Example 1

1. *Community-wide turnover*

is, for undertaking A, ECU 8 000 million and for undertaking B ECU 400 million.

2. *Turnover in one (and the same) Member State X*

is, for undertaking A (ECU 6 000 million), 75% of its Community-wide turnover and is, for undertaking B (ECU 200 million), 50% of its Community-wide turnover.

3. *Conclusion*

In this case, although undertaking A achieves more than two-thirds of its Community-wide turnover in Member State X, the proposed concentration would fall under the scope of the Regulation due to the fact that undertaking B achieves less than two-thirds of its Community-wide turnover in Member State X.

Example 2(a)

1. *Community-wide turnover*

of undertaking A, is ECU 2 400 million and for undertaking B, ECU 400 million.

2. *Turnover in one (and the same) Member State X*

is, for undertaking A, ECU 2 100 million (i.e. 87.5% of its Community-wide turnover); and, for undertaking B, ECU 300 million (i.e. 75% of its Community-wide turnover).

3. *Conclusion*

In this case, each of the undertakings concerned achieves more than two-thirds of its Community-wide turnover in one (and the same) Member State X; the proposed concentration would not fall under the scope of the Regulation.

Example 2(b)

Conclusion

In this case, the two-thirds rule would not apply due to the fact that undertakings A and B achieve more than two-thirds of their Community-wide turnover in different Member States X and Y. Therefore, the proposed concentration would fall under the scope of the Regulation.

Annex II

Holidays in 1990

		B	DK	D	GR	E	F	IRL	I	L	NL	P	UK
New Year:	1.1.	x	x	x	x	x	x	x	x	x	x	x	x
New Year:	2.1.												x[1]
Carnival Monday:	26.2.			x									
St Patrick:	19.3.							x					x[2]
Maundy Thursday:	12.4.		x			x							
Good Friday:	13.4.		x	x	x	x		x			x	x	x
Easter Monday:	16.4.	x	x	x	x		x	x	x	x	x		x
Anniversary of the Liberation:	25.4.								x				
Liberty Day:	25.4.										x		
The Queen's Birthday:	30.4.										x		
Labour Day:	1.5.	x		x	x	x			x	x		x	
May holiday:	7.5.												x
Armistice 1945:	8.5.						x						
General Prayer Day:	11.5.		x										
Ascension:	24.5.	x	x	x			x			x	x		
Spring holiday:	28.5.												x
Whit Monday:	4.6.	x	x	x	x		x	x		x	x		
Constitution Day:	5.6.		x										
Corpus Christi:	14.6.			x[3]								x	
Orangeman's Day:	12.7.												x[2]
St James:	24.7.					x							
First Monday in August:	6.8.								x				x[1]
Friedenfest:	8.8.			x[4]									
Assumption:	15.8.	x		x[5]	x	x			x	x		x	
Summer Bank holiday:	27.8.												x
Republic Day:	5.10.											x	
National holiday:	12.10.					x							
Bank holiday:	29.10.							x					
All Saints:	1.11.	x		x[6]		x	x		x	x		x	
All Souls:	2.11.	x											
Dynasty Day:	15.11.	x											
Repentance Day:	21.11.			x									
Constitution Day:	6.12.					x							
Christmas:	25.12.	x	x	x	x	x	x	x	x	x	x	x	x
Second day of Christmas:	26.12.	x	x	x	x			x	x	x			x

---

[1]   Scotland.
[2]   Northern Ireland.
[3]   Baden-Württemberg, Bayern, Hessen, Nordrhein-Westfalen, Rheinland-Pfalz, Saarland.
[4]   City of Augsburg (Bayern).
[5]   Saarland and Bayern, Bayern, public holiday in administrative districts with a predominantly Catholic population.
[6]   Baden-Württemberg, Bayern, Nordrhein-Westfalen, Rheinland-Pfalz, Saarland.

Commission

New Year's Day	1 January
Day after New Year's Day	2 January
Holy/Maundy Thursday	12 April
Good Friday	13 April
Easter Monday	16 April
Labour Day	1 May
Anniversary of the declaration by Robert Schuman	9 May
Ascension Day	24 May
Day after Ascension Day	25 May
Whit Monday	4 June
Assumption Day	15 August
All Saints' Day	1 November
All Souls' Day	2 November
Christmas	24 December
	25 December
	26 December
	27 December
	28 December
	29 December
	30 December
	31 December

Commission notice regarding restrictions ancillary to concentrations (90/C 203/05)

I — Introduction

1. Council Regulation (EEC) No 4064/89 of 21 December 1989 on the control of concentrations between undertakings ('the Regulation')[1] states in its 25th recital that its application is not excluded where the undertakings concerned accept restrictions which are directly related and necessary to the implementation of the concentration, hereinafter referred to as 'ancillary restrictions'. In the scheme of the Regulation, such restrictions are to be assessed together with the concentration itself. It follows, as confirmed by Article 8(2), second subparagraph, last sentence of the Regulation, that a decision declaring the concentration compatible also covers these restrictions. In this situation, under the provisions of Article 22, paragraphs 1 and 2, the Regulation is solely applicable, to the exclusion of Regulation No 17[2] as well as Regulations (EEC) No 1017/68,[3] (EEC) No 4056/86[4] and (EEC) No 3975/87.[5] This avoids parallel Commission proceedings, one concerned with the assessment of the concentration under the Regulation, and the other aimed at the application of Articles 85 and 86 to the restrictions which are ancillary to the concentration.

2. In this notice, the Commission sets out to indicate the interpretation it gives to the notion of 'restrictions directly related and necessary to the implementation of the concentration'. Under the Regulation such restrictions must be assessed in relation to the concentration, whatever their treatment might be under Articles 85 and 86 if they were to be considered in isolation or in a different economic context. The Commission endeavours, within the limits set by the Regulation, to take the greatest account of business practice and of the conditions necessary for the implementation of concentrations.

This notice is without prejudice to the interpretation which may be given by the Court of Justice of the European Communities.

II — Principles of evaluation

3. The 'restrictions' meant are those agreed on between the parties to the concentration which limit their own freedom of action in the market. They do not include restrictions to the detriment of third parties. If such restrictions are the inevitable consequence of the concentration itself, they must be assessed together with it under the provisions of Article 2 of the Regulation. If, on the contrary, such restrictive effects on third parties are separable from the concentration they may, if appropriate, be the subject of an assessment of compatibility with Articles 85 and 86 of the EEC Treaty.

4. For restrictions to be considered 'directly related' they must be ancillary to the implementation of the concentration, that is to say subordinate in importance to the main object of the concentration. They cannot be substantial restrictions wholly different in nature from those which result from the concentration itself. Neither are they contractual arrangements which are among the elements constituting the concentration, such as those establishing economic unity between previously independent parties, or organizing joint control by two undertakings of another undertaking. As integral parts of the concentration, the latter arrangements constitute the very subject matter of the evaluation to be carried out under the Regulation.

---

[1] OJ L 395, 30.12.1989, p. 1.
[2] OJ 13, 21.2.1962, pp. 204-62.
[3] OJ L 175, 23.7.1968, p. 1.
[4] OJ L 378, 31.12.1986, p. 1.
[5] OJ L 374, 31.12.1987, p. 1.

Also excluded, for concentrations which are carried out in stages, are the contractual arrangements relating to the stages before the establishment of control within the meaning of Article 3, paragraphs 1 and 3 of the Regulation. For these, Articles 85 and 86 remain applicable as long as the conditions set out in Article 3 are not fulfilled.

The notion of directly related restrictions likewise excludes from the application of the Regulation additional restrictions agreed at the same time which have no direct link with the concentration. It is not enough that the additional restrictions exist in the same context as the concentration.

5. The restrictions must likewise be 'necessary to the implementation of the concentration', which means that in their absence the concentration could not be implemented or could only be implemented under more uncertain conditions, at substantially higher cost, over an appreciably longer period or with considerably less probability of success. This must be judged on an objective basis.

6. The question of whether a restriction meets these conditions cannot be answered in general terms. In particular as concerns the necessity of the restriction, it is proper not only to take account of its nature, but equally to ensure, in applying the rule of proportionality, that its duration and subject matter, and geographic field of application, do not exceed what the implementation of the concentration reasonably requires. If alternatives are available for the attainment of the legitimate aim pursued, the undertakings must choose the one which is objectively the least restrictive of competition.

These principles will be followed and further developed by the Commission's practice in individual cases. However, it is already possible, on the basis of past experience, to indicate the attitude the Commission will take to those restrictions most commonly encountered in relation to the transfer of undertakings or parts of undertakings, the division of undertakings or of their assets following a joint acquisition of control, or the creation of concentrative joint ventures.

III — Evaluation of common ancillary restrictions in cases of the transfer of an undertaking

A — Non-competition clauses

1. Among the ancillary restrictions which meet the criteria set out in the Regulation are contractual prohibitions on competition which are imposed on the vendor in the context of a concentration achieved by the transfer of an undertaking or part of an undertaking. Such prohibitions guarantee the transfer to the acquirer of the full value of the assets transferred, which in general include both physical assets and intangible assets such as the goodwill which the vendor has accumulated or the know-how he has developed. These are not only directly related to the concentration, but are also necessary for its implementation because, in their absence, there would be reasonable grounds to expect that the sale of the undertaking or part of an undertaking could not be accomplished satisfactorily. In order to take over fully the value of the assets transferred, the acquirer must be able to benefit from some protection against competitive acts of the vendor in order to gain the loyalty of customers and to assimilate and exploit the know-how. Such protection cannot generally be considered necessary when *de facto* the transfer is limited to physical assets (such as land, buildings or machinery) or to exclusive industrial and commercial property rights (the holders of which could immediately take action against infringements by the transferor of such rights).

However, such a prohibition on competition is justified by the legitimate objective sought of implementing the concentration only when its duration, its geographical field of application, its subject matter and the persons subject to it do not exceed what is reasonably necessary to that end.

2. With regard to the acceptable duration of a prohibition on competition, a period of five years has been recognized as appropriate when the transfer of the undertaking includes the goodwill and know-how, and a period of two years when it includes only the goodwill. However, these are not absolute rules; they do not preclude a prohibition of longer duration in particular circumstances, where, for

example, the parties can demonstrate that customer loyalty will persist for a period longer than two years or that the economic life-cycle of the products concerned is longer than five years and should be taken into account.

3. The geographic scope of the non-competition clause must be limited to the area where the vendor had established the products or services before the transfer. It does not appear objectively necessary that the acquirer be protected from competition by the vendor in territories which the vendor had not previously penetrated.

4. In the same manner, the non-competition clause must be4. limited to products and services which form the economic activity of the undertaking transferred. In particular, in the case of a partial transfer of assets, it does not appear that the acquirer needs to be protected from the competition of the vendor in the products or services which constitute the activities which the vendor retains after the transfer.

5. The vendor may bind himself, his subsidiaries and commercial agents. However, an obligation to impose similar restrictions on others would not qualify as an ancillary restriction. This applies in particular to clauses which would restrict the scope for resellers or users to import or export.

6. Any protection of the vendor is not normally an ancillary restriction and is therefore to be examined under Articles 85 and 86 of the EEC Treaty.

B — Licences of industrial and commercial property rights and of know-how

1. The implementation of a transfer of an undertaking or part of an undertaking generally includes the transfer to the acquirer, with a view to the full exploitation of the assets transferred, of rights to industrial or commercial property or know-how. However, the vendor may remain the owner of the rights in order to exploit them for activities other than those transferred. In these cases, the usual means for ensuring that the acquirer will have the full use of the assets transferred is to conclude licensing agreements in his favour.

2. Simple or exclusive licences of patents, similar rights or existing know-how can be accepted as necessary for the completion of the transaction, and likewise agreements to grant such licences. They may be limited to certain fields of use, to the extent that they correspond to the activities of the undertaking transferred. Normally it will not be necessary for such licences to include territorial limitations on manufacture which reflect the territory of the activity transferred. Licences may be granted for the whole duration of the patent or similar rights or the duration of the normal economic life of the know-how. As such licences are economically equivalent to a partial transfer of rights, they need not be limited in time.

3. Restrictions in licence agreements, going beyond what is provided above, fall outside the scope of the Regulation. They must be assessed on their merits according to Article 85(1) and (3). Accordingly, where they fulfil the conditions required, they may benefit from the block exemptions provided for by Regulation (EEC) No 2349/84 on patent licences[1] or Regulation (EEC) No 559/89 on know-how licences.[2]

4. The same principles are to be applied by analogy in the case of licences of trademarks, business names or similar rights. There may be situations where the vendor wishes to remain the owner of such rights in relation to activities retained, but the acquirer needs the rights to use them to market the products constituting the object of the activity of the undertaking or part of an undertaking transferred.

In such circumstances, the conclusion of agreements for the purpose of avoiding confusion between trademarks may be necessary.

---

[1]   OJ L 219, 16.8.1984, p. 15.
[2]   OJ L 61, 4.8.1989, p. 1.

C — Purchase and supply agreements

1. In many cases, the transfer of an undertaking or part of an undertaking can entail the disruption of traditional lines of internal procurement and supply resulting from the previous integration of activities within the economic entity of the vendor. To make possible the break up of the economic unity of the vendor and the partial transfer of the assets to the acquirer under reasonable conditions, it is often necessary to maintain, at least for a transitional period, similar links between the vendor and the acquirer. This objective is normally attained by the conclusion of purchase and supply agreements between the vendor and the acquirer of the undertaking or part of an undertaking. Taking account of the particular situation resulting from the break up of the economic unity of the vendor such obligations, which may lead to restrictions of competition, can be recognized as ancillary. They may be in favour of the vendor as well as the acquirer.

2. The legitimate aim of such obligations may be to ensure the continuity of supply to one or other of the parties of products necessary to the activities retained (for the vendor) or taken over (for the acquirer). Thus, there are grounds for recognizing, for a transitional period, the need for supply obligations aimed at guaranteeing the quantities previously supplied within the vendor's integrated business or enabling their adjustment in accordance with the development of the market.

Their aim may also be to provide continuity of outlets for one or the other of the parties, as they were previously assured within the single economic entity. For the same reason, obligations providing for fixed quantities, possibly with a variation clause, may be recognized as necessary.

3. However, there does not appear to be a general justification for exclusive purchase or supply obligations. Save in exceptional circumstances, for example resulting from the absence of a market or the specificity of products, such exclusivity is not objectively necessary to permit the implementation of a concentration in the form of a transfer of an undertaking or part of an undertaking.

In any event, in accordance with the principle of proportionality, the undertakings concerned are bound to consider whether there are no alternative means to the ends pursued, such as agreements for fixed quantities, which are less restrictive than exclusivity.

4. As for the duration of procurement and supply obligations, this must be limited to a period necessary for the replacement of the relationship of dependency by autonomy in market. The duration of such a period must be objectively justified.

IV — Evaluation of ancillary restrictions in the case of a joint acquisition

1. As set out in the 24th recital, the Regulation is applicable when two or more undertakings agree to acquire jointly the control of one or more other undertakings, in particular by means of a public tender offer, where the object or effect is the division among themselves of the undertakings or their assets. This is a concentration implemented in two successive stages; the common strategy is limited to the acquisition of control. For the transaction to be concentrative, the joint acquisition must be followed by a clear separation of the undertakings or assets concerned.

2. For this purpose, an agreement by the joint acquirers of an undertaking to abstain from making separate competing offers for the same undertaking, or otherwise acquiring control, may be considered an ancillary restriction.

3. Restrictions limited to putting the division into effect are to be considered directly related and necessary to the implementation of the concentration. This will apply to arrangements made between the parties for the joint acquisition of control in order to divide among themselves the production facilities or the distribution networks together with the existing trade marks of the undertaking acquired in common. The implementation of this division may not in any circumstances lead to the coordination of the future behaviour of the acquiring undertakings.

4. To the extent that such a division involves the break-up of a pre-existing economic entity, arrangements that make the break-up possible under reasonable conditions must be considered ancillary. In this regard, the principles explained above in relation to purchase and supply arrangements over a transitional period in cases of transfer of undertakings should be applied by analogy.

V — Evaluation of ancillary restrictions in cases of concentrative joint ventures within the meaning of Article 3(2), subparagraph 2 of the Regulation

This evaluation must take account of the characteristics peculiar to concentrative joint ventures, the constituent elements of which are the creation of an autonomous economic entity exercising on a long-term basis all the functions of an undertaking, and the absence of coordination of competitive behaviour between the parent undertakings and between them, and the joint venture. This condition implies in principle the withdrawal of the parent undertakings from the market assigned to the joint venture and, therefore, their disappearance as actual or potential competitors of the new entity.

A — Non-competition obligations

To the extent that a prohibition on the parent undertakings competing with the joint venture aims at expressing the reality of the lasting withdrawal of the parents from the market assigned to the joint venture, it will be recognized as an integral part of the concentration.

B — Licences for industrial and commercial property rights and know-how

The creation of a new autonomous economic entity usually involves the transfer of the technology necessary for carrying on the activities assigned to it, in the form of a transfer of rights and related know-how. Where the parent undertakings intend nonetheless to retain the property rights, particularly with the aim of exploitation in other fields of use, the transfer of technology to the joint venture may be accomplished by means of licences. Such licences may be exclusive, without having to be limited in duration or territory, for they serve only as a substitute for the transfer of property rights. They must therefore be considered necessary to the implementation of the concentration.

C — Purchase and supply obligations

If the parent undertakings remain present in a market upstream or downstream of that of the joint venture, any purchase and supply agreements are to be examined in accordance with the principles applicable in the case of the transfer of an undertaking.

Commission notice regarding the concentrative and cooperative operations under Council Regulation (EEC) No 4064/89 of 21 December 1989 on the control of concentrations between undertakings [1] (90/C 203/06)

I — Introduction

Article 3(1) of Council Regulation (EEC) No 4064/89 ('the Regulation') contains an exhaustive list of the factual circumstances which fall to be considered as concentrations. In accordance with the 23rd recital, this term refers only to operations that lead to a lasting change in the structures of the participating undertakings.

By contrast, the Regulation does not deal with operations whose object or effect is the coordination of the competitive activities of undertakings that remain independent of each other. Situations of this kind are cooperative in character. Accordingly, they fall to be assessed under the provisions of Regulations No 17,[2] (EEC) No 1017/68,[3] No 4056/86[4] or No 3975/87.[5] The same applies to an operation which includes both a lasting structural change and the coordination of competitive behaviour, where the two are inseparable.

If the structural change can be separated from the coordination of competitive behaviour, the former will be assessed under the Regulation and the latter, to the extent that it does not amount to an ancillary restriction within the meaning of Article 8(2), second subparagraph of the Regulation, falls to be assessed under the other Regulations implementing Articles 85 and 86 of the EEC Treaty.

2. The purpose of this notice is to define as clearly as possible, in the interests of legal certainty, concentrative and cooperative situations. This is particularly important in the case of joint ventures. The same issue is raised in other forms of association between undertakings such as unilateral or reciprocal shareholdings and common directorships, and of certain operations involving more than one undertaking, such as unilateral or reciprocal transfers of undertakings or parts of undertakings, or joint acquisition of an undertaking with a view to its division. In all these cases, operations may not fall within the scope of the Regulation, where their object or effect is the coordination of the competitive behaviour of the undertakings concerned.

3. This notice sets out the main considerations which will determine the Commission's view to what extent the aforesaid operations are or are not caught by the Regulation. It is not concerned with the assessment of these operations, whether under the Regulation or any other applicable provisions, in particular Articles 85 and 86 of the EEC Treaty.

4. The principles set out in this notice will be followed and further developed by the Commission's practice in individual cases. As the operations considered are generally of a complex nature, this notice cannot provide a definitive answer to all conceivable situations.

5. This notice is without prejudice to the interpretation which may be given by the Court of Justice or the Court of First Instance of the European Communities.

---

[1] OJ L 395, 30.12.1989, p. 1.
[2] OJ 13, 21.2.1962, pp. 204-62.
[3] OJ L 175, 23.7.1968, p. 1.
[4] OJ L 378, 31.12.1986, p. 4.
[5] OJ L 374, 31.12.1987, p. 1.

II — Joint ventures within Article 3 of the Regulation

6. The Regulation in Article 3(2) refers to two types of joint venture: those which have as their object or effect the coordination of the competitive behaviour of undertakings which remain independent (referred to as 'cooperative joint ventures') and those which perform on a lasting basis all the functions of an autonomous economic entity and which do not give rise to coordination amongst themselves or between them and the joint venture (referred to as 'concentrative joint ventures'). The latter are concentrations and as such are caught by the Regulation. Cooperative joint ventures fall to be considered under other regulations implementing Articles 85 and 86.[1]

A — Concept of joint venture

7. To define the term 'joint venture' (JV) within the meaning of Article 3(2), it is necessary to refer to the provision of Article 3(1)(b) of the Regulation. According to the latter, JVs are undertakings that are jointly controlled by several other undertakings, the parent companies. In the context of the Regulation the term JV thus implies several characteristics:

1. Undertaking

8. A JV must be an undertaking. That is to be understood as an organized assembly of human and material resources, intended to pursue a defined economic purpose on a long-term basis.

2. Control by other undertakings

9. In the context of the Regulation, a JV is controlled by other undertakings. Pursuant to Article 3(3) of the Regulation, control means the possibility of exercising, directly or indirectly, a decisive influence on the activities of the JV; whether this condition is fulfilled can only be decided by reference to all the legal and factual circumstances of the individual case.

10. Control of a JV can be based on legal, contractual or other means, within which the following elements are especially important:

(i) ownership or rights to the use of all or some of the JV's assets,

(ii) influence over the composition, voting or decisions of the managing or supervisory bodies of the JV,

(iii) voting rights in the managing or supervisory bodies of the JV,

(iv) contracts concerning the running of the JV's business.

3. Joint control

11. A JV under the Regulation is jointly controlled. Joint control exists where the parent companies must agree on decisions concerning the JV's activities, either because of the rights acquired in the JV or because of contracts or other means establishing the joint control. Joint control may be provided for in the JV's constitution (memorandum or articles of association). However, it need not be present from the beginning, but may also be established later, in particular by taking a share in an existing undertaking.

12. There is no joint control where one of the parent companies can decide alone on the JV's commercial activities. This is generally the case where one company owns more than half the capital or assets of

---

[1] See footnotes 2 to 5, p. 304.

the undertaking, has the right to appoint more than half of the managing or supervisory bodies, controls more than half of the votes in one of those bodies, or has the sole right to manage the undertaking's business. Where the other parent companies either have completely passive minority holdings or, while able to have a certain influence on the undertaking, cannot, individually or together, determine its behaviour, a relative majority of the capital or of the votes or seats on the decision-making bodies will suffice to control the undertaking.

13. In many cases, the joint control of the JV is based on agreements or concertation between the parent companies. Thus, a majority shareholder in a JV often extends to one or more minority shareholders a contractual right to take part in the control of the JV. If two undertakings each hold half of a JV, even if there is no agreement between them, both parent companies will be obliged permanently to cooperate so as to avoid reciprocal blocking votes on decisions affecting the JV's activity. The same applies to JVs with three or more parents, where each of them has a right of veto. A JV can even be controlled by a considerable number of undertakings that can together muster a majority of the capital or the seats or votes on the JV's decision-making bodies. However, in such cases, joint control can be presumed only if the factual and legal circumstances — especially a convergence of economic interests — support the notion of a deliberate common policy of the parent companies in relation to the JV.

14. If one undertaking's holding in another is, by its nature or its extent, insufficient to establish sole control, and if there is no joint control together with third parties, then there is no concentration within the meaning of Article 3(1)(b) of the Regulation. Articles 85 or 86 of the EEC Treaty may however be applicable on the basis of Regulation No 17 or other implementing Regulations (see III.1).

B — Concentrative joint ventures

15. For a joint venture to be regarded as concentrative it must fulfil all the conditions of Article 3(2), subparagraph 2, which lays down a positive condition and a negative condition.

1. Positive condition: joint venture performing on a lasting basis all the functions of an autonomous economic entity

16. To fulfil this condition, a JV must first of all act as an independent supplier and buyer on the market. JVs that take over from their parents only specific partial responsibilities are not to be considered as concentrations where they are merely auxiliaries to the commercial activities of the parent companies. This is the case where the JV supplies its products or services exclusively to its parent companies, or when it meets its own needs wholly from them. The independent market presence can even be sufficient if the JV achieves the majority of its supplies or sales with third parties, but remains substantially dependent on its parents for the maintenance and development of its business.

17. A JV exists on a lasting basis if it is intended and able to carry on its activity for an unlimited, or at least for a long, time. If this is not the case there is generally no long-term change in the structures of the parent companies. More important than the agreed duration are the human and material resources of the JV. They must be of such nature and quantity as to ensure the JV's existence and independence in the long term. This is generally the case where the parent companies invest substantial financial resources in the JV, transfer an existing undertaking or business to it, or give it substantial technical or commercial know-how, so that after an initial starting-up period it can support itself by its own means.

18. A decisive question for assessing the autonomous character of the JV is whether it is in a position to exercise its own commercial policy. This requires, within the limits of its company objects, that it plans, decides and acts independently. In particular, it must be free to determine its competitive behaviour autonomously and according to its own economic interests. If the JV depends for its business on facilities that remain economically integrated with the parent companies' businesses, that weakens the case for the autonomous nature of the JV.

19. The JV's economic independence will not be contested merely because the parent companies reserve to themselves the right to take certain decisions that are important for the development of the JV, namely those concerning alterations of the objects of the company, increases or reductions of capital, or the application of profits. However, if the commercial policy of the JV remains in the hands of the parent undertakings, the JV may take on the aspect of an instrument of the parent undertakings' market interests. Such a situation will usually exist where the JV operates in the market of the parent undertakings. It may also exist where the JV operates in markets neighbouring, or upstream or downstream of, those of the parent undertakings.

2. Negative condition: absence of coordination of competitive behaviour

20. Subject to what is said in the first paragraph of this notice a JV can only be considered to be concentrative within the meaning of Article 3(2), subparagraph 2 of the Regulation, if it does not have as its object or effect the coordination of the competitive behaviour of undertakings that remain independent of each other. There must not be such coordination either between the parent companies themselves or between any or all of them on the one hand and the JV on the other hand. Such coordination must not be an object of the establishment or operation of the JV, nor may it be the consequence thereof. The JV is not to be regarded as concentrative if as a result of the agreement to set up the JV or as a result of its existence or activities it is reasonably foreseeable that the competitive behaviour of a parent or of the JV on the relevant market will be influenced. Conversely, there will normally be no foreseeable coordination when all the parent companies withdraw entirely and permanently from the JV's market and do not operate on markets neighbouring those of the JVs.

21. Not every cooperation between parent companies with regard to the JV prevents a JV from being considered concentrative. Even concentrative JVs generally represent a means for parent companies to pursue common or mutually complementary interests. The establishment and joint control of a JV is, therefore, inconceivable without an understanding between the parent companies as concerns the pursuit of those interests. Irrespective of its legal form, such a concordance of interests is an essential feature of a JV.

22. As regards the relations of the parent undertakings, or any one of them, with the JV, the risk of coordination within the meaning of Article 3(2) will not normally arise where the parent undertakings are not active in the markets of the JV or in neighbouring or upstream or downstream markets. In other cases, the risk of coordination will be relatively small where the parents limit the influence they exercise to the JV's strategic decisions, such as those concerning the future direction of investment, and when they express their financial, rather than their market-orientated, interests. The membership of the JV's managing and supervisory bodies is also important. Common membership of the JV's and the parent companies' decision-making bodies may be an obstacle to the development of the JV's autonomous commercial policy.

23. The dividing line between the concordance of interests in a JV and a coordination of competitive behaviour that is incompatible with the notion of concentration cannot be laid down for all conceivable kinds of case. The decisive factor is not the legal form of the relationship between the parent companies and between them and the JV. The direct or indirect, actual or potential effects of the establishment and operation of the JV on market relationships, have determinant importance.

24. In assessing the likelihood of coordination of competitive behaviour, it is useful to consider some of the different situations which often occur:

(a) JVs that take over pre-existing activities of the parent companies;

(b) JVs that undertake new activities on behalf of the parent companies;

(c) JVs that enter the parent companies' markets;

(d) JVs that enter upstream, downstream or neighbouring markets.

(a) JVs that take over pre-existing activities of the parent companies

25. There is normally no risk of coordination where the parent companies transfer the whole of certain business activities to the JV and withdraw permanently from the JV's market so that they remain neither actual nor potential competitors — of each other nor of the JV. In this context, the notion of potential competition is to be interpreted realistically, according to the Commission's established practice.[1] A presumption of a competitive relationship requires not only that one or more of the parent companies could re-enter the JV's market at any time: this must be a realistic option and represent a commercially reasonable course in the light of all objective circumstances.

26. Where the parent companies transfer their entire business activities to the JV, and thereafter act only as holding companies, this amounts to complete merger from the economic viewpoint.

27. Where the JV takes on only some of the activities that the parent companies formerly carried on independently, this can also amount to a concentration. In this case, the establishment and operation of the JV must not lead to a coordination of the parent companies' competitive behaviour in relation to other activities which they retain. Coordination of competitive behaviour between any or all of the parent companies and the JV must also be excluded. Such coordination is likely where there are close economic links between the areas of activity of the JV on one side and of the parent companies on the other. This applies to upstream, downstream and neighbouring product markets.

28. The withdrawal of the parent companies need not be simultaneous with the establishment of the JV. It is possible — so far as necessary — to allow the parent companies a short transitional period to overcome any starting-up problems of the JV, especially bottlenecks in production or supplies. This period should not normally exceed one year.

29. It is even possible for the establishment of a JV to represent a concentration situation where the parent companies remain permanently active on the JV's product or service market. In this case, however, the parent companies' geographic market must be different from that of the JV. Moreover, the markets in question must be so widely separated, or must present structures so different that, taking account of the nature of the goods or services concerned and of the cost of (first or renewed) entry by either into the other's market, competitive interaction may be excluded.

30. If the parent companies' markets and the JVs are in different parts of the Community or neighbouring third countries, there is a degree of probability that either, if it has the necessary human and material resources, could extend its activities from the one market to the other. Where the territories are adjacent or very close to each other, this may even be assumed to be the case. At least in this last case, the actual allocation of markets gives reason to suppose that it follows from a coordination of competitive behaviour between parent companies and the JV.

(b) JVs that undertake new activities on behalf of the parent companies

31. There is normally no risk of coordination in the sense described above where the JV operates on a product or service market which the parent companies individually have not entered and will not enter in the foreseeable future, because they lack the organizational, technical or financial means or because, in the light of all the objective circumstances, such a move would not represent a commercially reasonable course. An individual market entry will also be unlikely where, after establishing the JV, the parent companies no longer have the means to make new investments in the same field, or where an additional individual operation on the JV's market would not make commercial sense. In both cases there is no competitive relationship between the parent companies and the JV. Consequently, there is no possibility of coordination of their competitive behaviour. However, this assessment is only true if the JV's market is neither upstream nor downstream of, nor neighbouring, that of the parent companies.

---

[1]   See the Thirteenth Report on Competition Policy, point 55 (1983).

32. The establishment of a JV to operate in the same product or service market as the parent companies but in another geographic market involves the risk of coordination if there is competitive interaction between the parent companies' geographic market and that of the JV.

(c) JVs that enter the parent companies' market

33. Where the parent companies, or one of them, remain active on the JV's market or remain potential competitors of the JV, a coordination of competitive behaviour between the parent companies or between them and the JV must be presumed. So long as this presumption is not rebutted, the Commission will take it that the establishment of the JV does not fall under Article 3(2), subparagraph 2 of the Regulation.

(d) JVs that operate in upstream, downstream or neighbouring markets

34. If the JV is operating in a market that is upstream or downstream of that of the parent companies, then, in general, coordination of purchasing or, as the case may be, sales policy between the parent companies is likely where they are competitors on the upstream or downstream market.

35. If the parent companies are not competitors, it remains to be examined whether there is a real risk of coordination of competitive behaviour between the JV and any of the parents. This will normally be the case where the JV's sales or purchases are made in substantial measure with the parent companies.

36. It is not possible to lay down general principles regarding the likelihood of coordination of competitive behaviour in cases where the parent companies and the JV are active in neighbouring markets. The outcome will depend in particular on whether the JV's and the parent companies' products are technically or economically linked, whether they are both components of another product or are otherwise mutually complementary, and whether the parent companies could realistically enter the JV's market. If there are no concrete opportunities for competitive interaction of this kind, the Commission will treat the JV as concentrative.

III — Other links between undertakings

1. Minority shareholdings

37. The taking of a minority shareholding in an undertaking can be considered a concentration within the meaning of Article 3(1)(b) of the Regulation if the new shareholder acquires the possibility of exercising a decisive influence on the undertaking's activity. If the acquisition of a minority shareholding brings about a situation in which there is an undertaking jointly controlled by two or more others, the principles described above in relation to JVs apply.

38. As long as the threshold of individual or joint decisive influence has not been reached, the Regulation is not in any event applicable. Accordingly, the assessment under competition law will be made only in relation to the criteria laid down in Articles 85 and 86 of the EEC Treaty and on the basis of the usual procedural rules for restrictive practices and abuses of dominant position. [1]

39. There may likewise be a risk of coordination where an undertaking acquires a majority or minority interest in another in which a competitor already has a minority interest. If so, this acquisition will be assessed under Articles 85 and 86 of the EEC Treaty.

---

[1] Judgment of the Court of Justice of the European Communities in Joined Cases 142 and 156/84 *BAT and Reynolds* [1987] ECR pp. 4566 and 4577.

2. Cross-shareholding

40. In order to bring their autonomous and hitherto separate undertakings or groups closer together, company owners often cause them to exchange shareholdings in each other. Such reciprocal influences can serve to establish or to secure industrial or commercial cooperation between the undertakings or groups. But they may also result in establishing a 'single economic entity'. In the first case, the coordination of competitive behaviour between independent undertakings is predominant; in the second, the result may be a concentration. Consequently, reciprocal directorships and cross-shareholdings can only be evaluated in relation to their foreseeable effects in each case.

41. The Commission considers that two or more undertakings can also combine without setting up a parent-subsidiary relationship and without either losing its legal personality. Article 3(1) of the Regulation refers not only to legal, but also to economic concentrations.

The condition for the recognition of a concentration in the form of a combined group is, however, that the undertakings or groups concerned are not only subject to a permanent, single economic management, but are also amalgamated into a genuine economic unit, characterized internally by profit and loss compensation between the various undertakings within the groups and externally by joint liability.

3. Representation on controlling bodies of other undertakings

42. Common membership of managing or supervisory boards of various undertakings is to be assessed in accordance with the same principles as cross-shareholdings.

43. The representation of one undertaking on the decision-making bodies of another is usually the consequence of an existing shareholding. It reinforces the influence of the investing undertaking over the activities of the undertaking in which it holds a share, because it affords it the opportunity of obtaining information on the activities of a competitor or of taking an active part in its commercial decisions.

44. Thus, common membership of the respective boards may be the vehicle for the coordination of the competitive behaviour of the undertakings concerned, or for a concentration of undertakings within the meaning of the Regulation. This will depend on the circumstances of the individual case, among which the economic link between the shareholding and the personal connection must always be examined. This is equally true of unilateral and reciprocal relationships between undertakings.

45. Personal connections not accompanied by shareholdings are to be judged according to the same criteria as shareholding relationships between undertakings. A majority of seats on the managing or supervisory board of an undertaking will normally imply control of the latter; a minority of seats at least a degree of influence over its commercial policy, which may further entail a coordination of behaviour. Reciprocal connections justify a presumption that the undertakings concerned are coordinating their business conduct. A very wide communality of membership of the respective decision-making bodies — that is, up to half of the members or more — may be an indication of a concentration.

4. Transfers of undertakings or parts of undertakings

46. A transfer of assets or shares falls within the definition of a concentration, according to Article 3(1)(b) of the Regulation, if it results in the acquirer gaining control of all or of part of one or more undertakings. However, the situation is different where the transfer conferring control over part of an undertaking is linked with an agreement to coordinate the competitive behaviour of undertakings concerned, or where it necessarily leads to or is accompanied by coordination of the business conduct of undertakings which remain independent. Cases of this kind are not covered by the Regulation: they must be examined according to Articles 85 and 86 of the EEC Treaty and under the appropriate implementing Regulations.

47. The practical application of this rule requires a distinction between unilateral and reciprocal arrangements. A unilateral acquisition of assets or shares strongly suggests that the Regulation is applicable. The contrary needs to be demonstrated by clear evidence of the likelihood of coordination of the parties' competitive behaviour. A reciprocal acquisition of assets or shares, by contrast, will usually follow from an agreement between the undertakings concerned as to their investments, production or sales, and thus serves to coordinate their competitive behaviour. A concentration situation does not exist where a reciprocal transfer of assets or shares forms part of a specialization or restructuring agreement or other type of coordination. Coordination presupposes in any event that the parties remain at least potential competitors after the exchange has taken place.

5. Joint acquisition of an undertaking with a view to its division

48. Where several undertakings jointly acquire another, the principles for the assessment of a joint venture are applicable, provided that within the acquisition operation, the period of joint control goes beyond the very short term. In this case the Regulation may or may not be applicable, depending on the concentrative or cooperative nature of the JV. If, by contrast, the sole object of the agreement is to divide up the assets of the undertaking and this agreement is put into effect immediately after the acquisition, then, in accordance with the 24th recital, the Regulation applies.

Commission Decision of 23 November 1990 on the implementation of hearings in connection with procedures for the application of Articles 85 and 86 of the EEC Treaty and Articles 65 and 66 of the ECSC Treaty[1]

Article 1

(1) The hearings foreseen in the provisions implementing Articles 85 and 86 EEC Treaty and Articles 65 and 66 ECSC Treaty are decided on by the Member of the Commission responsible for competition and conducted by the Hearing Officer.

(2) Implementing provisions in the sense of paragraph (1) are:

(a) Regulation No 99/63/EEC of the Commission of 25 July 1963 on the hearings provided for in Article 19(1) and (2) of Council Regulation No 17;[2]

(b) Regulation (EEC) No 1630/69 of the Commission of 8 August 1969 on the hearings provided for in Article 26(1) and (2) of Council Regulation (EEC) No 1017/68 of 19 July 1968;[3]

(c) Commission Regulation (EEC) No 4260/88 of 16 December 1988 on the communications, complaints and applications and the hearings provided for in Council Regulation (EEC) No 4056/86 laying down detailed rules for the application of Articles 85 and 86 of the Treaty to maritime transport;[4]

(d) Commission Regulation (EEC) No 4261/88 of 16 December 1988 on the complaints, applications and hearings provided for in Council Regulation (EEC) No 3975/87 laying down the procedure for the application of the rules on competition to undertakings in the air transport sector;[5]

(e) Article 36(1) ECSC Treaty.

(3) Administratively the Hearing Officer shall belong to the Directorate-General for Competition. To ensure his independence in the performance of his duties, he shall have the right of direct access, as defined in Article 6 below, to the Member of the Commission with special responsibility for competition.

(4) Where the Hearing Officer is unable to act, the Director-General, in concert with the Hearing Officer, shall designate another official, who is in the same grade and is not involved in the case in question, to carry out the duties described herein.

Article 2

(1) The Hearing Officer shall ensure that the hearing is properly conducted and thus contribute to the objectivity of the hearing itself and of any decision taken subsequently. He shall seek to ensure in particular that in the preparation of draft Commission decisions in competition cases due account is taken of all the relevant facts, whether favourable or unfavourable to the parties concerned.

---

[1]   This text replaces the one published in the Annex of the Thirteenth Report on Competition Policy (1983).
[2]   OJ 127, 20.8.1963, p. 2268/63.
[3]   OJ L 209, 21.8.1969, p. 11.
[4]   OJ L 376, 31.12.1988, p. 1.
[5]   OJ L 376, 31.12.1988, p. 10.

(2) In performing his duties he shall see to it that the rights of the defence are respected, while taking account of the need for effective application of the competition rules in accordance with the regulations in force and the principles laid down by the Court of Justice.

Article 3

(1) Where appropriate in view of the need to ensure that the hearing is properly prepared, and particularly that questions of fact are clarified as far as possible, the Hearing Officer may, after consulting the appropriate director, supply in advance to the firms concerned a list of the questions on which he wishes them to explain their point of view.

(2) For this purpose, after consulting the director responsible for investigating the case which is the subject of the hearing, he may hold a meeting with the parties concerned and, where appropriate, the Commission staff, in order to prepare for the hearing itself.

(3) For the same purpose he may ask for prior written notification of the essential contents of the intended statement of persons whom the undertakings concerned have proposed for hearing.

Article 4

(1) After consulting the director responsible, the Hearing Officer shall determine the date, the duration and the place of the hearing, and, where a postponement is requested, he shall decide whether or not to allow it.

(2) He shall be fully responsible for the conduct of the hearing.

(3) In this regard, he shall decide whether fresh documents should be admitted during the hearing, whether persons should be heard and whether the persons concerned should be heard separately or in the presence of other persons summoned to attend.

(4) He shall ensure that the essential content of the statement made by each person heard shall be recorded in minutes which shall be read and approved by that person.

Article 5

The Hearing Officer shall report to the Director-General for Competition on the hearing and the conclusions he draws from it. He may make observations on the further progress of the proceedings. Such observations may relate among other things to the need for further information, the withdrawal of certain objections, or the formulation of further objections.

Article 6

In performing the duties defined in Article 2 above, the Hearing Officer may, if he deems it appropriate, refer his observations direct to the Member of the Commission with special responsibility for competition, at the time when the preliminary draft decision is submitted to the latter for reference to the Advisory Committee on Restrictive Practices and Dominant Positions.

Article 7

Where appropriate, the Member of the Commission with special responsibility for competition may decide, at the Hearing Officer's request, to attach the Hearing Officer's final report to the draft decision submitted to the Commission, in order to ensure that when it reaches a decision on an individual case it is fully apprised of all relevant information.

I — Competition policy towards enterprises —
List of Decisions, Notices and Judgments

1. Decisions pursuant to Articles 85 and 86 of the EEC Treaty

Decision of 12 January 1990 on a proceeding under Article 85 of the EEC Treaty 'Alcatel/Ant'   OJ L 32, 3.2.1990

Decision of 23 March 1990 on a proceeding under Article 85 of the EEC Treaty 'Moosehead/Whitbread'   OJ L 100, 20.4.1990

Decision of 26 June 1990 on a proceeding under Article 86 of the EEC Treaty 'Metaleurop'   OJ L 179, 12.7.1990

Decision of 13 July 1990 on a proceeding under Article 85 of the EEC Treaty 'Elopak/Metal Box-Odin'   OJ L 209, 8.8.1990

Decision of 27 July 1990 on a proceeding under Article 85 of the EEC Treaty 'Konsortium ECR 900'   OJ L 228, 22.8.1990

Decision of 15 October 1990 on a proceeding under Article 85 of the EEC Treaty 'Cekacan'   OJ L 299, 30.10.1990

Decision of 28 November 1990 on a proceeding under Article 85 of the EEC Treaty 'Bayer Dental'   OJ L 351, 15.12.1990

Decision of 12 December 1990 on a proceeding under Article 85 of the EEC Treaty 'KSB/Goulds/Lowara/ITT'   OJ L 19, 25.1.1991

Decision of 19 December 1990 on a proceeding under Article 85 of the EEC Treaty 'D'Ieteren — Huiles pour moteurs'   OJ L 20, 26.1.1991

Decision of 19 December 1990 on a proceeding under Articles 85 and 86 of the EEC Treaty 'Sodium carbonate'   OJ L 20, 26.1.1991

2. Notices pursuant to Articles 85 and 86 of the EEC Treaty

(a) Pursuant to Article 19(3) of Council Regulation No 17

'CGVL/Sicasov' (seeds)	OJ C 6, 11.1.1990
'Bayer/Gist-Brocades'	OJ C 57, 8.3.1990
'Shotton/Maybank' 'Shotton/Davidsons'	OJ C 106, 28.4.1990
'Alupower Chloride'	OJ C 152, 21.6.1990
'Jahrhundertvertrag'	OJ C 159, 29.6.1990
'Reorganization of the electricity industry in England and Wales'	OJ C 191, 31.7.1990
'Sippa'	OJ C 226, 11.9.1990
'Reorganization of the electricity industry in Scotland'	OJ C 245, 29.9.1990
'UER' — Eurovision system	OJ C 251, 5.10.1990
'IATA Passenger Agency Programme'	OJ C 267, 23.10.1990
'Eirpage'	OJ C 294, 24.11.1990
'IATA Cargo Agency Programme'	OJ C 320, 20.12.1990
'Yves Saint-Laurent Parfums'	OJ C 320, 20.12.1990

(b) Pursuant to Article 5(2) of Council Regulation (EEC) No 3975/87

'Sabena/British Midland Airways Ltd'	OJ C 29, 8.2.1990
'BA/KLM/SWA'	OJ C 82, 31.3.1990
'Aer Lingus/Lufthansa'	OJ C 108, 1.5.1990
'DHL/Lufthansa, JAL and Nisso Iwai'	OJ C 258, 22.9.1990

(c) Pursuant to Article 12(2) of Council Regulation (EEC) No 4056/86

'Agreement 1237'	OJ C 59, 9.3.1990
'Gulfway'	OJ C 130, 29.5.1990
'Eurocorde Agreements'	OJ C 162, 3.7.1990
'Eurotunnel'	OJ C 176, 17.7.1990

3. Decisions pursuant to Articles 65 and 66 of the ECSC Treaty

Decision of 12 January 1990 on a proceeding under Article 66 of the ECSC Treaty approving a merger resulting from the acquisition by Hoesch Rohstoff GmbH of all the shares in Schrott-Handelsgesellschaft mbH held by FAG Kugelsfischer-Georg Schäfer KGaA — Bull. EC 1-1990

Decision of 26 January 1990 on a proceeding under Article of the ECSC Treaty authorizing BHP-Utah International Exploration Inc. and Meekatharra (NI) Ltd, Belfast, Ireland to set up a joint venture, Ballymoney Coal Venture — Bull. EC 1-1990

Decision of 30 January 1990 on a proceeding under Article 66 of the ECSC Treaty authorizing Krupp Stahl AG to acquire 50% of the capital of Esta GmbH, Wilnsdorf, Germany — Bull. EC 1-1990

Decision of 22 March 1990 on a proceeding under Article 66 of the ECSC Treaty authorizing Société des Aciéries de Montereau, Compagnie Française des Ferrailles, Etablissement Marchetto and Etablissements Vendrand to set up a joint venture, Société Monterelaise de Broyage, Montereau, France — Bull. EC 3-1990

Decision of 23 March 1990 on a proceeding under Article 66 of the ECSC Treaty authorizing Usinor-Sacilor to acquire Allevard Finance, a holding company which controls Allevard Industries, France — Bull. EC 3-1990

Decision of 23 March 1990 on a proceeding under Article 66 of the ECSC Treaty authorizing Usinor-Sacilor through its subsidiary Ugine ACG to acquire all the shares in Sait Srl and Castelli Inox Service Srl — Bull. EC 3-1990

Decision of 26 March 1990 on a proceeding under Article 66 of the ECSC Treaty authorizing the acquisition by Ruhrkohle Handel GmbH of trading interests of BP-Stromeyer in the area of solid fuel for household and small business use — Bull. EC 3-1990

Decision of 26 March 1990 on a proceeding under Article 66 of the ECSC Treaty authorizing Thyssen AG to acquire the capital of Otto Wolff AG — Bull. EC 3-1990

Decision of 17 April 1990 on a proceeding under Article 66 of the ECSC Treaty authorizing Hoesch Rohstoff GmbH, Eisen und Metall AG, C. H. Scholz KG and Fa. Jürgen Karle to set up a joint venture — Bull. EC 4-1990

Decision of 23 May 1990 on a proceeding under Article 66 of the ECSC Treaty authorizing the acquisition of the entire issued share capital of C. Walker and Sons (Holdings) Ltd, Blackburn, United Kingdom — Bull. EC 4-1990

Decision of 8 June 1990 on a proceeding under Article 66 of the ECSC Treaty authorizing Ilva to acquire control of Zinzor Italia and Lavezzari Lamiere Sud — Bull. EC 5-1990 / OJ L 131, 23.5.1990

Decision of 26 June 1990 on a proceeding under Article 66 of the ECSC Treaty authorizing Stinnes Stahlhandel GmbH to acquire all the shares in Baustahl Schröder GmbH	Bull. EC 6-1990
Decision of 18 July 1990 on a proceeding under Article 65 of the ECSC Treaty concerning an agreement and concerted practices engaged in by European producers of cold-rolled stainless steel flat products	Bull. EC 7-1990 OJ L 220, 15.8.1990
Decision of 27 July 1990 on a proceeding under Article 65 of the ECSC Treaty authorizing the setting-up of Laminés Marchands Européens, a joint venture of Usinor-Sacilor, Cockerill-Sambre and Arbed, and various mergers connected with the transaction	Bull. EC 7-1990
Decision of 27 July 1990 on a proceeding under Article 66 of the ECSC Treaty authorizing Thyssen Handelsunion AG and Francisco Ros Casares SA to set up a joint venture Thyssen Ros Casares SA	Bull. EC 7-1990
Decision of 27 July 1990 on a proceeding under Article 66 of the ECSC Treaty authorizing Sollac SA to acquire all the share capital of Société des Forges de Basse-Indre and CMB Acier	Bull. EC 7-1990
Decision of 27 July 1990 on a proceeding under Article 66 of the ECSC Treaty authorizing British Steel to acquire certain assets and liabilities of Klöckner Stahl GmbH, Mannstädt-Werke and all the equity of a number of companies whose activities are related to those of Klöckner Stahl GmbH Mannstädt-Werke	Bull. EC 7-1990
Decision of 27 July 1990 on a proceeding under Article 66 of the ECSC Treaty authorizing Usinor-Sacilor SA to acquire all the shares in Merlin SA	Bull. EC 7-1990
Decision of 27 July 1990 on a proceeding under Article 66 of the ECSC Treaty authorizing Usinor-Sacilor SA to acquire 35% of the shares of Béraud-Sudreau SA	Bull. EC 7-1990
Decision of 27 July 1990 on a proceeding under Article 66 of the ECSC Treaty authorizing a merger between Sheerness Steel Company plc and Mayer Parry Recycling Ltd	Bull. EC 7-1990
Decision of 27 July 1990 on a proceeding under Article 66 of the ECSC Treaty authorizing Acerinox SA, Spain and Armco Inc., USA, to set up a joint venture Acerinox-Armco-Europa SA	Bull. EC 7-1990
Decision of 21 August 1990 on a proceeding under Article 65 of the ECSC Treaty authorizing TradeArbed Participations sarl and Salzgitter Stahl GmbH to set up a joint venture AP-Steel UK Ltd	Bull. EC 8-1990
Decision of 21 August 1990 on a proceeding under Article 66 of the ECSC Treaty authorizing Sidmar NV and Klöckner Stahl GmbH to set up a joint venture Sikel NV	Bull. EC 8-1990

Decision of 15 October 1990 on a proceeding under Article 66 of the ECSC Treaty authorizing Hoesch Aktiengesellschaft to acquire control of Gwent Steel Ltd	Bull. EC 10-1990
Decision of 20 November 1990 on a proceeding under Article 66 of the ECSC Treaty authorizing Thyssen AG to acquire shares in Austin Trumann Group Ltd	Bull. EC 11-1990
Decision of 4 December 1990 on a proceeding under Article 66 of the ECSC Treaty authorizing the creation of a joint venture by Usinor-Sacilor and ASD in the United Kingdom	Bull. EC 12-1990
Decision of 11 December 1990 on a proceeding under Article 66 of the ECSC Treaty authorizing British Steel plc to acquire certain assets and liabilities of Link 51 Ltd	Bull. EC 12-1990
Decision of 12 December 1990 on a proceeding under Article 66 of the ECSC Treaty authorizing Stinnes Intercarbon AG & Co. to acquire all the shares in Stromeyer GmbH	Bull. EC 12-1990
Decision of 17 December 1990 on a proceeding under Article 66 of the ECSC Treaty authorizing Usinor-Sacilor SA and Mannesmann Röhrenwerke AG to set up a joint venture Europipe SA	Bull. EC 12-1990
Decision of 17 December 1990 on a proceeding under Article 66 of the ECSC Treaty authorizing Usinor-Sacilor to acquire all the shares in Carimi srl, Italy	Bull. EC 12-1990
Decision of 19 December 1990 on a proceeding under Article 66 of the ECSC Treaty authorizing Riva Prodotti Siderurgici SpA to acquire 50 % of the shares in Rifinsider SpA, Genoa, Italy	Bull. EC 12-1990
Decision of 19 December 1990 on a proceeding under Article 66 of the ECSC Treaty authorizing Usinor-Sacilor to acquire 49 % of Service Acier Rhenan	Bull. EC 12-1990

4. Decisions pursuant to Article 6 of Council Regulation (EEC) No 4064/89[1]

Decision of 7 November 1990, Renault/Volvo	OJ C 281, 9.11.1990
Decision of 21 November 1990, AG/Amev	OJ C 304, 4.12.1990
Decision of 28 November 1990, ICI/Tioxide	OJ C 304, 4.12.1990
Decision of 10 December 1990, Arjomari/Wiggins Teape	OJ C 321, 21.12.1990
Decision of 17 December 1990, Promodes/Dirsa	OJ C 321, 21.12.1990
Decision of 20 December 1990, Cargill/Unilever	OJ C 327, 29.12.1990

---

[1]   Council Regulation (EEC) No 4064/89 of 21 December 1989 on the control of concentrations between undertakings.

5. Judgments of the Court of Justice

Judgment of 11 January 1900 in Case C-277/87 *Sandoz v Commission*	OJ C 28, 7.2.1990
Judgment of 13 February 1990 in Cases T-113/89, 114/89 and 116/89 *Omni-Partijen Akkoord*	OJ C 15, 23.1.1991
Judgment of 12 December 1990 in Case C-270/86 *Paris Court of Appeal*	OJ C 12, 18.1.1991
Judgment of 8 February 1990 in Case C-279/87 *Tipp-Ex*	OJ C 71, 21.3.1990
Judgment of 10 July 1990 in Case T-51/89 *Tetrapak*	OJ C 193, 2.8.1990
Judgment of 10 July 1990 in Case T-64/91 *Automec*	OJ C 194, 3.8.1990
Judgment of 13 December 1990 in Case C-347/88 *National monopoly*	OJ C 17, 25.1.1991

II — Competition policy and government assistance to enterprises

1. Aid cases in which the Commission raised no objection

Federal Republic of Germany

8.1.1990	Measures to promote participation by SMEs in trade fairs and exhibitions (Hessen)
8.1.1990	Aid for investors and copyright protection (Schleswig-Holstein)
8.1.1990	Programme for new enivronmental technologies (Schleswig-Holstein)
8.1.1990	Product innovation measures (Schleswig-Holstein)
8.1.1990	Aid for special advisory activities (Schleswig-Holstein)
8.1.1990	Acquisition of shareholdings (Schleswig-Holstein)
15.1.1990	Programme for the Westkueste and Landesteil Schleswig regions (Schleswig-Holstein)
17.1.1990	Energy research project
17.1.1990	Efficient use of energy and renewable energy sources
19.1.1990	Action programme to 1995 for Bremen and Bremerhaven (Innovation Fund)
31.1.1990	Programme of cooperative projects
7.2.1990	Guidance for enterprises (North Rhine-Westphalia)
13.2.1990	Strategy guidance and rationalization programme for small and medium-sized enterprises (Bavaria)
28.2.1990	Aid for the construction of multi-storey buildings in Berlin
28.2.1990	Programme for renewable energy resources
28.2.1990	Aid for energy research
28.2.1990	Aid for technological projects
2.3.1990	Aid for chemical fibres industry (Du Pont de Nemours Deutschland GmbH)
13.3.1990	Promotion of information technologies
19.3.1990	Law on the transfer of counter-guarantees (Berlin)
28.3.1990	Utilization of solar energy
28.3.1990	Credit programme (Rheinland-Pfalz)
28.3.1990	Aid for small hydroelectric plants (Bavaria)
4.4.1990	Aid for vocational training (Saarland)
4.4.1990	Aid for the long-term unemployed
10.4.1990	Amendment of scheme to promote the production and more efficient use of energy
26.4.1990	Counter-guarantees for credit and investment companies
26.4.1990	Aid for manure processing (North Rhine-Westphalia)

3.5.1990	Aid to shipbuilding
8.5.1990	Extension of ERP (European recovery programme) to GDR
29.5.1990	Aid to World Trade Centre (Ruhr basin — Gelsenkirchen)
31.5.1990	National common interest programme: promotion of guidance and service activities (Schleswig-Holstein)
5.6.1990	Special programme for Bremen under the joint Federal Government/*Länder* programme: improvement of regional economic structures
5.6.1990	Aid to promote investments in environmental protection
6.6.1990	Programme for the promotion of enterprises and self-managed projects on a cooperative basis
13.6.1990	Grants awarded by Saarland
20.6.1990	Shipbuilding aid to Sürken Werft Papenburg
20.6.1990	FRG measures to assist economic conversion in the GDR
20.6.1990	Measures to assist small and medium-sized enterprises
25.6.1990	HLT regional programme (Hesse) (*de minimis* amendment)
2.7.1990	Operational programme target area 2: aid for enterprises in the municipalities of Kreis Heinzberg
3.7.1990	Environmental technology scheme (Bremen)
6.7.1990	Policial and economic action programme to 1995 (Bremen and Bremerhaven)
6.7.1990	Operational programme target area 2: additional aid under the joint Federal Government/*Länder* programme (Saarland)
9.7.1990	Operational programme for Bremen and Bremerhaven
11.7.1990	Aid to small and medium-sized enterprises for environmental guidance (Bavaria)
17.7.1990	Preparation of Bremen's economy for the Community internal market (Bremen)
18.7.1990	Shipbuilding aid to Elsflether Werft
18.7.1990	Aid to a manufacturer of synthetic fibres
18.7.1990	Amendment of small businesses scheme (Bayern)
25.7.1990	General guarantee measures (Lower Saxony)
25.7.1990	Aid for GDR
25.7.1990	Aid to the motor-vehicle manufacturing industry (DBAG Stuttgart)
25.7.1990	Pilot schemes for the development of environmental protection technologies (Bremen and Bremerhaven)
26.7.1990	Regional structural programme (Baden-Württemberg)
30.7.1990	Guidance aid for small bakeries (North Rhine-Westphalia)
2.8.1990	Guidance aid for small craft industries granted by the Munster Chamber of Trade
4.9.1990	Aid to the textile firm Nino AG
5.9.1990	Investment aid for Bremer Werkzeug und Maschinen, Dortmund

11.9.1990	Extension of district heating network
11.9.1990	Aid for the microelectronics project EU 127 'Jessi'
18.9.1990	Regional programme of the *Land* North Rhine-Westphalia
18.9.1990	Development agency at Bochum
19.9.1990	Preparation of Bremen's economy for the Community internal market
21.9.1990	Aid for SMEs — Hamburg
26.9.1990	Aid for the rational and environmentally compatible use of energy (Hesse)
26.9.1990	19th general plan under the joint Federal Government/*Länder* programme for improving regional economic structures
26.9.1990	Schlömes Werft — Guinea Bissau
26.9.1990	Aid to Lufthansa
1.10.1990	Environmental programme: reduction of effluent discharges in North Rhine-Westphalia
1.10.1990	Programme to promote renewable energy sources in markets
15.10.1990	Eureka project EU-9 'HDTV'
15.10.1990	Eureka project EU-8 'Cosine (Rare)'
15.10.1990	Eureka project EU-147 'Digital audio broadcasting system'
17.10.1990	Aid to Bruker Franzen for metrological instruments (Bremen special programme)
18.10.1990	ERP economic plan for 1991
18.10.1990	Operational programme for Berlin: target area 2
24.10.1990	New directive on guarantees (Schleswig-Holstein)
24.10.1990	Measures to assist research and information technology
5.11.1990	Aid for technological improvements and innovation in enterprises (Hamburg)
8.11.1990	Aid for renewable energy (Lower Saxony)
12.11.1990	Aid for SMEs
20.11.1990	Schwerpunkt Ökologie
22.11.1990	Federal aid for the economy of the former GDR ('Rationalisierungs-Kuratorium der Deutschen Wirtschaft')
22.11.1990	Investment guarantees in Thuringia (Hesse)
22.11.1990	Aid for investments by Bavarian SMEs in the former GDR (Bavaria)
22.11.1990	Investment guarantees in the former GDR (Bavaria)
22.11.1990	SME consultation programme in Saxony and Thuringia (Bavaria)
22.11.1990	Tax concessions granted by the FRG on former GDR products
22.11.1990	Restructuring of consultation sector
22.11.1990	Investment aids in the FRG and former GDR
22.11.1990	Measures in the education sector under the social security system in the former GDR

22.11.1990	Municipal, Federal *Länder* and East German *Länder* programme
22.11.1990	Housing modernization programme
22.11.1990	ERP programme (federal)
22.11.1990	Extension of all West German aids to East Germany
22.11.1990	Extension of the programme for improving regional economic structures to the former GDR
22.11.1990	Measures to assist the economic conversion of the former GDR
28.11.1990	Technology applications scheme (Rheinland-Pfalz)
28.11.1990	Target programme 2 and 5B
30.11.1990	Operational programme for Berlin
5.12.1990	Law on electricity supply (Einspeisunggesetz)
11.12.1990	Guidance for SMEs concerning on-line research (Hamburg)
11.12.1990	Amendment to Law on the transfer of counter-guarantees
12.12.1990	Solvency guarantees and ERP loan guarantees for loan insurance associations in the former GDR
12.12.1990	Guarantee measures (Schleswig-Holstein)
17.12.1990	Product quality measures
18.12.1990	Solvency guarantees and ERP loan gurantees for loan insurance associations in the former GDR
18.12.1990	Aid award under the Bremen special programme to Atlas Copco
18.12.1990	Draft FUF innovation programme (Bremen)
19.12.1990	Guidance for SMEs (Hamburg)
21.12.1990	Extension of aid scheme for Berlin
21.12.1990	Scheme to promote technology and innovation in enterprises
21.12.1990	Enterprises and technology; GWK: Criteria for the acquisition of holdings (Schleswig-Holstein)
21.12.1990	Guidance scheme for small businesses by the Chamber of Trade (Saarland)
21.12.1990	Guidance for SMEs on environmental technology (Berlin)

Belgium

14.2.1990	'Prototypes' schemes
13.3.1990	Investment aid for Novoboch
10.4.1990	Privatization of Intermills
2.5.1990	New directives for the application of the law of 30 December 1970 (Walloon region)
8.5.1990	Aid co-financed by ERDF: AIDE programme (Walloon region)
4.7.1990	Shipbuilding aid to Namèche

16.7.1990	Resider — CCA target 2 — endogenous potential. Promotion of technological innovation (Walloon region)
25.7.1990	Acquisition of holding in Alz
31.8.1990	Budget of the 'aid' scheme for the Resider regions in Wallonia
14.9.1990	Employment aid (Walloon region)
19.9.1990	Aid for operational programmes (Flemish region)
26.9.1990	Amendment of the directives for the application of the law of 30 December 1970
14.11.1990	R & D aid to Fina Research SA (law of 30 December 1970)
5.12.1990	Aid to Donnay SA (Walloon region)
17.12.1990	Law of 4 August 1978: aid for SMEs (Walloon region)

Denmark

17.1.1990	Exemption measure for anti-pollution equipment on 'clean cars'
26.2.1990	Inclusion of Kallumborg in development areas
13.3.1990	State guarantee for guarantee funds for wind-generated energy
10.4.1990	Cooperation network
2.5.1990	Aid to shipbuilding (Danske Statsbaner — Scandinavian Ferry Lines)
25.7.1990	Aid to shipbuilding
12.12.1990	Aid for environmental protection in eastern Europe
17.12.1990	Promotion of trade and industry

Spain

31.1.1990	Aid for the promotion of stable employment
14.2.1990	Aid for the technological park of Málaga
21.3.1990	Measures to promote tourism
28.3.1990	Structural reform of commercial distribution in Andalusia
28.3.1990	Aid for SMEs (Canary Islands)
4.4.1990	Measures to promote rural tourism (Asturias)
6.4.1990	Aid for the production of trade catalogues
6.4.1990	Aid for famous exhibitions and fairs in the region of Castilla la Mancha
2.5.1990	Investment aid
6.6.1990	Six different aid schemes
18.6.1990	Aid for small and medium-sized enterprises
20.6.1990	Aid for the renewal and modernization of public transport vehicles
20.6.1990	1990 programme for quality improvement

20.6.1990	Steel — social aid for J. M. Aristrain SA
20.6.1990	Steel — social aid for E. Orbegozo SA
4.7.1990	Aid for Construcciones Aeronáuticas SA
6.7.1990	Quality improvement measures (Basque Country)
6.7.1900	Investment aid (Basque Country)
17.7.1990	Aid for the Andalusian Development Institute (IFA)
18.7.1990	Two series of measures to promote industrial quality
18.7.1990	Various aid schemes
25.7.1990	Six series of employment aids (Canary Islands)
25.7.1990	Investment aid, target area 2 (Madrid)
25.7.1990	Eight series of employment aids (Basque Country)
25.7.1990	Seven series of employment aids (Estremadura)
25.7.1990	National regional aid scheme in the Madrid and Asturias regions
2.8.1990	Measures to assist the hotel industry (Basque Country)
2.8.1990	Aid to tourism (Basque Country)
6.8.1990	Measures to assist tourism (La Rioja)
6.8.1990	Aid granted by Rioja to eight schemes of minor importance
6.8.1990	Aid to publishers
11.9.1990	1990 technological modernization programme
11.9.1990	Aid for technological modernization in the industrial sector
11.9.1990	Aid to the Rioja region
12.9.1990	Aid for SMEs (Andalusia)
18.9.1990	Aid for training in tourism (Valencia)
18.9.1990	Aid for the creation of enterprises by the young long-term unemployed or women
18.9.1990	Aid for vocational training (Valencia)
18.9.1990	Measures to assist the temporary employment of persons aged over 25 in long-term unemployment (Valencia)
18.9.1990	Measures to assist the employment of university graduates without employment (Valencia)
26.9.1990	Creation of an industrial, energy and technological base for the environment
26.9.1990	Aid for the promotion of trade missions (Andalusia)
26.9.1990	Eureka project EU-180 'Enosa, Crilaser SA'
10.10.1990	Training and employment aids (Castilla-Leon)
31.10.1990	Measures to assist tourism (Castilla-Leon)
14.11.1990	Aid for cooperatives and mutual societies
14.11.1990	Aid for aquaculture (Castilla-Leon)

23.11.1990	National training and vocational integration plan
28.11.1990	Improved marketing, manufacture and promotion of products of the community of Estremadura
28.11.1990	Measures to assist spa resorts (Estremadura)
28.11.1990	Aid for the region of Catalonia
11.12.1990	Aid to vocational training in SMEs
17.12.1990	Employment aid for migrant workers
17.12.1990	Various aid schemes (Catalonia)
11.12.1990	Aids for rubber processing (Cikautxo S. Coop)
11.12.1990	Co-generation of electricity — Gequisa SA
11.12.1990	Aid to the fibreboard and wood-processing industry
21.12.1990	Financial measures to assist investment projects (Melilla)
21.12.1990	Aid to enterprises to promote job creation (Melilla)
21.12.1990	Measures to assist enterprises in creating stable employment
21.12.1990	Raising of regional aid ceiling in the Decampoo area (Cantabria)

France

17.1.1990	Fuel retailers modernization fund levy scheme
31.1.1990	Paper and wood sector levy scheme
26.2.1990	Aid for radio broadcasting
28.2.1990	Tax exemption in Corsica
13.3.1990	Environmental aid (Air Quality Agency)
28.3.1990	Reclassification of PAT zones Aid for R & D: Anvar scheme
2.4.1990	State aids to co-finance Community support measures
2.5.1990	Aid for R & D
8.5.1990	Aid to Eureka project EU-127 'Jessi'
20.6.1990	Industrial redevelopment fund
22.6.1990	Fresh contributions for steel conversion companies
9.7.1990	Setting-up of diversification fund managed by Sodinor in north-eastern area of Lille
18.7.1990	Transfer of financial resources to a new alloy production unit (Usinor-Sacilor)
25.7.1990	R & D aid for the TGV (high-speed train)
25.7.1990	Tax credit for research
7.8.1990	Integrated Mediterranean programme for Corsica
20.8.1990	Conversion measures for the Lavelanet area
11.9.1990	Parafiscal charge for the Committee for the development of the furniture industries

20.9.1990	Measures by Charbonnages de France in Modena
28.9.1990	Aid for the setting-up of nurseries: enterprises providing services to SMEs and craft industries
10.10.1990	Refinancing of research and technology fund
24.10.1990	Aid for R & D Puma project
14.11.1990	Clock and watch industry levy scheme
14.11.1990	Investment by Exxon Chemicals
28.11.1990	Concrete and terracotta products levy scheme
28.11.1990	Measures covered by the ERDF under the multi-fund scheme for Réunion
12.12.1990	Clean cars and energy conservation (Peugot and Renault)
17.12.1990	Leather industry levy scheme
17.12.1990	Saab Scania SA — Angers

Greece

4.7.1990	Amendment of Law No 1262/82 on the Greek regional aid scheme (Thrace)
17.12.1990	Amendment of Law No 1262/82

Ireland

17.1.1990	National industrial development programme
2.8.1990	Certified international financial services custom house docks site (Dublin)
28.11.1990	Verolme Cork Dockyard

Italy

14.2.1990	Eureka project EU-204
29.3.1990	Assistance under the Technological Innovation Fund
10.4.1990	Payment of first instalment to Finsider
18.4.1990	Measures to assist research in 1990
6.6.1990	R & D aid: special fund for applied research — RAI Roma, Telettra Milano
6.6.1990	Aid for research: special fund for applied research — Itasiel Sidercad Genova Eureka EU-130
6.6.1990	Amendment and addition to Law No 127/80: quarry mining
20.6.1990	Aid for research: special fund for applied research — Eureka EU-189
20.6.1990	Aid for research: special fund for applied research — Auselda AED Group SpA, Rome, Eureka EU-58
20.6.1990	Aid for research: special fund for applied research — Alfa Romeo Avio SpA, Naples, Eureka EU-33

20.6.1990	Measures to promote tourism in the Marches
28.6.1990	Development of tourism in Piedmont
5.7.1990	Application of Law No 46/82: Technological Innovation Fund — Berco SpA
18.7.1990	Aids for the hotel and tourism industry
18.7.1990	Measures to assist the Sardinian craft industry (Sardinia)
25.7.1990	Aid for the Bolzano steelworks (part)
2.8.1990	Measures to assist tourism in Liguria
2.8.1990	Eureka-78 project: microbiological equipment for cement — Agra SrL, Genoa and Ravenna
2.8.1990	Eureka-110 project 'Mithra': Sepa, Elkron and Pianelli & Traversa
2.8.1990	Eureka-154 project 'Factory of the future': Fidia SpA, Turin
2.8.1990	Eureka-179 project 'Integrated environmental programme for ADA': Intecs Systems Olivetti
2.8.1990	Eureka-194 project 'Industrial application for the assessment of high-power lasers' — RTM and CISE
2.8.1990	Eureka-213 project 'Hipulse': Galileo & Irvin Elettronica
10.8.1990	Aid in the telecommunications sector: Law No 46/82 Technological Innovation Fund — Face Standard SpA
11.9.1990	Eureka-20 project: European advanced software technology (EAST)
18.9.1990	Aid to the electronics industry: Technological Innovation Fund, Law No 46/82 — Selenia SpA
22.10.1990	Application of Law No 46/82: Technological Innovation Fund — Videocolour SpA
28.11.1990	Investment aid for SMEs: target area 2 — ERDF
28.11.1990	Aid for the selective elimination, recycling and utilization of waste (Sardinia)
12.12.1990	Energy conservation under Law No 308/82
12.12.1990	Measures to promote tourism on the Adriatic coast
13.12.1990	Aid granted under Law No 46/82: Technological Innovation Fund — Foch SpA
17.12.1990	Steel conversion areas
17.12.1990	Grants to assist the craft industry in the Marches
17.12.1990	Grants to assist the craft industry in Latium
20.12.1990	Aid co-financed under the second phase of the IMP programme — Tuscany
21.12.1990	Sicilian draft law concerning the craft industry

Netherlands

31.1.1990	Aid to manure producers
22.2.1990	Aid in the form of guarantees, loans and grants
28.3.1990	Promotion of technology in the business world

28.3.1990	Loans for technical development
29.3.1990	Draft law on tax concessions for investments by small enterprises
2.5.1990	Measures to promote the rational use of energy
8.5.1990	1990 refinancing of the BTIP scheme
5.6.1990	Promotion of technology in enterprises
11.6.1990	Amendment of the law on the media
20.6.1990	Extension of the investment grants scheme in shipbuilding
20.6.1990	Experimental measures to assist SMEs
4.7.1990	Programme to promote technology in the business world
4.7.1990	Investment aid for energy conservation schemes in buildings
18.7.1990	Aid for cleaner and quieter lorries and buses
23.7.1990	Modification of aid for R & D
24.7.1990	Regional aid for investment grants
26.9.1990	Pilot and demonstration schemes concerning the exchange of electronic data
30.11.1990	Measures to encourage innovation
13.12.1990	Modification of State guarantees scheme for holding companies
17.12.1990	Regional policy 1991-94
17.12.1990	Scheme to promote environmental technologies
17.12.1990	Scheme to encourage energy savings in industry

Portugal

19.1.1990	Aid for social communication organizations
31.1.1990	Measures to assist the National Scientific and Technological Research Council (JNCT)
28.3.1990	Measures to promote the craft industry in the Azores
10.4.1990	Restructuring of the industrial sector: Pedip programme No 3
2.5.1990	Award of aid for electronic components
20.6.1990	Aid for young entrepreneurs
5.9.1990	Aid for employment and training
10.10.1990	Multi-fund operational programme — SIAT and Siappi
24.10.1990	Aid for commercial modernization
13.11.1990	Aid for vocational training
5.12.1990	Extension of aid programme for the wool industry
17.12.1990	Aid for the Seteneva shipyard (Mitrena Setubal)

United Kingdom

4.1.1990	Aid for Norbrook Laboratories in Northern Ireland
17.1.1990	Durham County Council (incentives scheme 1 and 2)
15.2.1990	Shropshire and Wrekin County Council
20.3.1990	Universal Steel Tube Company
21.3.1990	Aid under the Inner Urban Areas Act to Richard Edward Ltd
28.3.1990	Aid to electricity from non-fossil fuels (Wales and England)
28.3.1990	Aid to the electricity industry (Scotland)
28.3.1990	Tyne and Wear Development Company: aid to industry
26.4.1990	Aid to the development of enterprises
17.5.1990	Assistance for research and development
28.6.1990	Aid to the creation of small businesses
28.6.1990	Humberside Port and Wharfs promotion — Glanford Borough Council and Humberside County Council
28.6.1990	Aid to job creation — Dunfermline District Council
18.7.1990	West Cumbria Development Fund and Agency: Copeland Borough Council
18.7.1990	Aid to productive investments
18.7.1990	Three awards of aid to the Gateshead Metropolitan Borough Council
18.7.1990	Three awards of aid to the South Tyneside Metropolitan Borough Council
18.7.1990	Three awards of aid to York City Council
18.7.1990	Four awards of aid to Newcastle upon Tyne City Council
18.7.1990	Scunthorpe Borough Council
18.7.1990	Barnsley Metropolitan Borough Council
18.7.1990	Selby City Council
18.7.1990	Five awards of aid to Sheffield Metropolitan Council
18.7.1990	Richmond District Council
25.7.1990	Programme for the development of property ownership
25.7.1990	Grants for rural businesses
25.7.1990	Bolsover District Council
25.7.1990	North Yorkshire County Council: grants to small enterprises
7.8.1990	Measures to assist small enterprises
7.8.1990	Humberside County Council: assessment of investments
13.8.1990	Research and development aid: Eureka project EU-130 Jessica — British Constructional Steel
11.9.1990	Grimsby District Council: King Edward Street, New Enterprise Centre

11.9.1990	Kirklees Metropolitan Council: Enterprise House, Dewsbury
18.9.1990	Wansbeck District Council
18.9.1990	Falkirk District Council
27.9.1990	Aid to Acme Housing Association Ltd under the 1978 Urban Areas Act
26.9.1990	North Tyneside Council
26.9.1990	Sunderland Borough Council
26.9.1990	Humberside County Council
26.9.1990	North East Innovation Centre Co. Ltd and Blyth Valley: business aids
26.9.1990	Five awards of aid to the Regional Council
26.9.1990	Stirling Enterprise and Economic Development Company
26.9.1990	Tyne and Wear Enterprise Ltd
26.9.1990	Sheffield City Council
10.10.1990	West Lindsay District Council industry aid scheme
10.10.1990	Four awards of aid to Nottinghamshire County Council
11.10.1990	Aid to promote tourism in Northern Ireland
15.10.1990	Aid for Lincolnshire County Council
24.10.1990	Aid for regional development and selective regional aid to D. B. Marshall
5.11.1990	Stirling District Council: Central Regional Council for Scotland
8.11.1990	Nottinghamshire County Council: Private-sector leveraged investment grant
10.11.1990	Support for small enterprises: Chesterfield Borough Council
10.11.1990	Great Grimsby Borough Council
15.11.1990	Kirklees; Wakefield; Selby; Northumberland; Gateshead Council
18.12.1990	Kirkcaldy District Council: aid for small enterprises
21.12.1990	Mansfield District Council
14.11.1990	Four awards of aid to Nottingham City Council
28.11.1990	North Derbyshire, Bassetlaw District Council
5.12.1990	Scottish Development Agency
17.12.1990	Local Enterprise Agencies

2. Aid cases in which the Commission decided to open the Article 93(2) EEC procedure

Federal Republic of Germany

10.4.1990	Aid to H. Reinhold KG — Bavaria
2.5.1990	Aid to Textilwerke Deggendorf GmbH (Bavaria)
26.9.1990	Flensburger Schiffbau Gesellschaft and Co. KG (shipyard)
10.10.1990	Aid to Nefab GmbH in the wood-processing sector
10.10.1990	Paper processing — Chukyo Europe GmbH

Belgium

10.4.1990	Aid to Volkswagen-Bruxelles SA
16.5.1990	Aid to DAF Trucks SA (Flemish region)
4.7.1990	Investment aid for Mactac SA
18.7.1990	Aid to Solvay SA
25.7.1990	Aid for the purchase of ships
25.7.1990	Funds for the promotion of industrial research in Flanders (FIOV)
26.9.1990	Investment aid for Wiggins-Teape
17.1.1990	Aid to shipbuilding

Spain

18.7.1990	Aid to the textile manufacturer Hytasa SA
18.7.1990	Aid to the footwear manufacturer Imepiel (extension)
25.7.1990	Aid to Cenemesa, Conelec and Cademesa
25.7.1990	National regional aid scheme in the Madrid region
25.7.1990	Aid to the textile manufacturer Intelhorce SA
28.11.1990	Aid for Catalonia

France

18.7.1990	Investment aid for Saint Gobain
17.12.1990	Aid for Pari Mutuel Urbain PMU (economic interest grouping)
17.12.1990	Regional aid in mainland France (part)
14.11.1990	Enterprise areas (resulting from appropriate measures)

Greece

20.6.1990   Aid to shipbuilding: Neorion Shipyards of Syros SA

Italy

18.7.1990   Aid in the forestry and papermaking sectors
25.7.1990   Interest subsidies on financing for industrial and commercial SMEs
25.7.1990   Various measures
28.11.1990   Aid to the manufacture of printed wrapping film (Mezzogiorno)

Netherlands

6.6.1990   Aid to experimental manure-processing projects
10.10.1990   Aid to the shipyard Van der Griessend Noord

United Kingdom

14.2.1990   Aid in the automobile sector concerning Toyota

3. Aid cases in which the Commission decided to open the procedure provided for in Article 6(4) of Decision No 322/89/ECSC

Spain

28.2.1990	Aid to Acerinox SA
4.7.1990	Aid to Extremena de Laminados SA

Italy

25.7.1990	Aid to the Bolzano steelworks (part)

4. Aid cases in which the Commission decided to close the Article 93(2) EEC procedure

Federal Republic of Germany

17.1.1990   Assistance for technologies of the future

20.6.1990   Aid for R&D in transport and traffic

26.9.1990   Werftenverbund Bremen

Belgium

4.7.1990   Aid to the pharmaceutical firm Smithkline Biologicals SA

18.7.1990   Guarantee granted by the Walloon Region to Tubemeuse

17.12.1990   Investment aid to Wiggins-Teape

Spain

28.2.1990   Mantequerias Arias SA

10.4.1990   Community framework on aid to the motor vehicle industry

25.7.1990   Aid to public transport in the Basque Country

24.10.1990   Aid to the steel undertaking Extremena de Laminados SA

France

14.2.1990   Cumulation of aids for different purposes

Greece

17.12.1990   Assistance granted by the Business Reorganization Organization to Fimisco

Italy

28.2.1990   Measures to assist mining policy (Decree-Law No 3435)

10.4.1990   Aid to Dalmine (Italian steel industry not covered by ECSC Treaty)

10.4.1990   Grants for CNR research contracts (National Research Council)

4.7.1990   R&D on alternative energy sources

14.11.1990   Setting-up of a stamping press at Foggia

17.12.1990   Law No 34 of 8.11.1984, Sicilian region

20.6.1990   Aid to shipbuilding (Law No 234/89)

Netherlands

22.5.1990   Aid for regional schemes
17.12.1990   Pilot manure-processing schemes

Portugal

28.2.1990   Aid to the chemical firm Quimigal

5. Aid cases in which the Commission decided to close the procedure provided for in Article 6(4) of Decision No 3484/85/ECSC

Spain

13.3.1990   Aid for environmental protection to Altos Hornos de Vizcaya

5.12.1990   Aid to the steel undertaking Acerinox SA

6. Aid cases in which the Commission took a negative final decision under Article 93(2) of the EEC Treaty

Federal Republic of Germany

18.7.1990   Aid to Hamburg to assist enterprises

1.8.1990 and   Aid to shipbuilding: guarantee granted to Gemersheim
12.12.1990

17.12.1990   Aid in the synthetic fibres sector to Heinrich Reinhold KG

Belgium

4.7.1990   Law of 23.8.1948: credit for the building of an LPG vessel and two refrigerator ships

Greece

2.5.1990   Aid to Halkis Cement Co.

Italy

20.6.1990   Tirreno and Siderpotenza steelworks

25.7.1990   Optical Sector

25.7.1990   Law No 120/87: aid for areas in the Mezzogiorno affected by natural disasters

25.7.1990   Aid to the Bolzano steelworks

United Kingdom

27.6.1990   Aid to the Rover Group

7. Judgments of the Court of Justice

Judgment (14.2.1990) in Case C-301/87
France v Commission

OJ C 61, 10.3.1990, p. 4

Judgment (21.2.1990) in Case C-74/89
Commission v Belgium

OJ C 85, 3.4.1990, p. 4

Judgment (21.3.1990) in Case C-142/87
Belgium v Commission

OJ C 101, 21.4.1990, p. 3

Judgment (22.3.1990) in Case C-347/87
Triveneta Zuccheri and Others v Commission
(agriculture)

OJ C 105, 27.4.1990, p. 5

Judgment (12.7.1990) in Case C-169/84
*Société CdF Chimie et Fertilisants and Société Chimique de
la Grande Paroisse v Commission*

OJ C 199, 8.8.1990, p. 5

Judgment (20.9.1990) in Case C-5/89
Commission v Germany

OJ C 261, 16.10.1990, p. 3

Judgment (6.11.1990) in Case C-86/89
Italy v Commission (agriculture)

OJ C 299, 28.11.1990, p. 3

III — Competition policy and government assistance in the agriculture sector

1. Aid cases in which the Commission raised no objection

Belgium

3.5.1990   Individual award in the potato sector

22.6.1990   Measures to control swine fever

Germany

22.1.1990   North Rhine-Westphalia: scheme to encourage flax-growing

24.1.1990   Bremen: manufacture of miscellaneous foodstuffs (Jacobs-Suchard Kaffeeveredelungs GmbH)

24.1.1990   Bremen: aid in the food-manufacturing sector (Coffein Compagnie Dr Scheele GmbH & Co.)

24.1.1990   Bremen: aid in the food-manufacturing sector (NACE 423) CR3 Kaffeeveredelung M. Hermsen GmbH & Co.

14.2.1990   Bavaria: aid for the construction of a marketing station for breeding animals

2.3.1990   Measures to assist the marketing of agricultural products

3.4.1990   Schleswig-Holstein: programme to control Aujeszky's disease in pigs

3.4.1990   Organic farming

5.4.1990   Hamburg: aid for the setting-up of a meat-cutting plant

6.4.1990   Bavaria: farm loan programme for the food sector

10.5.1990   Lower Saxony: grassland conservation

14.5.1990   Bavaria: housing programme for farmers

14.5.1990   Bavaria: farm loan programme

28.5.1990   Bavaria: slurry programme

28.5.1990   Bavaria: measures to assist programmes relating to branded products in certain agricultural sectors

6.6.1990   Lower Saxony: cider production (plant and machinery)

6.6.1990   Baden-Württemberg: premiums for maintaining horses

12.6.1990   Lower Saxony: aid for the construction of a cheese factory

19.6.1990   Saarland: aid for the marketing of agricultural products and foodstuffs

22.6.1990   Rhineland Palatinate: measures to improve agricultural structures

25.6.1990   Schleswig-Holstein: improvement of the efficiency of agricultural structures

4.7.1990	Bavaria: measures to improve agriculture
20.7.1990	Hesse: environmental protection
20.7.1990	Schleswig-Holstein: measures concerning the improvement, processing and marketing of milk and milk products
24.7.1990	Measures to improve agricultural structures
2.8.1990	Rhineland Palatinate: meat quality (beef)
6.8.1990	Hesse: aid measures following storm damage between January and March 1990 to private forests
9.8.1990	Aid following storm damage to private forests between January and March 1990
6.9.1990	Improvement of the efficiency of agricultural structures (1990/91 marketing year)
6.9.1990	Hesse: soil analyses
6.9.1990	Hesse: measures to reduce soil analysis costs
10.9.1990	Bavaria: training programme (marketing of agricultural products)
11.9.1990	Hesse: aid for training
4.10.1990	Lower Saxony: measures to encourage the transfer of agricultural holdings
4.10.1990	Hamburg: investment aid for Roesch & Eggers GmbH
18.10.1990	Lower Saxony: measures to control atrophic rhinitis, Aujeszky's disease and infectious rhinotracheitis in cattle
24.10.1990	North Rhine-Westphalia: improving agricultural structures
24.10.1990	Rhineland Palatinate: regional programme for mountain areas
24.10.1990	Hesse: measures to encourage the use of farm machinery
30.10.1990	Rhineland Palatinate: measures to encourage the leasing or purchase of areas used to calculate the reference quantities for milk deliveries
30.10.1990	Bavaria: aid for publicity measures for agricultural products
8.11.1990	Baden-Württemberg: environmental protection measures
13.11.1990	Hesse: aid to encourage the sale of agricultural products
3.12.1990	Improving the efficiency of agricultural structures in certain less-favoured areas
3.12.1990	Aid for the setting-up of a stock-farming station
11.12.1990	Draft law on funds to assist forestry
17.12.1990	Measures to improve agricultural structures and protect the coastline
30.12.1990	Bavaria: improving agricultural structures (1991)

Denmark

5.2.1990	Aid to promote the development of agricultural products
13.3.1990	Aid for forestry consultants
2.4.1990	Aid for the marketing of agricultural products

9.4.1990	Buyers' groups (small growers)
6.6.1990	Planting of hardwood trees in classified forests
18.6.1990	Organic farming
24.7.1990	Measures to assist farming
31.7.1990	Aid to young farmers
8.11.1990	Aid for organic fruit-growing
19.12.1990	Aid for young farmers

Spain

22.1.1990	Asturias: measures to facilitate land acquisition
22.1.1990	Asturias: measures to facilitate forestry production
2.2.1990	Aid for measures to control mites
19.2.1990	Aid for agriculture and fishing (agriculture only)
20.2.1990	Investment aid for a cheese factory at Villaviciosa
20.2.1990	Investment aid for a cheese factory at Ribera de Arriba
20.3.1990	Land reform in Andalusia and Extremadura
9.4.1990	Aragon: aid for primary irrigation facilities
20.4.1990	Aid for the Bilbao slaughterhouse
3.7.1990	Asturias: aid in the agri-foodstuffs sector
18.7.1990	Castile-Leon: aid for sheepfarming
18.7.1990	Castile-Leon: aid for the purchase of boars
18.7.1990	Castile-Leon: pig-insemination scheme
18.7.1990	Castile-Leon: aid for sugarbeet growers
18.7.1990	Castile-Leon: aid for training courses for farmers, co-financed by the European Social Fund
24.7.1990	Castile-Leon: aid for the employment of technical staff in arable-farming and stockfarming cooperatives
3.8.1990	Improvement of the conditions under which agricultural and fishery products are processed and marketed
11.9.1990	Castile-Leon: aid for the restructuring of the Rueda, Ribera del Duero, Toro and Bierzo vineyards
11.9.1990	Castile-Leon: measures to assist stockfarms
14.9.1990	Catalonia: funding for agriculture and fishing
14.9.1990	Castile-Leon: aid to sheepfarmers
14.9.1990	Catalonia: aid in the farming, fisheries and forestry sectors
14.9.1990	Catalonia: funding for agriculture and fishing

20.9.1990	Castile-Leon: aid for the purpose of cattle
20.9.1990	Castile-Leon: measures to assist stockfarmers (transport of animals to slaughterhouses)
27.9.1990	Asturias: measures to improve agricultural holdings
24.10.1990	Valencia: aid for local job-creation schemes in agriculture
12.11.1990	Castile-Leon: aid for breeders of small animals
3.12.1990	Aid for rabbit farmers
18.12.1990	Canary Islands: aid to improve the structure of agricultural holdings

France

12.1.1990	Special aid to cereal growers adversely affected by heavy rainfall in the spring of 1988
30.1.1990	Agricultural debt relief fund
16.5.1990	Aid to increase sheep numbers in Normandy
16.5.1990	Aid for farmers in the south-west who were adversely affected by the storms in July 1989
14.6.1990	Aid for the disposal of wine alcohol
25.6.1990	Aid granted to certain producers of alcohol
4.7.1990	Measures to assist farmers who were adversely affected by drought
2.8.1990	Granting of special loans to CUMAs (agricultural machinery users' cooperatives)
22.8.1990	Aid and parafiscal charge to assist the CIVDN (Comité Interprofessionnel des Vins Doux Naturels — Joint-Trade Committee on Natural Sweet Wines)
22.8.1990	Aid and parafiscal charge to assist the CIVC (Comité Interprofessionnel du Vin de Champagne — Joint-Trade Committee on Champagne)
24.8.1990	Aid and parafiscal charge to assist certain trade organizations in the wine-growing sector
24.8.1990	Aid for pig producers in mountain-farming areas
3.10.1990	Measures planned to assist farmers hit by drought
5.10.1990	Parafiscal charges used to fund the BNIP (Bureau National Interprofessionnel du Pruneau — National Interbranch Prune Agency)
30.10.1990	Subsidized long-term loans for land deals

Greece

10.5.1990	Measures to assist crop and livestock farmers who suffered fire losses in 1988
19.7.1990	Measures to assist farmers who suffered fire losses in 1988
24.8.1990	Draft decision of the Prices and Incomes Committee on the granting of aid to farmers on the island of Rhodes
8.10.1990	Measures to assist farmers in Vafiochorion, where crops were damaged by floods in August 1988

Italy

5.2.1990	Sicily: Decision of the CIPE (Join-Ministerial Committee on Economic Planning) on public aid for beef carcasses
5.2.1990	Sicily: measures to promote and market agricultural products
8.2.1990	Aid for sheepfarmers
12.2.1990	Lazio: aid to compensate for frost damage to olive trees in 1984 and 1985
19.3.1990	Liguria: emergency aid to assist the collection, processing and health checks on cow's milk
3.4.1990	Liguria: measures to assist agricultural cooperatives (reducing the financial costs of improvement loans)
4.5.1990	Sicily: measures to assist agriculture
28.5.1990	Lazio: measures to assist organic farming
12.6.1990	Aid for advertising firms
25.6.1990	Provisions amending and supplementing regional Law No 10/78
3.7.1990	Apulia: measures to assist the relaunch of agricultural cooperatives
24.7.1990	Measures to assist the disposal of wine alcohol
24.7.1990	Veneto: regional farming and forestry development programme (1990-94)
24.7.1990	Sicily: aid to promote the advertising of Sicilian products
13.8.1990	Measures to promote Italian ham in France
13.8.1990	Production of bioethanol (from beet molasses)
14.8.1990	Umbria: production and testing of organic products
18.12.1990	Measures to support ham prices
18.12.1990	Fruli-Venezia Giulia: aid for silkworm production
21.12.1990	Sicily: laws on agriculture

Luxembourg

10.5.1990	Premium for the birth of foals of the Ardennais breed

Netherlands

12.2.1990	Investment aid (environmental projects)
21.5.1990	Scheme to encourage the cessation of farming and improve agricultural structures
4.6.1990	Structural improvement (pigmeat sector)
2.8.1990	Cessation of farming and structural improvement in agriculture
30.10.1990	Aid for environmental-protection projects in agriculture

United Kingdom

15.2.1990	Investment aid (environmental projects)
19.2.1990	Measures to control migratory geese (Isle of Islay)
19.2.1990	Farm and conservation grant scheme
13.3.1990	Northern Ireland: specific award in the poultrymeat sector (Fleming Poultry Ltd, Ballymoney)
19.3.1990	Scotland: aid for replacement planting of raspberry canes of the Glen Clova variety
30.4.1990	Nitrate-sensitive area pilot scheme
3.5.1990	Gypsum grant scheme
10.5.1990	Investment aid (development project)
25.6.1990	Aid granted following storm damage
4.7.1990	Specific award (aid granted to Beaumond Butchers and Chad Food Products)
4.7.1990	Specific award (aid granted to Headley Food Services)
24.7.1990	Aid granted following storm damage
2.8.1990	Specific award (aid granted to Country Fayre Traditional Foods)
2.8.1990	Seed potato scheme
2.8.1990	Amendment to farm improvement scheme
2.8.1990	Crop arrangements for 1990
3.8.1990	British Egg Industry Council
6.8.1990	Home-grown Cereals Authority levies
22.8.1990	Meat and Livestock Commission
22.8.1990	Meat and Livestock Commission levy
27.8.1990	Specific award (aid granted to Kerry Food Ltd)
31.8.1990	Specific award (poultrymeat processing — aid granted to Celia Clyne Catering)
31.8.1990	Specific award (poultrymeat processing — aid granted to W. A. Turner)
11.9.1990	Specific award (poultrymeat processing — aid granted to Marshall Limited)
14.9.1990	North-West development scheme
9.10.1990	Measures to assist forestry
18.10.1990	Apple and Pear Research Council
24.10.1990	Isle of Man (basic slag scheme)
30.10.1990	Specific award (D. B. Marshall (Newbridge Ltd) — Coatbridge Poultry Processing)
3.12.1990	Countryside premium scheme

2. Aid cases in which the procedure provided for in Article 93(2) of the EEC Treaty was initiated

Belgium

23.5.1990	Compulsory charge to fund a pigmeat-promotion scheme	OJ C 162/90, 3.7.1990

Germany

19.4.1990	Baden-Württemberg: Directive B of the regional environmental programme	OJ C 121/90, 17.5.1990
12.12.1990	Hesse: measures to reduce the pressure of agriculture on the environment	OJ C 45/91, 21.2.1991
18.12.1990	Rhineland-Palatinate: storage aid for wine	OJ C 32/91, 7.2.1991

Spain

17.5.1990	Castile-La Mancha: investment aid (yoghurt production)	OJ C 135/90, 2.6.1990
5.10.1990	Measures to encourage the cultivation of varieties of potatoes used by the starch industry	OJ C 270/90, 26.8.1990

France

7.3.1990	Reimbursement of the parafiscal storage charge in the cereals sector	OJ C 74/91, 20.3.1991
14.5.1990	Measures to boost and modernize strawberry production	OJ C 170/90, 12.7.1990
1.6.1990	Aid and parafiscal charge to assist the CNIH (Comité National Interprofessionnel de l'Horticulture Florale, Ornementale et des Pépinières — National Joint-Trade Committee for Flower-Growing and Nurseries)	OJ C 170/90, 12.7.1990
5.12.1990	Aid and parafiscal charge to assist Entav (Etablissement National Technique Interprofessionnel pour l'Amélioration de la Viticulture — National Joint-Trade Technical Centre for the Promotion of Wine-Growing)	OJ C 91/91, 25.3.1991

Italy

6.2.1990	Sicily: measures to promote the marketing of agricultural products and improve agricultural cooperation	OJ C 32/90, 10.2.1990
19.4.1990	Sardinia: aid for agricultural holdings hit by drought in 1988-89	OJ C 111/90, 5.5.1990
1.6.1990	Aid granted by AIMA in 1986-87	OJ C 169/90, 11.7.1990
28.12.1990	Aid granted to a manufacturer of cereal products, Italgrani SpA	OJ C 315/90, 14.12.1990

Netherlands

23.2.1990	Price charged to horticulturists for natural gas in 1989-94	OJ C 103/90, 25.4.1990

3. Aid cases in which the procedure provided for in Article 93(2) of the EEC Treaty was closed

Spain

4.4.1990	Galicia: specific award (Lácteos de Galicia SA)	OJ C 111/90, 5.5.1990
17.5.1990	Navarre: Regional Law on improving the efficiency of agricultural structures	
25.6.1990	Murcia: aid to agriculture in Lorca	OJ C 229/90, 14.9.1990
27.12.1990	Aid in the olive oil sector	OJ C 58/91, 7.3.1991

Italy

2.7.1990	Aid to pecorino cheese	OJ C 165/90, 6.7.1990

Luxembourg

1.6.1990	Aid and parafiscal charge to assist the Wine-Growers' Mutual Fund	OJ C 156/90, 27.6.1990

4. Aid case in which the Commission adopted a negative final decision under Article 92(3)(a) of the EEC Treaty

Belgium

1.6.1990   Application of the economic expansion law of 12 July 1959 in respect of investment in the Couplet sugar refinery at Brunehaut-Wez

5. Aid case in which the procedure provided for in Article 93(1) of the EEC Treaty was initiated to examine an existing aid scheme

Denmark

2.7.1990   Aid and parafiscal charge to assist the fruit-growers' and horticulturists' fund — existing scheme of operating aid to plant-propagation stations

6. Judgments of the Court of Justice

Judgment (6.11.1990) in Case C 86/89 *Italy* v *Commission*

Aid for the use of rectified concentrated grape must — Application for the cancellation of a Commission decision (OJ L 94, 9.4.1989, p. 38)

Judgment (22.3.1990) in Case C 347/87 *Eight sugar firms* v *Commission*

Aid to Italian sugar dealers — Application for the cancellation of a Commission Decision (OJ L 313, 4.11.1987, p. 24)

IV — List of studies published in 1990 and to be published

Document

Title	Research institute	Expert
Aid element of government R&D contracts	Segal Quince and Wicksteek Ltd Cambridge	R. Quince

Competition law in the Member States

§ 1 — Legislative developments in the Member States

1. In Belgium, no changes were made in 1990 to the Law of 27 May 1960 on protection against abuse of economic power. The draft law on concerted practices, abuses of dominant positions and mergers[1] was agreed in principle by the Belgian Council of Ministers on 9 February. It was then submitted to the Council of State for scrutiny.

The draft was amended to take account of the Council of State's Opinion on 9 April. The new version was resubmitted to the Council of Ministers, which approved it on 27 July. The draft was then tabled before the Chamber of Representatives, by whose Committee on Economic Affairs it will be examined during the coming months.

2. After the passing of the Competition Act (Statute No 370 of 7 June 1989), which came into force in Denmark on 1 January 1990, the Monopolies and Restrictive Practices Supervision Act of 1955 and the Prices and Profits Act of 1974 were repealed; furthermore, the Monopolies Control Authority resigned, to be replaced by the Competition Board.

The Competition Act is administered by the Competition Board, which comes under the Ministry of Industry. An executive committee has been appointed to prepare cases for the Competition Board.

Under the Competition Act decisions made by the Competition Board can be brought before the Competition Appeals Tribunal. The Competition Appeals Tribunal consists of a Chairman and two members; it hears appeals against decisions to the extent laid down in the Competition Act. An appeal must be lodged with the Appeals Tribunal within four weeks of the decision being notified to the party concerned. A decision made by the Appeals Tribunal may be brought before the High Court within eight weeks of the decision being notified to the party concerned.

The Competition Act has a general industrial policy aim. The purpose of the Act is to promote competition and hence strengthen the efficiency of production and distribution of goods and services.

It applies to all economic activity, including business activity subject to control or approval by the public authorities, which was not covered by the Monopolies Act. It also applies to financial institutions, insurance companies and other business activity in the financial sector.

In order to fulfil the purpose of the Act, the Competition Board must make a point of ensuring transparency, i.e. make it easier for manufacturers, dealers and consumers to have access to information about the various aspects of competition.

An important means of ensuring transparency is to publish reports on prices and competition, partly through the general publications of the Competition Board and partly by publishing more thorough investigations into branches of trade etc. Enterprises which are the subject of an investigation must be informed of the report before it is published, and any comments made by the enterprises must on request be published in conjunction with the report.

The Competition Board may, furthermore, publish topical information about prices, discounts, bonuses, etc. It may thus for a period of up to two years at a time order an enterprise or association to submit regular information on such matters as prices, profits, business terms, and financial and organizational relations.

In accordance with the principle of transparency, the public has extensive access to information on competition questions. However, information about technical matters, including research, production

---

[1]   Nineteenth Competition Report, point 98; Seventeenth Competition Report, point 112.

methods and products, may not be published. Enterprises are obliged to supply all information which the Competition Board considers necessary to its activities. Agreements and decisions by which a dominant influence may be exerted on a certain market are subject to notification to the Competition Board and the notified information is accessible to the public.

If transparency does not suffice to create competition, the Competition Board can attempt to influence the parties' conduct through negotiation and, if this fails, may order the total or partial annulment of agreements, decisions, stipulations or business terms. The essential condition for intervention is the existence of an anti-competitive practice on a certain market which adversely affects competition and efficiency.

An order may also include an obligation to supply goods or services to specified buyers.

If an anti-competitive practice means that a price or profit clearly exceeds that which would be obtainable on a competitive market, the Competition Board may stipulate maximum prices, maximum profits or calculation requirements. Any intervention in relation to prices or profits presupposes that the other means provided for in the Act have not been successful in terminating the harmful effects on competition.

As already indicated, The Competition Act also applies to public undertakings and corporations. However, the intervention measures of the Act do not apply to this type of business activity. The Competition Board may nevertheless approach the competent public authority and point out the potentially anti-competitive effects of the practice in question. Such communications must be published.

Under the Act enterprises or associations are not allowed to require observance of minimum prices by subsequent resellers. Infringement of this prohibition is punishable by fine. If justified by valid reasons the Competition Board may grant exemptions from the prohibition. The Board has granted exemptions for books and periodicals and for sheet music. The prohibition as regards prices on tobacco products is to be repealed with effect from 1 January 1991.

The Competition Act does not include any merger control provisions, and an assessment of the competition aspects of mergers by reference to the Competition Act must be based on whether the mergers influence efficiency of production and distribution of goods and services. Under the Commercial and Savings Bank Act intended mergers of banks must be submitted to the Minister for Industry for his approval.

Reference was made during the preparatory work on the Competition Act to increasing internationalization and its importance to competition in Denmark, including the interaction with the Commission of the European Communities as regards the application of the competition rules laid down in Articles 85 and 86 of the EEC Treaty — the application of which is administered by the Competition Board in Denmark.

3. The Fifth Amending Law amending the German Law against restraints of competition entered into force on 1 January 1990. [1] There were no other legislative changes.

4. In Greece no legislative changes were made to Law 703/77 on monopolies, oligopolies and the protection of free competition. Nevertheless, a draft amendment to the existing law was submitted to Parliament for adoption.

5. The changes in competition legislation in Spain in 1990 can be considered from both an organizational and a substantive point of view.

As regards the organizational aspect, Royal Decree 177/90 of 9 February 1990 incorporates the Competition Protection Service (Servicio de Defensa de la Competencia) referred to in Law 16/89 of 17 July 1989 on the protection of competition [2] into the Directorate-General for the Protection of Competition (Dirección General de Defensa de la Competencia) and creates within the latter a new unit, the sub-Directorate-General for Control of the Structures of Competition (Subdirección General de

---

[1]   Nineteenth Competition Report, point 97.
[2]   Nineteenth Competition Report, point 101.

Control de las Estructuras de Competencia). The Directorate-General now consists of the following units, each having the functions indicated:

(i) The sub-Directorate-General for Investigations and Monitoring (Subdirección General de Instrucción y Vigilancia). This is responsible for investigating and following up current cases with a view both to imposing penalties and to granting authorizations; monitoring implementation of the Resolutions of the Competition Protection Tribunal (Tribunal de Defensa de la Competencia); providing information and making proposals in relation to agreements and restrictive practices; and collaborating with the Commission of the European Communities both as regards the application in Spain of the Community competition rules and as regards attendance at committee meetings and hearings in competition cases.

(ii) The sub-Directorate-General for Studies and Registration in connection with the Protection of Competition (Subdirección General de Estudios y Registro de Defensa de la Competencia). This is responsible for keeping the Competition Protection Register; studying and examining the various sectors of the economy, analysing the competitive situation and the amount of competition there and uncovering any restrictive practices; proposing measures to overcome the obstacles resulting from the restrictions detected; providing information and making proposals regarding the degree of competition in domestic and foreign markets and any other questions relating to the protection of competition; cooperating in competition matters with foreign organizations and international institutions; and attending meetings of the EEC with a view to drawing up Community legislation in this field.

(iii) The sub-Directorate-General for Control of the Structures of Competition. This is responsible for providing information and making proposals in relation to concentrations and associations of undertakings; providing information to the 'Comisión Informadora sobre Fusiones de Empresas'; detecting and reporting on any merger or takeover, whether planned or already executed, which affects or may affect the Spanish market; analysing and reporting on any voluntarily notified merger operation; reporting on State aids to the Minister for Economic and Financial Affairs; and, lastly, collaborating with the EC Commission in connection with the Community Regulation on merger control and with foreign organizations in relation to company mergers.

As to the substantive aspect, work continued in 1990 on two preliminary draft Royal Decrees for implementing Law 16/89 on the protection of competition: a preliminary draft Royal Decree approving the procedure to be followed before competition protection bodies in individual authorization cases, and a preliminary draft Royal Decree approving the procedure to be followed before competition protection bodies in cases of economic concentration.

6. There were no legislative changes in the field of competition policy in Ireland during 1990. However, legislation to give effect in domestic law to provisions similar to Articles 85 and 86 of the EEC Treaty is at an advanced stage of preparation. It is anticipated that this legislation can be enacted by the Irish Parliament in 1991.

7. The Luxembourg Law of 17 June 1970 on restrictive trade practices, which was amended as regards investigatory powers by the Law of 20 April 1989,[1] did not undergo any further changes in 1990. It is worth noting, however, that a draft law amending certain provisions of the Law of 27 November 1986 regulating certain commercial practices and penalizing unfair competition is being prepared. The amendments are to take account of two factors:

(i) a reasoned opinion of the EC Commission of 30 October 1989 on two provisions of the Law (advertising by reference to the price previously charged, incentive marketing);

(ii) the judgment of the European Court of Justice of 7 March 1990 in Case 362/88 (advertising by reference to the price previously charged and duration of that advertising).

The Department for Small Firms is sponsoring the changes. The draft amending law will be submitted to the legislature and the EC Commission will be consulted.

---

[1] Nineteenth Competition Report, point 104.

8. In the Netherlands, the Law of 15 November 1989[1] amending the Law on economic competition with regard to resale price maintenance entered into force on 15 June 1990. The Law prohibits collective resale maintenance, although exemptions may be allowed where required by the general interest. Individual resale price maintenance is prohibited in respect of such goods as are to be specified by administrative measure.

9. In Portugal, Decree-Laws 329/90 and 346/90 were published on 23 October and 3 November 1990 respectively. Article 11 of the first, and Article 20 of the second, Decree-Law render applicable to the provision of services in the value-added telecommunications sector and to complementary services the rules laid down in the Law on the protection of competition (Decree-Law 422/83 of 3 December 1983), derogating in this respect from the exemption normally granted to the telecommunications sector on the basis of Article 36(1)(b).

10. Two Acts were passed in 1990 in the United Kingdom which have a bearing on competition law and policy.

(1) The Courts and Legal Services Act 1990, which includes the following provisions:

(i) the Act sets out the provisions under which rights of audience in the courts and rights to conduct litigation will be recognized. Rights currently held by solicitors and barristers are deemed to be approved already. The Act's provisions set out the procedures under which those rights can be extended and other bodies can apply to be designated as 'authorized bodies' so that their members can have similar rights. The rules of new applicants must be submitted to the Director-General of Fair Trading (DGFT), who will advise on whether the proposed rules have potential or actual anti-competitive effects. Amendments to the existing rules of the Law Society (in relation to solicitors) or the General Council of the Bar (in relation to barristers), or of any new authorized body, are subject to a similar procedure. There is also provision for the existing rules of the Law Society or the General Council of the Bar to be challenged on the grounds that they would not have been approved had they been submitted under the terms of the Act.

(ii) Existing legal barriers to solicitors and barristers entering into multidisciplinary or multinational practices are removed. The Law Society and the General Council of the Bar remain able to make rules which prohibit their members from entering into such practices, subject if necessary to scrutiny by the DGFT under a procedure similar to that outlined above.

(iii) Conveyancing services are to be extended, under the auspices of the Authorized Conveyancing Practitioners Board. The Board is required to promote the development of competition in the provision of conveyancing services and to supervise the conveyancing activities of authorized practitioners. The Board's proposed rules and regulations and the Lord Chancellor's regulations on the conduct of the new conveyancers must be sent to the DGFT, who will advise on any potential anti-competitive effects.

(iv) There is a prohibition on offering residential property loans on condition that the borrower must accept other services (to be specified in the Regulations). Where a package of services is offered to the borrower, the borrower is to be given adequate information (including the cost) on the separate services which it comprises.

(2) The Broadcasting Act 1990 introduces a new regulatory framework for television, sound radio and cable broadcasting.

The Act gives the DGFT two new responsibilities:

(i) He is required to monitor BBC compliance with a duty to take at least 25% of their new TV programmes (in certain categories) from independent programme makers, as from the beginning of 1993.

---

[1]   Nineteenth Competition Report, point 105.

(ii) The DGFT must examine the networking arrangements between regional television companies. Networking is a system of cooperative scheduling, commissioning and broadcasting of television programmes by regional television companies (Channel 3, a new regional service, will replace the existing independent television broadcasting service from January 1993). The Act requires the DGFT to report on the new networking arrangements and to say whether any anti-competitive effects meet the exemption criteria in Article 85(3) of the EEC Treaty, interpreted in the UK context. He may also specify any modifications to the arrangements necessary to remove anti-competitive effects. The DGFT's conclusions may be appealed to the Monopolies and Mergers Commission.

As foreshadowed in the Nineteenth Competition Report,[1] Regulations were made bringing into effect a statutory system of voluntary prenotification to the DGFT of proposed mergers and a system of charging fees for merger control.

Regulations were also made to enable the UK authorities to perform their function under Council Regulation No 4064/89, which came into effect on 21 September, and to make changes to the Fair Trading Act 1973 consequent upon the Regulation.

Four orders were made under the Electricity Act 1989[1] exempting certain agreements in the electricity industry from the provisions of the Restrictive Trade Practices Act 1976.

---

[1]   Nineteenth Competition Report, point 107.

§ 2 — Application of Community law by national courts

1. Of the recent judgments delivered by the Belgian courts concerning the application of Articles 85(1) and 86 of the EEC Treaty, three are particularly interesting for the principles they contain.

(i)   A judgment of 21 December 1989 of the Brussels Court of Appeal concerning the suspension of contractual relations between a travel agency and the Belgian branch of Singapore Airlines, due first to the fact that the travel agency did not adhere to the minimum tariffs prescribed, and secondly to the fact that it sold airline tickets to French nationals flying from Brussels. With regard to the application of the competition rules set out in the EEC Treaty, the Court, after noting that the European Court of Justice had expressly stated that transport was subject to the Treaty's general competition rules (including Articles 5, 85 and 86), held that, by requiring the appellant (the travel agency) to observe prescribed prices, the respondent (the airline) had restricted competition between travel agencies and affected trade between Member States in so far as agents in one Member State were free to sell tickets to customers residing in other Member States. As a result, the respondent had failed to fulfil the requirements of Article 85 of the Treaty and had infringed Article 54 of the Law on trade practices.

(ii) A judgment of 19 March 1990 of the President of the Brussels Commercial Court in connection with a dispute between an intermediary specializing in trade in cars intended for export (mainly to Italy) and an importer of Italian cars, involving instructions from the latter to members of his network to refuse to sell second-hand vehicles to the intermediary in the absence of an order placed by a private individual, the end-user of the vehicle, as in the case of the sale of new cars.

As regards the application of Community competition law, the President of the Court considered that Regulation (EEC) No 123/85, which legitimized selective motor vehicle distribution agreements containing a clause requiring intermediaries to have prior written authority from the end-user, applied only to new vehicles and that it should be interpreted narrowly as it derogated from Article 85.

He therefore held that the importer's prohibition on his dealers selling freely, at the prices offered to the public, second-hand vehicles to the intermediary constituted a definite barrier to trade between Member States.

(iii) A judgment of 17 July 1990 of the President of the Brussels Commercial Court in response to a complaint by a charter airline about a joint venture agreement between Belgian, Dutch and British airlines involving the Belgian company which operated the fleet of aircraft belonging to, and exploited the traffic rights held by, the Belgian airline, of which that company was a subsidiary. The essential purpose of the agreement was to develop Brussels as another European 'hub' airport and pave the way for cooperation between the three airlines on certain intercontinental routes which were extensions of intra-Community links, the partner companies remaining, however, independent of one another and retaining their own markets.

With regard to the application of Community law, the President pointed out that the agreement concluded by the three partners (each of which had a sizeable share of the Community market and pursued the same economic objective) was likely, as it stood, to affect trade between Member States and distort competition at Community level. The partners already had the opportunity of occupying the economically most worthwhile take-off and landing slots without hindrance from other carriers. Furthermore, there were as yet no Community rules on slot allocation, and when the Belgian legislation had entered into force and other Community carriers such as the plaintiff, having obtained the necessary operating licence, at last had access to the market, a good many of the best slots would have gone, being already allocated to the company concerned and to each of its partners.

The President concluded that competition in the field of take-off and landing slots had been distorted before it even existed.

2. In the Federal Republic of Germany, since the Fifth Amending Law came into force, courts with jurisdiction to hear competition cases are required to inform the Federal Cartel Office (Bundeskartell-amt) of all civil actions brought before them concerning the application of Articles 85 and 86 of the EEC Treaty. The Federal Cartel Office does not, however, have a complete view of the application of the Community competition rules by the civil courts, it being impossible to determine whether all courts are already applying the new rules. German courts are still hesitant to base a decision on the Community competition rules.

The Federal High Court (Bundesgerichtshof) held that a pricing arrangement whereby Volkswagen dealers were in fact obliged to abide by the prices recommended, in theory on a non-binding basis, by the manufacturer did not qualify for block exemption having regard to Article 6, point 2 of Regulation (EEC) No 123/85 (judgment of 8 May 1990, KZR 23/88).

The Karlsruhe Higher Regional Court (Oberlandesgericht) held in a definitive judgment that a long-term agreement for the supply of motor oil was not covered by Article 85(1) of the Treaty (judgment of 17 April 1989, GU 33/90). The Court based its decision on the lack of proof of the cumulative effects of agreements of the same type which, according to the theory on the subject developed by the European Court of Justice, might affect trade between Member States.

A number of courts of first instance had occasion to deal with the question of the compatibility of agreements for the supply of drinks, and in particular beer, with Article 85 of the Treaty, and with a series of questions connected with Regulation (EEC) No 1984/83. In this respect a preliminary ruling is still awaited from the European Court of Justice on the questions referred to it by the Frankfurt/Main Higher Regional Court on 13 July 1989. [1]

3. In France, the Paris Court of Appeal delivered four judgments during 1990 in actions concerning the compatibility of motor vehicle distribution agreements with the Community provisions concerning the exemption of distribution agreements (Regulation (EEC) No 1983/83). [2]

The Bordeaux Court of Appeal examined the practices of a firm of undertakers enjoying a local monopoly in the light of the interpretation of Article 85 given on this point by the European Court of Justice. [3]

For the record, the Council of State handed down on 24 October 1990 a decision recognizing the primacy of Community law over French law, even where the latter was more recent, and in an opinion delivered on 23 October the Competition Council examined the validity of inter-trade agreements in the sugar sector in the light of Regulation (EEC) No 1785/81 and the competition rules.

4. In the Netherlands, the President of the Roermond Court held on 21 September 1989 that a contractual obligation to sell certain sorts of beer should be discharged in good faith. In the President's view, this meant that the agreement should be in keeping with the spirit of Regulation (EEC) No 1984/83, as expressed in recitals 13, 14 and 15 of that Regulation. The President ordered the party concerned to suspend the sale of a type of beer not covered by the agreement, failing which he would be liable to payment of a daily fine. (The outcome would probably have been different had the interests at stake been weighed against each other, but for that a judge sitting in chambers was not the proper forum.)

In a judgment delivered on 24 November 1989, the High Court upheld a decision of the Amsterdam Court to the effect that purchasers who, even without a written agreement, take account of restrictions which go beyond those permitted by Regulation (EEC) No 1984/83 are guilty of concerted practices prohibited by Article 85(1) of the Treaty. In the case in point, besides accepting a prohibition on manufacturing or selling products competing with certain ceramic products intended for a special decor, the other parties to the contract had also accepted from the supplier a tacit obligation not to sell any other products intended for that special decor.

---

[1]   Nineteenth Competition Report, point 109.
[2]   Judgment of 14 June 1990 (*SA Loisirs Auto* v *Volvo France*).
       Judgment of 27 April 1990 (*Sté Nantes Sud Auto* v *Sté VAG France*).
       Judgment of 6 April 1990 (*Sté Le Cardinal* v *BMW France*).
       Judgment of 10 May 1990 (*SA Corade* v *Sté Macallan Glenlivet*).
[3]   Judgment of 23 January 1990.

In a judgment delivered on 8 March 1990, the President of the Amsterdam Court held that a refusal to admit a mail-order house into a selective distribution network was not contrary to Article 85(1) of the Treaty in view of the manufacturer's small market share. The Court dismissed the defendant's argument that the relevant market consisted only of expensive perfumes and beauty products.

In a judgment of 14 March 1990, the President of the Zwolle Court held that a beer-supply agreement which fell within the scope of Regulation (EEC) No 1984/83 was not covered by the prohibition provided for in Article 85(2) of the Treaty as it conferred special economic and financial advantages.

The defendant had granted the plaintiff an unsecured loan as part of the agreement. The debt had been discharged by means of a set-off arrangement involving the quantity rebates payable.

On 1 June 1990 the High Court made a reference to the European Court of Justice for a preliminary ruling concerning an exclusive purchasing agreement between a retailer and a wholesaler containing a non-competition clause. The Court was seeking answers to questions relating to the anti-competitive nature of the agreement and the possibility of trade between Member States being affected as a result.

European Communities — Commission

XXth Report on Competition Policy

Luxembourg: Office for Official Publications of the European Communities

1991 — 362 pp. — 16.2 × 22.9 cm

ISBN 92-826-2314-9

Catalogue number: CM-60-91-410-EN-C

Price (excluding VAT) in Luxembourg: ECU 25

The Report on Competition Policy is published annually by the Commission of the European Communities in response to the request of the European Parliament made by a Resolution of 7 June 1971. This Report, which is published in conjunction with the General Report on the Activities of the Communities, is designed to give a general view of the competition policy followed during the past year. Part One covers general competition policy. Part Two deals with competition policy towards enterprises. Part Three is concerned with competition policy and government assistance to enterprises and Part Four with the development of concentration, competition and competitiveness.